W9-COG-426

Kidnap

Kidnap

Inside the Ransom Business

Anja Shortland

OXFORD
UNIVERSITY PRESS

OXFORD
UNIVERSITY PRESS

Great Clarendon Street, Oxford, OX2 6DP,
United Kingdom

Oxford University Press is a department of the University of Oxford.
It furthers the University's objective of excellence in research, scholarship,
and education by publishing worldwide. Oxford is a registered trade mark of
Oxford University Press in the UK and in certain other countries

© Anja Shortland 2019

The moral rights of the author have been asserted

First Edition published in 2019
Impression: 1

Published in the United States of America by Oxford University Press
198 Madison Avenue, New York, NY 10016, United States of America

British Library Cataloguing in Publication Data
Data available

Library of Congress Control Number: 2018945171

ISBN 978-0-19-881547-1

Printed and bound in Great Britain by
Clays Ltd, Elcograf S.p.A.

Links to third party websites are provided by Oxford in good faith and
for information only. Oxford disclaims any responsibility for the materials
contained in any third party website referenced in this work.

For Andrew

Acknowledgements

This book is based on many long conversations with a wide range of industry insiders. I am extremely grateful that you decided to trust me, told me about your world, and allowed me to share some of your experiences. It has been fascinating to watch and listen to you solving some of the trickiest trade problems in the world to bring kidnap victims safely back to their families and friends. You chose to remain anonymous, but I hope this book does justice to the amazing work you do.

I greatly appreciate the support of my admired colleagues. Conversations with Paul Aligica, Lee Benham, Lisa Bernstein, Peter Boettke, David Fielding, Diego Gambetta, Gillian Hadfield, Jeffrey Howard, Tom Keatinge, Peter Leeson, Mike Munger, Mark Pennington, Todd Sandler, and Edward Stringham convinced me that I had stumbled upon something exciting and helped to direct and sharpen my analysis. My mentor Ben Bowling knew that I wanted to write this book before I did. David Skarbek and Federico Varese lent support and gave advice throughout. Part I is largely based on my joint work with Federico. Thank you, David, for your thoughtful comments on the first draft of this book—I didn't enjoy rewriting it, but I am glad I did.

My editor Adam Swallow has kept me on track with his positivity, mischievous sense of humour, gentle chiding, and excellent coffee. Thank you for making it such fun to write my first book. Sir Nicholas Bayne, Liam Morrissey, and a further (anonymous) referee read and commented in detail on the entire book, while Per Gullestrup, Ali M. Ali, and others helped with specific chapters. Matthias Baumann drew the maps for Chapter 3. Thank you for your wisdom, guidance, and for helping me to communicate better.

'It takes a village to raise a child.' My village has raised a book as well as two beautiful kids. I thank my friends, family, neighbours, co-authors, and colleagues for their patience and support as I focused single-mindedly on completing my first book. J. S. Bach and W. A. Mozart kept me (more or less) sane: thank you for the music, Christine Williams, Roland Rosner, and Camilla Darling. I am most grateful for the enthusiastic support of my children, who were only too pleased to tell their impressed classmates: 'Daddy (an Egyptologist) studies mummies—but our mummy is a pirate!' My parents and father-in-law were always ready to drop anything to hold the fort during research trips, conferences, or simply for much-needed downtime. Thank you.

It is both my nature and my job to be puzzled and to puzzle things out. I have seen and heard some strange, some disturbing, and many wonderful things. I thank my husband for his encouragement and practical assistance in my academic adventures. This book is dedicated to him.

Contents

List of Figures

Endorsements

Using jargon-free prose and impeccable analytical clarity this book portrays the business logic of the protagonists of kidnap—the kidnappers, their protectors, the hostages, and the insurers—vividly illustrating it with many real-life cases replete with unexpected twists. Whether you are afraid of being kidnapped, eager to sell insurance, working hard to deter or catch kidnappers, or even just a social scientist eager to understand what makes kidnapping fail or thrive, this treatise, the first of its kind, will prove supremely enlightening.

Diego Gambetta
European University Institute and Oxford University.
Author of *Engineers of Jihad*,
Codes of the Underworld and *The Sicilian Mafia*

What do you get when you combine the intrigue of the international kidnap-for-ransom business and solid nuanced economic theory? A great read and deep insights into how extra-legal markets really work.

Gillian Hadfield
University of Toronto

The business and economic dynamics of kidnap-for-ransom are highly complex, but in this new book—unique in this field—Shortland provides a masterful deconstruction and explanation of the trickiest trade. Shortland lifts the veil on a highly complex world, revealing the ecosystem of motivations and competing interests that allow an orderly market to operate in the most disorderly of environments.

Tom Keatinge
Director,
Centre for Financial Crime & Security Studies, RUSI

Negotiation with criminals; a fortune at stake; emotions on the redline; lives hanging in the balance. What couldn't go wrong with kidnap-for-ransom? In this gripping new book, Anja Shortland analyses the ransom business from the inside. Her discovery is startling and brilliant:

a self-governing marketplace of cooperation and order. Outstanding and original, *Kidnap* is mandatory reading for students of (anti-)social order.

Peter T. Leeson
George Mason University.
Author of *The Invisible Hook: The Hidden Economics of Pirates and WTF?! An Economic Tour of the Weird*

Rigorous analysis which is needed not just in this field but also in cyber, art crime and all those areas where the lack of international policing leaves the private sector to find its own solutions... Meticulous research and clear conclusions of great importance to policy makers and those engaged in the prevention and mitigation of ransom attacks.

Julian Radcliffe OBE
Founding Director of Control Risks and
Chairman of the Art Loss Register

This outstanding book enlightens readers on the modern workings of the ransom business with its stakeholders—the kidnappers, the insurers, the governments, and the victims and their families. The author applies economic reasoning in a clear, clever, and insightful manner. In doing so she puts a perplexing problem into sharp focus. This must-read book addresses a crucial political problem in an engaging way.

Todd Sandler
University of Texas at Dallas.
Author of *Terrorism: What Everyone Needs to Know*

1

Kidnap for Ransom as a Business

> The most exciting phrase to hear in science, the one that heralds new discoveries, is not 'Eureka!' (I found it!) but 'That's funny...'
>
> Attributed to Isaac Asimov[1]

The Trickiest Trade in the World

Every year, thousands of people are kidnapped to be ransomed back to their families, employers, or governments. The trade in human lives is a well-established business in many areas of the world and practised by criminals, rebels, and terrorists alike. According to the leader of Al Qaeda in the Arabian Peninsula: 'Kidnapping hostages is an easy spoil...which I may describe as a profitable trade and a precious treasure.'[2] However, to anyone who has read or watched a film about a hostage crisis or ransom negotiation—such as *Ransom*, *Captain Phillips*, or *All the Money in the World*—the description of kidnap for ransom as an 'easy spoil' seems odd. Any economist, manager, or business analyst would agree: the trade in hostages is the trickiest trade in the world! There are so many obstacles to the successful resolution of a hostage crisis, that the safe return of any hostage seems like a miracle.

Let's look at the problems one by one. The first challenge is a logistical one: acquire a live hostage and convey them to a place from which the ransom negotiation can be safely conducted. The pirates in *Captain Phillips* fell at this first hurdle. From then on, the hostage needs to be guarded, fed, and if necessary treated for medical problems. Dead bodies are difficult to sell. The next challenge is equally complex: how do you price a hostage? Many people are kidnapped opportunistically—perhaps dragged out of their car at a roadblock, hijacked with their yacht, or abducted at knife-point in a dodgy area of town. So, the kidnappers have to find out the identity of the victim, who to approach for the ransom, and how much the victim is 'worth' to each. There are usually several parties who could take charge of the negotiation or contribute to the ransom: the immediate family, rich friends or relatives, the victim's employer, or even their government. Throughout the book I use the term stakeholders to denote the people or groups who offer assistance to retrieve the hostage. The stakeholders are not going to volunteer full financial information to the criminals: subject to retrieving a live hostage, they would like to hide as many assets as possible from the kidnappers. In the negotiation, both parties have every reason to suspect the worst of each other. Perhaps the police are preparing a rescue operation and the ransom negotiation only serves to buy time and collect information. Maybe the hostage is already dead. Yet, for a successful commercial resolution the parties have to communicate, cooperate, and agree an affordable price that persuades the kidnappers to release the hostage.

Complex information problems are often resolved by bartering. Usually there are social norms to help smooth this process, such as turn-taking, focal points (such as fifty-fifty), and convergence of offers over time. Once a price has been agreed it is often a matter of honour not to renegotiate it later. Bartering over hostages can be anarchic, however. Criminals make and break rules according to their own interest. If a kidnap is a one-off interaction, it is worth 'wringing the towel dry'—that is extracting the maximum ransom the buyers can raise. Kidnappers have a whole arsenal of tools for psychological combat at their disposal: long silences, reports of ill health, threats, torture, mutilations, mock executions, and even murder. They can try anything to encourage the buyers to reveal their hidden assets.

If a price is agreed, the next problem arises: how do you pay the ransom? Banks cannot handle criminal transactions and kidnappers generally demand to be paid in used, unmarked, small-denomination notes. Whoever drops them off puts themselves at risk—and a hired courier may prefer to abscond with the ransom rather than deliver it. In the meantime, the kidnapper fears surveillance or an ambush at the specified rendezvous point. This would be the prime opportunity for the police to strike and make an arrest. The kidnappers' (justifiable) distrust and caution generally makes it impossible to verify a successful hand-over. What if the courier says he dropped the ransom in the designated dustbin and the kidnappers claim they never got it? You cannot prove whether the courier, the police, a curious passer-by, or the kidnappers themselves are in possession of the ransom.

Assuming that this hurdle has also been cleared and the kidnappers admit that they have received the ransom, is it really in their interest to release a live hostage? Might the hostage reveal useful information to the police? Will the kidnappers meet their former victim again at an identity parade or in court? If the hostage 'disappears' this would be avoided. Or perhaps there was something about the drop-off that suggested that there was more money to be made? Is it worth starting over—or selling the hostage on to a more sophisticated gang? Kidnappers will only release hostages if they think it is in their own interest do so.

By Murphy's law, 'anything that can go wrong, will go wrong'. Media reports of kidnappings strongly suggest that this is a deeply dysfunctional market. If you read the news, it seems that many people die in bungled kidnap attempts. Hostages disappear without a trace, or their broken bodies are dumped to be found by grieving relatives and friends. Some families scrape together multiple ransoms before the kidnappers turn ominously silent. Some hostages are cruelly and humiliatingly murdered in public spectacles. Others perish in rescue attempts. The few survivors give harrowing accounts of their time in captivity: tormented by fear, violent threats, and perhaps torture, mutilations, and mock executions. Post-traumatic stress disorder and survivor's guilt are common. How can we reconcile these observations with the ubiquity of kidnap for ransom as a 'profitable trade'?

The Puzzling Kidnap for Ransom Business

What do the data tell us? Official kidnap statistics are patchy and biased. Abductions are only reported if there is a local police presence, the police officers are not suspected of being complicit in the kidnapping, and people reporting the incident expect a net benefit from doing so. The local authority may not be keen to flag up a kidnapping problem that might reduce their city's attractiveness for tourism and investment. For these reasons, only a minority of kidnap cases are ever recorded in official statistics.[3] Media coverage has a different bias. Commercial media outlets tend to focus on emotional drama: tense or drawn-out negotiations, daring rescue bids, and kidnaps gone sensationally wrong. Editors are rarely interested in short, smoothly resolved kidnappings. There is also self-censorship. It would be unwise for a victim's family to advertise that they paid a substantial ransom for the safe return of a loved one. Such information might attract the attention of other kidnappers—or the police.

Several security consultancies closely monitor kidnaps around the world to help their customers manage their risks. Analysing the outcomes of abductions where the kidnappers demand some sort of concession in return for the hostage (financial or otherwise), they reckon that in around 90 per cent of cases the hostages return alive.[4] The large majority of kidnap victims are successfully ransomed.[5] This is an astonishing success rate, given the difficulties in trading hostages and the inherent bias against reporting successful resolutions. Moreover, the security consultancy Control Risks reported that in 2016, 81 per cent of kidnaps lasted less than a week and only 4 per cent exceeded four weeks.[6] Clearly, the hostage trade functions surprisingly well in the large majority of cases. How can such a difficult market operate so successfully?

Private Governance

Social scientists studying how underground and criminal markets work would offer two possible explanations. The market may be self-governing, meaning that it is in the interest of the transaction partners to develop rules and norms to structure the trade.[7] These rules are generally self-enforcing: it is in everyone's best interest to obey the rules, even without third-party enforcement. One might expect such spontaneous, bottom-up rule design to operate in the market for hostages. The abduction is generally the most dangerous part of a kidnap for ransom operation. It could be worth developing a norm of limited violence on both sides. For example, crews and naval vessels tried their best to prevent Somali pirates from boarding ships. If this was unavoidable, the sailors hid in a secure area awaiting rescue. But as soon as the intruders had a single hostage under their control, resistance ceased and the ship was steered to Somalia for ransoming. Crew members who complied were largely left in peace, but sailors who resisted were made to suffer. Captains under attack knew they could choose between either risking injuries, fatalities, and the total loss of the ship or the boredom of waiting to be ransomed. Ship-owners certainly knew what they preferred: a commercial resolution.

Building a reputation for punishing non-compliers can be costly in the short run, but in the long run kidnappers, hijackers, and their victims benefit from norms of limited violence. The reputational solution to the problem of costly crew resistance has a long tradition in maritime piracy. Eighteenth-century merchants knew what their options were when their pursuer hoisted the 'Jolly Roger': you can fight back, but if your defence fails, you walk the plank.[8] Similarly, in Yemen kidnapping is traditionally non-violent. In thirty-six kidnappings of foreign nationals in Sana'a in Yemen between 2010 and 2014, only seven victims were hurt. In four of the cases that turned violent, the victim had employed close protection officers or a police escort. All of these abductions led to fatalities.[9] Although foreigners may feel safer with an armed bodyguard, they risk paying the ultimate price for breaking the social norm.

Kidnapping gangs could also gather information on the hostages' financial position before the kidnap. This reduces the underlying information problems and hence the bargaining period. For example, Naxalite insurgents in India mostly abduct family members of people who are known to have come into an inheritance or sold a major asset. Similarly, the Revolutionary Armed Forces of Colombia (FARC) collected detailed financial data on the firms operating in their territory. If the total amount to be bargained over is common knowledge, it is easier to apportion the surplus between the two sides.

When gangs repeatedly abduct local people, the trade ceases to be a one-off interaction. If the community shares information about the past behaviour of kidnapping gangs, it can become financially rewarding to develop a reputation for the decent treatment of hostages and keeping one's word. Survival expert Larry Busch writes about Mexican kidnapping gangs: 'The criminal groups carrying out these kidnappings are successful because they have a reputation for bargaining in good faith.... they have built credibility: if the ransom is paid, the hostage is released.'[10] In cultures where hostage-taking is an established way of resolving intercommunity conflict, such as in the tribal areas of Yemen, hostages traditionally have the social status of a guest.[11] If you or a loved one are likely to become hostages, it makes sense to treat your hostages as you wish to be treated yourself. But would these local norms necessarily be applied to outsiders? Reputational solutions rely on repeated interaction or good information flow. We might expect social norms to break down if the victim is a foreigner; especially if the financial rewards for rule-breaking are potentially large.

We also know that there are highly effective enforcement institutions governing criminal and illicit markets. In the formal economy, traders rely on the courts and the police to resolve disputes and enforce contracts. Criminals and consumers of illegal goods (such as drugs) cannot turn to the police when their trade partners cheat them. Instead, these markets are governed informally: by mafias, drug cartels, or prison gangs.[12] The extra-legal authority orders criminal and underground markets for profit: usually it takes a percentage cut from each successful transaction. It is therefore in its interest to create and enforces rules that maximize its 'tax base'. Again, this is something we can observe in the market for hostages. Informal authorities—such as sheikhs and tribal elders—often intercede on behalf of hostages. The overlong captivity of the Chandler couple, taken from their yacht by Somali pirates, ended when locals and diaspora clan members lost patience with the 'temperamental and crass' thugs: squeezing a retired couple for millions they simply did not have. Clan elders told the pirates that they would no longer tolerate their 'embarrassing' behaviour and facilitated the release.[13] A sadistic or murderous kidnapper who puts off tourists and threatens businesspeople in mafia-controlled territory is more likely to be called to order by the Godfather than by the police. But even an underfunded, corrupt, and out-of-control police force will eventually be deployed against violent kidnappers when political pressure mounts.[14] Thus, if the victim's family knows who to appeal to and it is in the financial interest of the authority (whether formal or informal) to respond, the market for hostages could run smoothly. A credible threat of rule enforcement discourages rule-breaking.

Existing academic research therefore identifies two possible reasons why the trade in hostages succeeds as often as it does: reputational solutions and extra-legal governance. Both of them work well for local-on-local kidnaps, where the necessary information circulates freely. People know how to behave if someone tries to abduct them, kidnappers broadly know how much the hostage 'worth', most kidnappers can be trusted to deal fairly, and families know who to appeal to when kidnappers turn rogue. Based on this analysis we would predict local-on-local kidnaps—which represent the majority of global kidnaps—to be resolved relatively smoothly, whereas transnational kidnaps would be the problematic ones. These are one-off events, with potentially huge sums of money at stake. When foreigners or the employees of foreign companies are abducted, kidnappers find it difficult to obtain and verify information about their hostage's financial position. Remembering the unfortunate victims of terrorist groups, we may even surmise that in these cases the reputational solution may be turned on its head: perhaps it is lucrative to kill at least a few hostages? How could a family or firm find, contact, and engage the support of a foreign extra-legal organization to act on behalf of their hostage? What if the informal authority is itself implicated in the kidnapping or ransoming? Are foreign hostages doomed?

The Puzzle of Transnational Kidnap Resolutions

We know that many people are willing to work and travel in areas with extreme kidnap risks. Journalists routinely report from war zones. Wherever oil and minerals are discovered, local opposition and rebel groups form—and many of them lend weight to their demands by kidnapping. Firms are building pipelines and roads right through territory held by insurgent groups—and often attract criminal attention, too. Aid is regularly delivered into conflict and disaster zones. After a peace deal, it is often a political necessity to rebuild key infrastructure before rebels capitalize on local grievances—even if the security situation is precarious. Intrepid academic colleagues research remote areas far beyond the reach of any government. Often the only other foreigners are courageous missionaries, who we know are regularly targeted by rebel movements. All employers have a legal obligation to exercise a reasonable duty of care in providing a safe workplace. Clearly, they cannot put their employees in harm's way and abandon them to an uncertain fate when they are abducted. What happens to the victims of transnational kidnaps?

Luckily, there are reliable data to answer this question. Firms, non-governmental organizations (NGOs), and charities whose employees are at risk often obtain kidnap insurance, as do many well-off families. If a kidnap occurs, they report the incident to a helpline and are immediately allocated a crisis response consultant to assist them in retrieving the hostage. Thus, both the crisis responder and kidnap insurers have excellent records of how the cases were resolved. Hiscox, the global market leader for kidnap insurance, retains the services of the security and crisis response consultancy Control Risks. Between 2000 and 2014, in 85.5 per cent of crises resolved by Control Risks, the hostages were safely released by their kidnappers, 6 per cent of hostages were rescued, and 6 per cent managed to escape. Only 2.5 per cent of cases resulted in the death of a hostage—and most of them were related to ill health or bungled escape or rescue attempts. Depending on the year range, the consultancy, and the specialists one talks to, death rates in hostage incidents fluctuate between 0.3 and 3 per cent. This compares to an estimated 10 per cent fatality rate in ransom kidnaps overall. So, on balance, transnational kidnaps—which should be the most complex to resolve—are the most likely to result in a successful resolution. One immediately surmises that this has something to do with the existence of kidnap insurance—and of professional crisis responders who order the transnational market for hostages.

Kidnap for Ransom Insurance

The previous section implied that the transnational market for hostages is so predictable and well ordered that firms can insure against hostage crises and thereby fulfil their duty of care to their at-risk employees. Or is it the other way around? Do insurers order the market for transnational hostages to create demand for and deliver a profitable insurance product?

If the market for kidnap insurance was highly concentrated and information flowed freely, it would be possible to sustain cooperative ransom negotiations and encourage kidnappers to build reputations, just as they do in local communities. Somebody could make it their business to find out about local informal rules and social norms and advise people in kidnap-prone locations accordingly—preferably before they get themselves into trouble. It would be worth finding out who governs the local criminal, illicit, and informal markets before posting people abroad. It might be worth cultivating these informal providers of governance a little—one might need their help later. However, the company's shareholders and the senior management would feel queasy about dealing directly with the economic underworld. So, we probably need specialists to conduct commercial and social inter-actions at the ragged intersection between the legal economy and the economic underworld.

But what if the market for hostages functions too well? What if the insured become complacent and let their guard down? Resolving a spiralling number of kidnap cases would erode insurers' profits. If kidnappers suspect that well-resourced insurance companies are involved, ransom demands are likely to explode. What if the insured are weak negotiators? The cost of reimbursing escalating ransoms in a kidnap hotspot would have to be passed back on to the customers via a higher insurance premium. But this would reduce demand for kidnap insurance. So, insurers also have to stabilize kidnapping. This looks like a highly complex undertaking. How would you start to build the insti-tutions to order such a tricky market? Industry insiders have a positive, can-do attitude to these challenges: 'Managing risk is the key to unlock-ing opportunity.'[15]

Governance at the Legal/Extra-legal Boundary

This book examines how special risks insurers selling kidnap for ransom insurance created a system of supporting services that underpin both the transnational trade in hostages and its insurance. I use the tools of economics to analyse each vital component in the system. We see a whole range of governance specialists at work: creating rules, dissemin-ating information, evaluating performance, spotting breaches of proto-col, and enforcing rules and norms. Many of these specialists operate entirely in the legal realm. Insurers discipline their customers with the governance devices of the formal economy: formal contracts and law courts. Laws and by-laws are also used to structure cooperation between insurers and between insurers and their service providers—though mostly the system works through informal peer monitoring. Occasionally the police and elite military forces intervene to punish rogue kidnappers.

Other agents in the system operate mostly in the shadow economy and the extra-legal realm. If firms want their staff to travel or conduct long-term business in rebel territory, they may need to square it with the local clan, tribe, or warlord. Even in Europe there are cities where it makes economic sense not to upset the mafia boss when building a new store or factory. Finally, there are the specialists for conducting business across the legal/extra-legal interface. For example, specialists for crafting protection contracts—or rather informal agreements that work like protection contracts but do not look corrupt or suspicious. Crisis responders help firms or families negotiate affordable ransoms that do not put others at risk. Mediators, ransom couriers, and air ambulance pilots will meet the kidnappers face to face, if necessary. And there are many, many more. Having analysed each component part in detail, I examine how the entire system works, how it adapts to different security environments, and how it responds to new challenges.

The idea that insurers order criminal markets to make crime insurable is intuitively attractive, but also a little worrying. Is this a co-dependent relationship? Are insurers in cahoots with criminals, not just mitigating but optimizing the threat level on which demand for their products relies? Indeed, occasionally critics voice such suspicions and accusations. 'Is the insurance industry a hidden cause of the growth in Somalia piracy?' asked the journalist Matthew Parris. He observed a 'whole network of agents and middlemen . . . used by insurers and shippers as a semi-formalized line of communication with the Somali pirates. Many careers and many fortunes—all of them perfectly legal—are now founded upon this racket.' He concluded that 'the policies [insurers] offer and pay-out are an inducement to piracy'. The headline? 'The Piracy Racket Begins Here in the City'.[16]

What exactly is the role of insurers in this system? Does kidnap for ransom insurance encourage kidnapping? Would people be safer if insurance did not exist? These questions should be at the back of our minds as we analyse this intricate, complex governance system—a wonderful testament to human ingenuity. I see a system that puts the welfare of the hostage centre stage—but also prevents ransom payments from escalating, so as not to put others at risk. Kidnap insurance and the services associated with it thereby facilitate international trade and investment, resource extraction, aid, development initiatives, research, and reporting from some of the most complex and hostile security environments in the world. Is this not in the public interest?

I consider the market for terrorist hostages as a counter-example: UN and domestic law forbid the transfer of money to proscribed organizations—and that includes ransoms. Insurers can neither facilitate nor reimburse ransoms paid to terrorists. Even so—there is a market for hostages held by terrorist groups, because some governments ransom their citizens and others tolerate private resolutions. Does this ungoverned market work better? Reports of multi-million-dollar ransoms, gruesome videos of torture and beheadings, and the number and size of 'no-go' areas for citizens of countries that refuse to negotiate with terrorists suggest otherwise.[17] If governments cannot govern—and how could they possibly govern transactions between legal entities and criminals or violent political rivals to the official government?— private governance is probably the lesser evil.

Roadmap

When I first studied the market for hostages, I was fascinated by transnational crisis resolution. How do you trade human beings across national and cultural boundaries? One day I realized that compared to the total number of insured people working, travelling, and living in kidnap-prone areas, the number of hostage crises is very low indeed. The world's leading crisis responder advertises its unrivalled experience of resolving kidnap and extortion cases all over the world. By early 2018, Control Risks had resolved more than 2,300 cases in 138 countries—in over 50,000 case days.[18] But the company has been in this business for over forty years! Other crisis responders advertise that their consultants have resolved 'hundreds' of cases. An understatement of the true figures? Apparently not—if anything there is double counting, as experienced consultants sometimes establish or move to new consultancies. The new firms just add up all their consultants' previous cases to advertise their total case experience. 'Do you want your open-heart surgery performed by an experienced surgeon, or by a junior doctor?' asked a senior consultant. 'Everyone tries to look as experienced as possible here.' The implication is that crisis resolution is Plan B—most hostage crises are avoided rather than resolved. Security consulting is much bigger business than crisis response, and to prevent kidnaps, security consultants often rely on the huge private security industry.

A meaningful analysis of kidnap for ransom insurance therefore has to consider the millions of potential hostage crises that never happened, as well as the thousands that have occurred. Part I of the book looks at hostage-taking from the perpetrator's point of view. Kidnapping looks intuitively attractive: 'Here are some rich kids, their families would give good money to retrieve them.' However, abducting people is relatively easy when compared to negotiating a significant ransom and concluding the deal without being caught. And if someone can credibly threaten well-off people with a kidnap, it is probably better to charge everyone protection money rather than squeezing a handful of victims dry every year. Moreover, if criminals squeeze too hard, the most attractive targets will probably harden their defences or leave altogether. If you know who creates the threat, kidnaps should be preventable by negotiation.

Part II of this book studies how specialist kidnap for ransom insurers prevent kidnaps and order the trade in the few hostage crises that occur. The market for kidnap insurance is small and highly concentrated. The vast majority of kidnap for ransom insurance is underwritten at Lloyd's of London, where the key underwriters have their desks within a few metres of each other. This facilitates smooth and discreet information exchange, peer monitoring, and informal governance solutions. I show how the governance system evolved in response to painful financial impulses. Every time hostage trades fail and losses mount, new solutions are proposed, tested, and the successful ones adopted. Today's system has rigorous and intelligent protocols for disciplining the insured. There are many options to create a positive business environment in which kidnaps are rare, even when there is no formal law enforcement, or the police force is corrupt. I devote two chapters to the vexing question of how to negotiate a ransom that does not trigger dozens of copycat abductions. Once a price has been agreed, we still need solutions to the logistical and enforcement problems of effecting the money-for-hostage exchange. The final chapter of Part II pulls the threads together and shows that the market for hostages only works because it is highly concentrated and tightly governed. The market for kidnap insurance is (reasonably) competitive, but the competitors are members of a club that sets and enforces rules to benefit and stabilize the market.

Having concentrated on why the market operates so successfully in difficult circumstances, Part III of the book looks at why hostages die. The private governance system does not manage to prevent every hostage death. Occasionally things go wrong. However, experienced crisis responders create clear incentives for criminals: murder and torture do not pay. Hostage maltreatment tends to escalate if stakeholders deviate from the tried and tested protocol. I then compare the largely cooperative outcomes achieved by the private governance system with the track record of government-negotiated hostage crises. Rather than focusing on the politics of 'terrorist' kidnaps, I contrast the set of economic incentives kidnappers face under each regime. I argue that the involvement of governments has created perverse incentives in the market for hostages and show that kidnappers make rational choices. The same group will cooperate under the private regime and settle for low ransoms but turn murderous and achieve multi-million-dollar ransoms when they negotiate with governments. I therefore argue that the (partially observed) UN ban on ransom payments to terrorists is counterproductive: it puts lives at risk and increases the returns to terrorist kidnaps.

This book will take you on a journey into a strange and fascinating world, where brokers and insurers in smart Saville Row suits, charismatic former special forces officers, intrepid adventurers, venerable sheikhs, and brutal warlords have learned to cooperate. Although everyone pursues their private interest, they have created a system that serves us all.

Part I
Why People are Kidnapped for Ransom

I had to bring machinery to a remote town, but the road was controlled by the FARC. I knew that if the FARC stopped me on the way, I would have to pay a US$2,000 tax. I did not want to do this, so we waited a few days until a procession in honour of the Virgin Mary used the road. We hired a float, hid the goods, and put a band on top. They played beautifully and nobody thought of stopping us. I was so pleased—but when I arrived in the town I realized that my friend had been kidnapped on the way. I drove after my friend immediately, taking the US$2,000 with me. Local people told me the way to the FARC camp in the forest. I was taken to an accountant to make the contract. The accountant was in a tent with a satellite phone and two computers. He consulted his database and demanded a US$10,000 fine. He knew everything about my company.

I was told to deliver the fine in small notes, some painkillers, and a pair of prescription glasses to an out-of-the-way farm in a few days' time. The accountant asked me for a tip and I got out US$100 from the huge bundle of peso notes in my pocket. The FARC said that my friend's car would be required for FARC business for a little while. My friend and I left immediately, and I raised the ransom in the next city as the local bank did not have enough cash. The bag with the ransom was large and heavy and an army helicopter helped me to deliver it. We hadn't expected to see my friend's car again, but it was found abandoned nearby a few days later. I never reported this to the police and from then on the mayor told me exactly how much the FARC wanted and I paid straight away.

* * *

When the manager of a medium-sized Colombian company first told me about his personal encounter with the FARC, I was astonished. He had gone straight to a rebel camp without any apparent concern for his own safety—rushing in to help his friend. He unconsciously used the words 'tax', 'contract', accountant', and 'fine' to describe a forced, extralegal transaction. He entered a rebel camp with a huge wad of pesos worth US$2,000 visibly bulging in his pocket and left with US$1,900 and his friend. Why were the rebels so sure he would pay the 'fine'? Why did the army help to deliver a ransom to the rebels—for a friend who was already free? And why did the mayor facilitate the tax-collecting efforts of the FARC? The only thing my acquaintance found surprising was how well informed the rebels were: the 'fine' eroded but did not eliminate his firm's profit from fulfilling its contract in the town. The fact that the friend's car turned up again was an unexpected bonus. My contact was amused by his subsequent transactions with the town's mayor, who believed that she was bugged. So, they met in a café and talked about the weather and local gossip, while she scribbled the FARC demands in the margins of his newspaper.

Most people think that kidnap for ransom is about extracting the maximum ransom in a tense, one-off trade. But this local businessman's recollection describes a very different type of economic interaction. Although a rebel group abducted his friend and released him for a ransom, the lasting impression is one of a state-like organization enforcing a tax demand by making an arrest. The manager knew exactly what he had done wrong, effectively admitted his guilt, and agreed to pay a sizeable fine. Local norms and institutions were strong enough for him to complete the transaction and facilitate his subsequent work in the city: further trouble was averted by paying protection money. People who understand how the local system works can therefore predict and prevent most abductions—and resolve kidnappings arising out of misunderstandings or poor communication with minimal economic disruption and psychological trauma. If experienced specialists ordered the interface with the local protector, kidnaps should become rare and peaceful commercial resolution would be the norm. In other words, kidnapping would become insurable.

To appreciate how kidnap for ransom insurance works, I therefore propose that we start by changing perspective. Let's look at kidnapping from the perpetrators' point of view and analyse their options in a rational choice framework. Most kidnapping problems occur in states where governments are challenged by insurgencies and organized crime. The 2018 Riskmap published by Control Risks highlighted extreme security risks in Iraq and Syria, Afghanistan and the Pakistan/Afghan border areas, Somalia, Yemen, western parts of Sudan, the Central African Republic, eastern areas of the Democratic Republic of the Congo, Libya, and northern Nigeria. There is a high risk of being kidnapped by Islamist militias in Mali and neighbouring countries. High kidnap risks also exist around every hub of the drug smuggling routes through central America.[1] This part of the book therefore analyses the role of rebels, cartels, and mafias in kidnap for ransom.

Mafias and rebel groups aim to control territory and are engaged in a long-term relationship with the local population. Randomly abducting local businesspeople and squeezing their families dry is probably counterproductive. Instead, the most common mafia business model is extortion, where the demand for a 'protection payment' is enforced with a range of violent threats. From the mafia literature, we are familiar with threats against property (ranging from glue in locks, smashing windows, and burning cars, to torching business premises) and the person (ranging from beatings to cold-blooded murder). But destroying assets and putting people in fear of their lives does more harm than good to an Olsonian 'stationary bandit' who wants to maximize his revenue in the long term.[2] Firms and well-off individuals will not locate or stay in a violent thug's territory. It is therefore in the stationary bandit's interest to limit violence—his own as well as that of others—to avoid eroding his tax base. A reputation for targeted kidnappings that are resolved peacefully at affordable prices can encourage 'tax' compliance without driving away the economic activities that fund the mafia or rebel organization. In rebel territory in Colombia, locals pay '*la vacuna*' as a matter of course: literally it is 'the vaccine' against kidnapping.

Chapter 2 introduces protection theory as a framework for analysing the behaviour of rebel groups and mafias. Protection theory stresses that anyone who wants to extract benefit from controlling a territory in the long term must provide security to the people under their rule. Nobody produces a surplus if the fruits of their labour are regularly plundered. People will not invest time and effort in production if they cannot keep their goods or trade them for a fair price. Protection theory therefore predicts that someone in a community should specialize in the production of violence: to protect the interests of producers and enforce contracts to facilitate trade. The protector thus provides a valued service to the community and is paid for this. How much—and with what degree of violence that payment is extracted—depends on the bargain between the ruler and the ruled. Protection theory encompasses any form of organized violence: ranging from organized crime at one end of the spectrum to democratic states at the other.

The main question addressed in Chapter 2 is under what conditions protectors—whose raison d'être is to keep people safe—kidnap *inside* their own territory. I propose that kidnap for ransom indicates a disequilibrium in the market for protection. If people do not know whether, how, or whom to pay, the protectors must reveal themselves and demonstrate their power. A targeted abduction is a powerful signal of a protector's reach and capability. Moreover, the ransom negotiation allows the protector to probe the victim's financial resources. Kidnapping thus resolves information problems in the market for protection.

Chapter 3 analyses when protectors provide shelter and services to criminals targeting people *outside* their territory. Those who control territory can massively raise the return to kidnapping by providing safe havens from which lengthy ransom negotiation can be conducted. A capable protector will ensure that hostages are treated decently and that kidnappers safely release live hostages after the ransom payment. An orderly market for hostages maximizes ransoms in the long term. Protectors can extract significant profits from protecting kidnapping gangs: they can charge the criminals for protection and the families for interceding on behalf of the hostages. However, harbouring kidnappers or pirates often creates considerable political and economic costs. In Chapter 3, I analyse the geography of Somali piracy to show why local and regional protectors rarely choose to support kidnappers.

By analysing kidnapping using protection theory, the puzzling observations in my Colombian acquaintance's story are all explained. The kidnap was the FARC's rational response to the attempted evasion of the expected protection payment. The US$2,000 payment would have been a small burden on the firm. It was still in the firm's interest to fulfil their contract and continue trading in the town after paying the US$10,000 'fine'. The town would benefit from the firm's investment—so the FARC cell chose the long-term protection relationship over making a quick buck from the hostage. The firm's manager indicated that he had learned his lesson—so the kidnappers released the hostage immediately. After the ransom was paid, everyone reverted to equilibrium behaviour: the firm paid the extortion money and the FARC did not harass them. The agents of the state simply accepted the situation. With specialist advice, such local solutions can also be extended to foreign firms, tourists, and NGOs. Part II of the book builds on the insights from protection theory developed in Part I. Boutique insurers at Lloyd's of London employ a range of specialists to gather information on the local power relationships between formal law enforcement and extra-legal protectors. This knowledge (combined with their past claims experience) enables special risk insurers to predict kidnap threats, help their clients eliminate the majority of these threats, and limit the damage arising from the relatively few kidnapping cases that do occur.

2

Understanding Patterns of Kidnapping

One night of anarchy does more harm than a hundred years of tyranny.

Iraqi and Syrian proverb

The implosion of the Venezuelan economy is [a] dynamic and evolving driver for kidnapping . . . With the devaluation of the Venezuelan bolivar, foreign cash is king and kidnapping has become a favoured method of acquiring it. Today, the growing reluctance of gangs to accept ransom payments in local currency has put high-net-worth individuals and anyone perceived to have access to foreign currency back in their crosshairs . . . [A]ffluent Caracas neighbourhoods such as Las Mercedes, La Castellana and Country Club have become staging grounds for brazen abductions.

Control Risks, 24 November 2016

Protection Theory and Kidnapping

What do the Italian mafia, Mexican drug cartels, Colombian rebels, Naxalite insurgents in India, Islamist movements such as the Taliban, ISIL (Islamic State of Iraq and the Levant)/Daesh, Abu Sayyaf, Boko Haram and Al Shabaab, and the clans on Somalia's Puntland and Galmuduq coast have in common?

All of them are (or were) infamous for kidnapping (or piracy). All these groups are also extra-legal organizations that share an important ambition with the state: to govern territory. There is great variation in the size of the territories these groups control. A mafia family may control just a small part of a city. Drug cartels seek to govern larger areas suitable for drug production or convenient smuggling routes, while rebels may aim to replace the current government or carve out a new state in a peripheral region. Different groups tap various sources of revenue, but all of them extort money from households, merchants, and firms in their territory. In addition, many also prey on domestic or international trade routes, pipelines, airports, or harbours. Some control access to natural resources or drugs.

Extra-legal organizations differ in how they interact with the local population. Where the state is absent, or perceived as corrupt or unresponsive to local needs, extra-legal groups often provide order and a measure of much-appreciated security to the wider population. In some cases, they offer services such as education, healthcare, and charity to the poor—and as a result have a degree of legitimacy among locals. Most people remember the infamous Colombian drugs boss Pablo Escobar for atrocious acts of violence and murder—but 'Pablito' remains a hero to many of Medellín's poor who benefitted from his charity.[3] Rebels can thus replace the state in the hearts and minds of the local population: what looks like 'extortion' to outsiders may be perceived by locals as a legitimate 'tax'. If national governments (or their international supporters) challenge extra-legal groups, the usual result is disorder and instability and, in some cases, civil war. Concurrently, we also often observe a surge in kidnapping.

In this chapter, I therefore analyse the role of a wide range of extra-legal groups in kidnap for ransom. At the country level, kidnap risks are strongly associated with the presence of extra-legal groups that challenge the government over territorial control. But at the local level, mafia and rebel presence does not predict crime. Kidnap hotspots are often highly localized. Even at the height of civil wars, some districts and municipalities rarely see kidnaps or other forms of crime. Interestingly, many of the most peaceful districts are tightly controlled by extra-legal groups. As a tourist, I have marvelled over the counter-intuitive exclamation of my local hosts in Naples or Palermo: 'It's perfectly safe here. It's mafia territory.' The Cali drug cartel's chilling campaign 'Cali limpa, Cali linda' (clean Cali, beautiful Cali) cruelly 'cleansed' central areas of the city of prostitutes, the homeless, and petty thieves.[4] Similarly, when ISIL/Daesh militias took over control of Raqqa, they not only found themselves in charge of organizing postal services and rubbish collections, but also of public order. The militants quickly devoted resources to policing and consumer protection—thereby demonstrating their ambition to create a functioning state.[5] Many Somali expats take their children on holiday in Somaliland. Although internationally unrecognized, Somaliland's government has created a more secure environment than the official government in Mogadishu, where kidnap risks are 'extreme'.[6] Rebels, traditional elites, and mafias can act as capable protectors and frightening kidnappers.

In this chapter I put forward the hypothesis that kidnapping hotspots develop where there is a disequilibrium in the market for protection. In equilibrium, everyone knows who to pay protection money to. Kidnaps only occur where people are unaware of the protector's existence, try to avoid, or cannot afford to be seen to be making protection payments. The next section introduces protection theory. I then classify different types of protectors and explore how they relate to the state in the protection theory framework. We will then examine the circumstances under which mafias, cartels, and rebel groups resort to violence and kidnapping.

Protection Theory

Every exchange contains a risk of predation, cheating, and unfulfilled promises. We work for a salary, which may or may not be paid at the end of the month. We pay online and in advance for goods and services. Will the seller dispatch my new computer? Does my bargain five-star holiday resort even exist? We buy goods and services whose quality or authenticity we are unable to ascertain. Did Picasso really paint this? Suppliers make huge investments into production lines—but will Siemens or BMW buy the products next year? We take the pills our doctors prescribe, but are they safe and will they help? If I have a baby, will the father contribute to its upbringing? When a curious child asks us why all of this (usually) works, we might answer that division of labour and exchange are based on 'trust'. But we don't trust blindly. We rely on rules, norms, and effective enforcement institutions that provide incentives for people to fulfil their obligations.[7]

But who makes and enforces these rules? If you grew up in the Global North, you tend to assume that it is 'the state'. There are laws, which demarcate the boundary between the legal and the illegal and set out the duties and obligations of people engaging in exchanges. The police, civil servants, and courts uphold standards, enforce contracts, and adjudicate in disputes. But people in 'failed states' and remote provinces of weak states also build houses, raise children, produce goods, trade, save, and invest. Clearly, governance can be provided privately and informally.

Protection theory describes the properties of 'protection' as a privately provided service. A 'protector' establishes a monopoly on violence in a territory. He defends the life, liberty, and property rights of individuals within his territory and orders exchanges between them.[8] Without the assurance that property rights will be respected, the weak have no incentive to produce a surplus. The cultivation of the nutritionally poor and toxic bitter cassava plant as a main food staple in the Democratic Republic of the Congo is an excellent example of a survival strategy in the absence of effective protection. The cassava tubers grow so deeply in the ground that they survive slash and burn attacks. Harvesting and preparing them is so labour-intensive that they are not worth looting. Congolese women spend many hours every day digging up, peeling, soaking, drying, pounding, sieving, and cooking cassava. This back-breaking labour just about ensures their families' survival—though the cyanide in the plant slowly poisons their children. A capable protector would transform their lives.

Reliable enforcement of property rights encourages people to engage in the production of higher-value goods and services. Protectors encourage specialization by facilitating trade and enforcing contracts, thereby reducing the incentive to cheat a weaker counterparty. The division of labour only became attractive because of the emergence of specialists enforcing promises and providing security. The protector has an absolute or comparative advantage in the production of violence. There are significant economies of scale. For example, it is cheaper to police a market than posting guards at each shop. In equilibrium, there is therefore only one protector in each domain. Protectors with a reputation for fierce and effective violence do not invite many challengers and rarely expend resources to demonstrate their might.

Of course, the protectors must be paid for this service. Because they have the monopoly on violence, protectors can set the price. Protection is potentially highly lucrative. It is not surprising that the Neolithic archaeological record shows that as soon as agriculture facilitated the production of significant surpluses we see unequal income distribution and hierarchy: the protector can take the lion's share of any surplus—if necessary by force. Yet, the protector does not take all the surplus, as a roving bandit would. In the long run, the stationary bandit can extract greater total revenue from the territory by protecting producers and limiting tax extraction.[9]

Protection Theory and State Formation

Economists, historians, and political theorists have used protection theory to explain the emergence of the modern state.[10] The political scientist Margaret Levi analyses the incentives of a predatory but rational ruler who has successfully established a monopoly on violence within his territory.[11] The ruler aims to maximize his profit from controlling territory in the long term. By creating monitoring and enforcement institutions, the ruler lowers transactions costs and raises the potential output of the territory. But people will only exert effort in production and trade if the ruler refrains from excessive taxation. The 'theory of plunder' states that for efficient tax collection, rulers must be able to commit to not taking away their subject's wealth if they fully comply with the tax demands.[12]

The ruler incurs a cost in raising revenue. It is costly to create compliance by direct one-on-one coercion. Also, unless the cost of exit is prohibitively high, people (and firms) vote with their feet if taxes are collected by violent thugs. The total profit from ruling the territory will rise considerably, if the ruler can encourage their subjects' acquiescence to paying taxes or tributes. Tax compliance is at best quasi-voluntary: people choose to pay taxes because they know they would be punished if they did not. In return for cost-saving compliance, people usually demand some additional benefits (as well as restraint) from their ruler. Modern states with their constitutions mandating checks and balances and redistribution (at least towards a minimal winning coalition) can be interpreted as the outcome of a process of bargaining between the ruler and the ruled. The form of government (tyranny, oligarchy, and democracies with various franchise rules) determines which proportion of the population the ruler must bargain with.[13]

At each point in time, the ruler makes a rough estimate whether the marginal costs of the current revenue-collecting strategy outweigh their return. If not, processes and institutions may be changed. The sociologist and historian Charles Tilly argues that external wars play an important role in the state-building process: during military conflicts the ruler's revenue needs escalate. Widening the tax base requires a bigger tax-collecting apparatus and bargaining with more social groups.[14] Wars can also be funded by borrowing, but lenders will insist on credible commitment mechanisms—'checks and balances'—to encourage the ruler to repay the loan rather than killing his creditors.[15]

When the ruler's hold on power becomes insecure, there are two alternatives: either agree to diluting power and sharing future revenues with those whose support he needs—or return to the ways of the roving bandit. In many European nations, rulers repeatedly chose to expand the electoral franchise, eventually leading to parliamentary democracies. If politicians administer the territory in their own rather than in the public interest, they can be replaced at the next election. However, massive capital flight from the poorest African nations and foreign rulers' luxurious *pieds-à-terre* in London, New York, and Geneva, demonstrate that state-building is not a one-way street. Over the last thirty years, Swiss banks have returned over US$2 billion of misappropriated funds from 'politically exposed persons' to plundered nations.[16] It is likely to be just the tip of the iceberg of elite theft.

Protection Theory and the Mafia

Protection theory has also been applied extensively in the study of crime.[17] The term 'organized crime' is widely used as a catch-all phrase for any grouping of criminals who cooperate to break the law on a regular basis. However, specialization and division of labour also occurs in criminal markets. Protection theory distinguishes between those who *produce* crime (e.g. thieves) or illegal goods (e.g. drugs, forgeries), those who *trade* illicit goods (smugglers, traffickers, and dealers), and those who *order* the market.[18] The groups that order the market provide governance: they create and enforce a set of rules and norms to regulate exchange in the criminal economy.[19] To distinguish the governance providers in criminal markets from other types of criminal enterprises, protection theory uses the term 'mafia'.

Mafias specialize in violence: they settle disputes by (lethal) force.[20] Mafia governance is generally perceived as violent and parasitic. The mafia business model is to demand 'protection payments' from local firms and better-off households—where the implied threat is created by the extortionists' own thugs. However, the sociologists Diego Gambetta and Federico Varese propose a more nuanced view of mafia governance.[21] They stress that mafias also provide genuine services to those they protect. Firms that pay the *pizzo* are not just protected from the mafia, but also from thieves, cheating counterparties, and (police) harassment. If the mafia's threat is credible and its services genuine, most people will comply and mafias rarely need to use violence.

When a government criminalizes the sale of drugs or alcohol or prohibits gambling and prostitution, consumer demand for these goods and activities does not disappear entirely. The illicit market may be smaller, but it continues to operate underground. People who are cheated, maltreated, or expropriated in these markets cannot turn to the state for redress. Mafias thus satisfy a genuine need for private order and enforcement. The economist James Buchanan argued that from a public policy perspective it may be desirable to have an extralegal organization—such as a mafia—ordering these criminal markets.[22] If drugs are sold monopolistically, then prices are higher and consumption lower than when many providers compete. Cut-throat competition between drug dealers generally involves the sale of adulterated drugs at rock-bottom prices—with terrible health implications. If different gangs compete for territory or market share, ordinary citizens become innocent victims in the crossfire of gang warfare. The deadly fallout of the Mexican 'war on drugs' in which tens of thousands of civilians are slain as criminals fight to replace killed or jailed former cartel bosses demonstrates the problem. The violence only stops when the power vacuum is filled. Unfortunately, if the market is illicit, the demand for governance cannot be supplied by state forces.

Once a mafia has acquired a reputation for reliably punishing non-compliers in one criminal market (e.g. drugs), this can be leveraged to order a whole range of criminal activities (e.g. prostitution, trafficking, and the sale of smuggled goods). In addition, mafias may provide arbitration services in grey and licit markets. Where the legal system is slow, expensive, and opaque, people and firms operating in the legal economy may also come to prefer mafia rulings—if they are quick, fair, and reliably enforced. If people have significant doubts about the legitimacy of the government and the impartiality and honesty of its officers, mafias can cross the legal/illegal divide and unlock licit trade and investment. People lending in informal credit markets rely on mafias to retrieve loans and punish defaulters. Knowing this, borrowers are less tempted to renege on their commitments. Private enforcement (however unpleasant) thus facilitates access to credit (and hence investment or consumption-smoothing) in areas that are notoriously underbanked.

Critics of protection theory argue that it paints too benign a picture of 'racketeering'. Mafia rule is not 'fair' or social welfare-maximizing. Those who pay for mafia protection gain an advantage at the expense of their competitors, encouraging others to also seek mafia protection. Where there is no demand for mafia 'protection', the mafioso's thugs create the threat against which companies and families need to insure.[23] Mafias also restrict competition, allowing protected firms to charge higher prices. For example, the Italian mafia was hired to enforce cartel agreements among firms: the credible threat of violence made defection from the agreement unattractive. Firms sheltered from competition rarely operate efficiently, but those beholden to the mafia are often forced to employ other mafia clients—regardless of whether this makes economic sense. Ultimately, the direct and indirect costs of mafia protection are born by customers who pay higher prices and those who cannot find or create jobs in the local economy due to mafia practices.

When viewed through the lens of protection theory, the distinction between states and mafias is no longer clear. Some governments closely resemble extortion rackets. These are sometimes referred to as 'kleptocracies'. Examples are Congo (Zaire) under Mobutu Sese Seko, Nicaragua under the Somozas, Haiti under the Duvaliers, Uganda under Idi Amin, and the Philippines during the Marcos presidency. In exchange for supporting the centre, local strongmen squeezed the local population for taxes and kick-backs—providing very limited services, rules, and enforcement institutions to underpin productive economic activity.[24] Yet, a dismal economic performance affects the protectors' bottom line and the stability of their rule. Unless the territory contains high-value natural resources, protectors have an interest in maintaining their tax base by protecting residents' economic activities.

Mafias, States, and Proto-states

Some governments fail to project power outside the capital. If there are serious state failures, the demand for governance and protection is often filled by private, extra-legal protectors. Like mafias, traditional providers of governance (such as religious and tribal elites), warlords, rebels, and secessionist insurgents are alternative providers of governance. They seek to control territory and maintain militias to defend it. Tax extraction by traditional informal protectors is often highly ritualized. Because compliance appears voluntary, it may not be immediately recognized as a protection payment.

In pre-colonial Africa, traders were expected to pay 'tribute' to chiefs and give significant 'gifts' to tribal elders before conducting business.[25] 'Gift-giving' and 'entertaining' remains an important part of business culture in many countries—and woe betide those who offend against the local etiquette. In the Middle East, travellers such as Wilfred Thesiger and Lawrence of Arabia employed local 'guides' to ensure their safe passage through tribal lands. Nowadays, tourists are well advised to join an organized tour. Many religious institutions were funded by tithes and temple offerings. Hindu temples in India still hold vast gold reserves.[26] *Sharia* law recognizes four different Islamic taxes. Three of them were originally punitive taxes, applied to residents and traders who refused to convert to Islam (*dhimmis*). The *jizya* was a per capita tax, the *kharaj* taxed non-Muslim landholdings and their produce, and the *ushr* was applied to foreign merchandise. For Muslims, the payment of *zakat* is a religious obligation: non-payment may be punishable by a fine, imprisonment, or death. Thus, Islamist rebels have a range of religiously legitimized tax instruments at their disposal. To scholars studying informal governance, all these arrangements look like protection payments.

Warlords, rebels, and insurgents often graft on to traditional forms of governance. Many start by ordering transactions in the 'grey' or 'parallel' economy—i.e. activities conducted outside the control of the state where market participants avoid taxes, duties, or other obligations. Some derive significant income from the unlicensed exploitation of natural resources.[27] As extra-legal groups grow, they erode state capacity and are drawn into adjudicating and protecting ever more exchanges. In areas of limited statehood, there is a large grey zone between protection and extortion. Rebel movements and traditional protectors differ from mafias in that the relationship between the protector and the protected is more reciprocal. Civilians may either support, passively obey, or resist rebel rule. The minimal requirement which people have of their protector is that their possessions and physical integrity are secure once they have paid protection money (or tax). If aspiring protectors are unable to deliver basic security, people only pay whoever directly threatens them. This is an expensive way to collect tax.

Rebels therefore aim to consolidate their rule to maximize their revenue—if not to line their own pockets then to raise funds for further campaigns to capture more territory. Rebels can gain legitimacy in the eyes of the population by providing more than (selective) security: the intuition is the same as Margaret Levis' argument regarding state formation. Rebels' advantages from governing territory are maximized by a combination of governance institutions (to raise total output), a tax regime that does not undermine effort or investment, and a mixture of sticks (violence) and carrots (services) to encourage quasi-voluntary compliance with the tax demands.

Most traditional forms of governance have therefore developed relatively sophisticated bodies of customary or religious law. Many rebel movements satisfy the demand for governance by convening courts for arbitration. The Frente Farabundo Martí of El Salvador, the Liberation Tigers of Tamil Eelam of Sri Lanka, the FARC of Colombia and the Revolutionary United Front of Sierra Leone all conducted trials in rudimentary courts, where a limited degree of due process was guaranteed.[28] In addition, some extra-legal groups actively participate in the provision of education, health, food, and infrastructure, while others leave civilian elites to organize their provision.[29] Revolutionary socialist and Marxist rebel movements captured the imagination of millions with the promise of radical social change—but also by providing free services in disadvantaged and remote regions before taking their fight to the cities. Highly lethal terror groups have often grown from organizations with a significant presence in social security provision and education among the neglected, poor, and disadvantaged.[30]

Thus, rebel movements are more than mafias, yet they are not quite states. Where local state provision is disappointing or corrupt, rebels can 'outgovern' the government. Where civilians feel that rebels are responsive to local needs, they will shelter, provide material support, and even join the rebels. When insurgents and terrorists are celebrated as 'freedom fighters' and 'nationalist heroes' by those living under their rule, one may surmise that the rebels have addressed deep failures of state governance. The US Army's Counterinsurgency Field Manual explicitly recognizes that successful asymmetric warfare not only requires military superiority, but outcompeting rebels in public service provision. 'Winning hearts and minds' means persuading the civilian population that their long-term interest lies in supporting the counterinsurgency—regardless of whether they approve of the presence of foreign soldiers.[31] Indeed, in Iraq US military leaders who listened carefully to local grievances and met civilian needs were significantly more successful in preventing rebel attacks.[32]

It therefore makes sense to think of various types of protectors as being on a continuum. All protectors are similar in their ambition to govern territory and establish a monopoly of violence within it. The key distinction is the degree to which those who govern are responsive and accountable to the local population. Those under mafia rule cannot change their ruler or appeal against their judgements. In democratic societies, citizens' rights are protected by codified rules enforced through an independent judiciary and citizens can replace their rulers at elections. This distinction puts mafias at one end of the spectrum and democratic states at the other. Warlords, rebel movements, traditional and religious elites, and autocratic states are somewhere in-between.[33]

Informal Protectors in Kidnap for Ransom

Kidnap and hijack for ransom can also be examined through the lens of protection theory. There is considerable scope for specialization within this business. The kidnappers are the *producers* of crime. For opportunistic kidnapping the main qualification is either physical strength or skill and experience with a weapon. For 'miracle fishing' at roadblocks a suitable location must be identified, but thereafter the main qualification is the physical skill (or strength in numbers) required to subdue the victims. For targeted kidnaps, extensive surveillance and planning are required to minimize the chances of the victim escaping or being killed or the raid being interrupted by security forces. People deliberately targeted for kidnapping are usually aware of the danger. The kidnappers must overcome any defensive measures put in place by the intended target, such as armed guards, armoured vehicles, and fortified compounds. Usually such kidnaps are carried out by multi-member armed gangs.

Ransoming hostages requires completely different skills. Street criminals with a VIP hostage face a dilemma: what next? To sell hostages back to their firm or family for a high price requires patience and experience in conducting covert negotiations. Each contact with the stakeholders gives away valuable information about the location of the hostage or those conducting the negotiation. The *trader* thus needs to have a communication strategy which minimizes his risk of apprehension. The criminal negotiator must ascertain what the victim might be worth and push the counterparty to settle towards the top of their price range. A trader in hostages will seek to build a reputation for returning live hostages at premium prices. To complete the deal, the trader needs to establish a secure payment mechanism. Ransom payments can be intercepted by the police or rival gangs and those delivering the ransom should themselves remain secure during the transaction. Finally, the released hostage should not be able to lead the police back to the trader's lair. The preponderance of 'express' kidnaps—where a minimal ransom is paid out by an ATM—demonstrates that a meaningful ransom negotiation is well beyond the skills set of the ordinary thug with a strong arm, sharp knife, or (replica) gun.[34]

From the description above, we see that a sophisticated hostage *trader* would greatly benefit from having a *protector*. A capable protector can offer a safe location to hold the hostage and from which to communicate without being apprehended. Police or military commanders need to weigh the human and financial cost of forcibly entering informally controlled territory against the benefits of an attempted rescue. The protector can affect this cost–benefit calculation in two ways. First, by always shooting hostages at the first sign of a rescue operation being mounted. Second, by ensuring that all traders operating from their territory treat their hostages well. This ensures that 'commercial resolution' of hostage crises will become the favoured option of the stakeholders, rather than involving the police. Finally, a protector in full control over his territory can smooth the ransom for hostage exchange. Opportunists, police, and rivals would not dare to enter the protector's territory to intercept the payment, but the messenger with the ransom will be protected from harassment. Often the messenger departs with the hostage as soon as the money has been counted. In many countries it is operationally irrelevant that the police know where the Boss, God-father, or Don lives: they would not dare to apprehend him anyway.

When we analyse kidnap for ransom in this way, we immediately realize that most of the power rests with the protector. If the protector wishes to kidnap, he can hire criminals or send his foot soldiers. The kidnapper himself is stuck with an awkward asset that is almost impossible to monetize. The trader cannot conduct his business in peace without a hostage and a safe haven. Without a protector, there won't be a secondary market for hostages either: the trade is vulnerable to cheating on both sides. The trader will prefer to hand over as little of the ransom as possible, but the violent kidnapper may take everything from him. Anticipating enforcement problems, the kidnapper may prefer a low but relatively secure quick payment at the ATM. However, protectors can enforce and adjudicate in the matter—or acquire the hostage themselves and employ a negotiator. If ransoms are an important source of funds, the protector will offer good prices for hostages to incentivize ordinary criminals and opportunists to exert greater effort in the production of hostages. They will reward the traders for squeezing more out of each hostage. But ultimately, most of the profit will remain with the protector.

By analysing kidnap for ransom through the lens of protection theory we have arrived at an interesting contradiction. On the one hand, the aim of the protector is to control and tax economic transactions in their territory. In the long run this is less costly if the protector provides valued services to the population and the protector's demands are perceived as being legitimate. Security, order, and fair dispute resolution are among the most valuable service a protector can offer. This clearly includes protecting citizens from being kidnapped. In equilibrium, everyone will pay 'taxes' to the protector, who in turn will neither kidnap nor permit anyone else to kidnap in his territory. On the other hand, protection theory suggests that protectors in full control of their territory are uniquely placed to extract the maximum benefit from kidnap for ransom. In the absence of a protector, abductions and hijackings will be very short and cheaply resolved—unless the thugs lose their nerve and shoot their hostages. The rest of this chapter analyses under what circumstances a protector will engage in kidnap for ransom.

Why Is Mafia Rule Violent?

The question of why mafia governance is often associated with violence was first formally analysed by the economist Alasdair Smith and the sociologist Federico Varese.[35] At the root of the problem is an information problem. For perfect quasi-compliance, people must be able to correctly identify the protector's agents collecting the protection payment. This works well in small territories and tight-knit communities: 'There's Uncle Pino and every month you have to give him an envelope with €2,000.'[36] If Uncle Pino falls out with the boss, this is communicated to the relevant mafia clients, or Pino leaves the territory. Often, he dies. In larger territories, the tax collector could wear the protector's uniform or insignia, so people know whom to pay. In Japan, the yakuza gangs are not illegal, and their members are instantly recognizable by their tattoos and missing digits.

If the protector rules openly, violence is largely unnecessary. As part of Colombia's 1998 peace talks, the government granted a 16,000 square mile sanctuary to FARC rebels to govern as they saw fit. A visiting journalist described it as follows: 'the rebels run their own fiefdom, dubbed Farclandia by most. Security forces are forbidden to enter, and the FARC are the law. Patrolling the streets of San Vicente, the biggest town in the zone and the capital of Farclandia, uniformed guerrillas can be seen browsing in the shops and imposing order. This is the safest place in the country.'[37] Similarly, a security consultant working in Mexico explained that in some cartel-controlled areas you can ignore extortion calls made by phone. 'You just pay the man in the passenger seat of the pick-up truck with 6 men openly bearing arms on the back.'[38] With such insouciant displays of power, there is no need for actual violence.

Kidnap statistics compiled by the Colombian Centre for National Memory record the annual number of kidnaps in over a thousand Colombian municipalities. The data show that kidnapping was rare in the FARC heartlands.[39] In 'Farclandia's' capital San Vicente only one kidnap was reported in 2001 and three in 2002. One of the latter was the infamous abduction of Colombia's Green Party presidential candidate Ingrid Betancourt. Her team had rashly decided to travel overland towards the FARC capital when their army helicopter ride was inexplicably cancelled. Local FARC operatives grasped this unexpected opportunity at the first roadblock. Protectors protect (paying) insiders, not outsiders.

Another excellent example of relative stability under a capable informal protector is the city of Medellín (Figure 2.1). Of 1,920 kidnaps recorded from 1971–2010, only eighty-eight occurred in the nineteen years from 1971 to 1989 when the city was controlled by Pablo Escobar's Medellín cartel. In 1990, when Colombian government forces cracked down on the cartel and hunted for Escobar, there were 108 kidnappings in a single year. In 1991 Escobar went to jail and Medellín became the world's murder capital with 381 deaths per 100,000 inhabitants.[40]

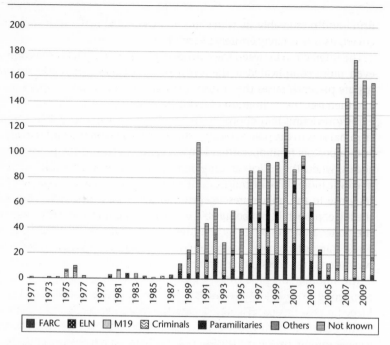

Figure 2.1. Annual number of kidnaps in Medellín municipality, Colombia

Source: Centro National de Memoria Historica SECUESTRO 1970–2010 dataset available at http://www.centrodememoriahistorica.gov.co/micrositios/informeGeneral/basesDatos. html (accessed March 2018).

Kidnapping occurred with frightening regularity over the next two decades. What explains this sea change?

Smith and Varese's model analyses situations where the informal protector (in their case the mafia) operates in the shadows. The collectors of protection payments must blend into the street scene. The extortion demand is set low enough that compliance is less costly than the expected cost of non-compliance. But if everyone unquestioningly pays whoever comes in the name of 'the boss', it is very tempting for impostors to also turn up on people's doorsteps and demand payment. While it would be unwise for the uninitiated to imitate a yakuza tattoo, anyone can don a hoodie or mutter darkly about 'the Godfather'. Households approached for multiple payments will eventually rebel against the excessive taxation and withhold the money. An impostor who is denied payment just disappears, but the mafia will punish the non-complier. This restores the full information equilibrium for the household or firm—and presumably its wider social circle. If the mafia must remain covert, its rule is rarely entirely peaceful.

The interaction between the extortion racket and its victims becomes even more complicated if there is a police presence in the territory. A state presence raises the enforcement cost of the protection racket—and therefore the willingness of its targets to pay. Instead of acquiescing, extortion victims may choose to report extortion demands, threats, and criminal acts to the police. Ideally, the police would prevent both mafias and impostors from operating. However, the mafia and the police may coexist where the police can only help with some (low) probability. This makes it more difficult but not impossible for the mafia to operate. In response to the police presence, the protector becomes more violent: the lower probability of being able to carry out a crime under the nose of the police must be offset by the higher expected cost of punishment. Thus, state intervention to erode mafia control can be counterproductive. Often it escalates rather than reduces violence.

The information problem gets even worse when there are multiple, competing extra-legal protectors (as well as impostors and the police). Medellín post-Escobar (Figure 2.1) and the terrible escalation of violence in the wake of Mexico's 'war on drugs' illustrate what happens when there is gang warfare over territory. There is no longer a reliable protector but plenty of people demanding protection money and punishing the non-compliers in the confused, hassled, and frightened population. Sudden eruptions of violence can also be observed in remote economic backwaters which suddenly attract massive investment, e.g. for oil or mining installations. Almost inevitably, rebel groups, criminal gangs, and perhaps local self-defence militias will appear in the area to divert some of the revenues towards themselves. The government will try to prevent this by sending soldiers to protect the investors and claim the revenues for the central fiscal budget (or the elite's 'special reserves' in Panama or Switzerland). It usually takes some time before the new protection arrangements are worked out. Sometimes one group wins, often there is revenue sharing. For example, the soldiers might guard the oil facility itself, one rebel group the pipeline, and another the contractors, while a third articulates the demands of the local community in a corporate social responsibility programme. We will return to this in Chapter 5. Figure 2.2 shows this pattern in an oil-rich Colombian municipality in the province of Casanare. Violence, murders, and kidnapping escalated from 1996 as an oil pipeline was constructed to commercially exploit the Cupiagua oilfields. As in Figure 2.1, once kidnapping erupts it is notable that multiple groups abducted hostages. Every aspiring protector punished the non-compliers, but people probably simply didn't know whom to pay—until there was a hostage situation.

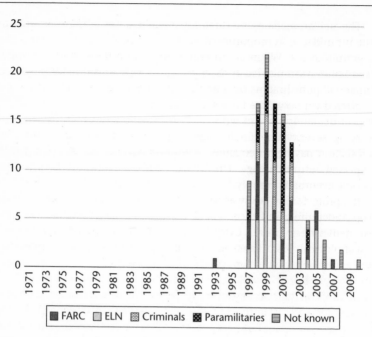

Figure 2.2. Annual number of kidnaps in Aguazul municipality, Colombia

Source: Centro National de Memoria Historica SECUESTRO 1970–2010 dataset available at http://www.centrodememoriahistorica.gov.co/micrositios/informeGeneral/basesDatos. html (accessed March 2018).

When Do Protectors Kidnap?

What kind of punishment will the informal protector inflict on non-compliers? On the one hand, the punishment must clearly distinguish between the mafioso and the impostor. If the mafia punishment is too difficult or dangerous for the impostor to imitate (bearing in mind that he will have both the police and the protector on his tail), it works as a credible signal that the extortion demand was made by a capable protector. The recipient knows how to act on this information. On the other hand, the cost of inflicting the punishment should not exceed the gain from improved 'tax' collection afterwards. Murdering people or destroying a victim's liveli-hood only works if it raises compliance among many others. If the problem is one of impostors, rather than one of general willingness to comply with mafia rule, very harsh penalties can easily backfire. Firms and high-net-worth individuals vote with their feet—often in large numbers—shrinking the protector's tax base.[41] Violence should therefore be used very judiciously.

The Sicilian mafia uses a carefully gradated approach. The severity of the intimidation is proportional to the resistance of the victim: it is not a gratuitous act. When an entrepreneur is unresponsive to the initial 'symbolic' warnings (such as glue in the locks), the mafia moves to 'material' punishments on a finely calibrated scale. Starting with a few shattered windows, the bosses' thugs progress to small robberies when repeat demands are also ignored. This may be followed by assaults of varying severity and finally vandalism or arson. At each point the protection payment demanded is lower than the material cost of the expected future damage. Unless the police can protect them, most people eventually comply.[42]

If a protector has ready access to sanctuary in which hostages can be kept indefinitely and cheaply, kidnap for ransom can be the ideal punishment strategy for an extortion racket. Kidnapping has a very high psychological cost. Targeted kidnappings send a strong signal that the extortion racket is both professional and powerful. However, unlike most other forms of violence, it does not destroy valuable assets. The firm can continue in business while the incident is resolved. If the stakeholders concede quickly, there is no need to escalate threats or violence. Compliant but poor local victims can be released immediately to raise their own ransom, saving everyone the hassle and unpleasantness of long incarcerations. The business-like efficiency experienced by my Colombian acquaintance in the FARC camp, and Somali pirates who often reassured frightened crew members that they would be on their way home as soon as the ship-owner stumped up a ransom, show that maltreatment is very much Plan B. If stakeholders are slow to respond and Plan B is implemented, we generally see a progressive escalation of threats and violence. If the survival of the hostage is crucial to the future success of his business or a firm's decision whether to remain in the area, he or she almost always survives. Otherwise, the final sanction is very much on the table. In Mexico, violent kidnapping gangs sometimes send back the bodies of chauffeurs and bodyguards kidnapped alongside their main targets to show they mean business. Or they kidnap a *paysan* alongside his boss for torture by proxy.[43]

There are two further reasons for using kidnap for ransom in an extortion context. First, a protector may not have sufficient information to set the rate of extortion at the revenue-maximizing level. Perhaps the group is new to an area, perhaps the victim has just arrived or is only there for a limited period. Just how rich is this peasant farmer—and what are his liquid assets? He does not want to be parted from his money and refuses to reveal his income. Will anyone important intercede on his behalf? How much protection money would you charge to a major

British construction company building a road or airport in your territory? What if the company is Chinese or Italian? How would the price
change if there were further projects down the line? A tax authority
would start by conducting an audit, but firms do not enter sensitive
conversations with informal protectors voluntarily. A careful ransom
negotiation can help to resolve such information problems.

Second, internationally active firms have become highly sensitive to
anything that might be interpreted as 'corruption'. Paying protection
money to rebels will require some explanation or creative accounting.
We will return to this issue in Chapter 5. However, most firms allow
their employees to pay a bribe to avoid an extra-legal detention. Paying
off the rogue policeman who threatens to arrest you for an imaginary
speeding offence is 'not corruption'. Neither is paying a (substantial)
ransom to retrieve abducted employees.

Kidnapping Indicates Disequilibrium in the Market for Protection

Protection theory provides us with a novel perspective to interpret
kidnap for ransom: kidnapping of residents is disequilibrium behaviour.
In equilibrium, protection is supplied monopolistically in the territory.
It does not matter whether the protector is the state or some form of
extra-legal organization. The revenue-maximizing ruler creates a credible threat of violence and sets taxes at a level that encourages compliance. With full information and perfect enforcement there is no need
for actual violence. However, if people don't believe that the demand for
protection money is enforceable, or they don't know whom (or how) to
pay, they refuse to do so, and the protector must act. Revenues and
customs write stiff letters, the mafia bosses' thugs throw bricks, and
rebels point guns. In certain circumstances, kidnapping will be the
sanction of choice for extra-legal protectors. It is analogous to a state's
decision to arrest and detain tax dodgers until they have paid their dues.

International kidnap statistics are dominated by local-on-local kidnaps: in 2016, just 5 per cent of kidnaps reported in the media involved
foreigners.[44] Protection theory explains why the large majority of local
cases are peacefully resolved. It also helps to explain why foreign firms
and NGOs can operate relatively undisturbed in the most challenging
security environments. If there is a capable protector, effective long-
term security arrangements can be made. The greatest kidnap risks
occur in areas that are contested by different groups—and for firms
which are inexperienced at negotiating the local power landscape. It

would be naïve to expect protection solely from the central government in countries like Somalia, Mali, Libya, Yemen, and Afghanistan. Sure, the minister may be very keen to offer you an 'elite' army unit to guard your remote facility—for a substantial sum of money. In fact, it will be impossible to refuse the offer—though quite possibly the teenagers who arrive with their (t)rusty Kalashnikovs look rather scared and not at all like the SAS or the Navy Seals. They also mislaid the night-vision goggles you were charged good money for. Perhaps it is even worse when the government dispatches a battalion of heavily armed paramilitaries who terrorize the local population—wreaking havoc with your carefully crafted human rights record.[45] In Chapter 5, we will examine how you keep everyone safe if the richest opportunities are right in the middle of rebel territory.

This chapter focused on the incentives of different types of protectors to kidnap residents or firms operating in their territory—and their ability to protect them from other groups who might contest their control. But many hostages are outsiders: tourists who strayed from the beaten path, aid workers rushing to a crisis zone, journalists who crossed an invisible battle line, ships hijacked in transit, oil workers just across an international border. Here ransoming is a one-off event rather than part of a long-term tax and protection relationship. The analysis developed so far has highlighted that strong protectors are uniquely placed to maximize the return to kidnapping. Should the protector prey on outsiders—or offer protection to criminals who do so? Safe havens would help hostage traders to squeeze the maximum from each case— and the protector can cream off much of this. On the other hand, abducting foreigners or pilfering in someone else's territories is unlikely to go unchallenged. There are also internal political costs to protecting criminals—how does taking 'dirty' money affect the protector's perceived legitimacy among the public (and foreign donors)? Chapter 3 will examine the protector's choice in this respect.

3

The Protector's Choice

> Without a reliable working relationship with local fishermen, busi-
> nessmen and elders, we cannot plan and execute our mission. They
> are always rewarded handsomely!
>
> Former Somali pirate[1]

Kidnapping Outsiders

Somalia. Two films dominate the general public's perception of this
troubled country. *Black Hawk Down* portrays the bloody battle of
Mogadishu. The humanitarian intervention with mission creep, which
culminated in a deadly firefight in 1993 that left eighteen US soldiers
dead and seventy-three wounded still shapes Western attitudes to intervention in African civil wars. *Captain Phillips* is a tense survival thriller
about a merchant mariner taken hostage by Somali pirates. From 2009 to
2013 piracy and international counter-piracy efforts dominated the news
coverage from Somalia. But people also became aware of the pervasive,
abject poverty in the country. Somalia languishes at or near the bottom of
every international league table of economic and social development
indicators. Civil war and state collapse explain much of this miserable
situation. Since a bloody uprising toppled Siad Barre's dictatorship in
1991, Somali society has been so deeply divided that it has been impossible to re-establish a central, stable, and functioning government in
Mogadishu. Millions of civilians were caught in the shifting battle lines
between warlords, clans, and Islamic militias. They suffered indiscriminate
killings, assassinations, hostage-taking, rape, torture, displacement, theft
of land and property, and forced labour. *Sharia* courts handed out cruel,
inhuman, and degrading punishments in summary trials. In 2008, the
Islamist group Al Shabaab was proscribed by the United States, adding the

keyword terrorism to the long list of Somalia's problems. Dadaab, the world's largest refugee camp, sheltered nearly half a million Somali refugees in 2011. Somalia serves as the principal textbook example of state failure, state collapse, warlord rule, and anarchy.

At first sight, the image of Somalia as a war zone pillaged by roving bandits fits well with piracy. When there is no state, no law, and no police, the boundaries between the legal and illegal are fluid. Guns and heavier weapons were easily available and there was an abundance of young men experienced in using them. Merchant ships were traditionally unarmed and their crews could easily be overpowered. However, Somali piracy was not a hit-and-run affair. Ships were hijacked for ransom with negotiations dragging on for months and sometimes for years. This required a supply infrastructure and regular contact with the land. How can you anchor a multi-million-dollar asset in plain view of the coast, if the land is anarchic? This puzzle has motivated much of my research on Somali piracy.[2]

Somali pirates knew how to keep hijacked ships safe. The Automated Information System (AIS) is mandatory for all international ships over 300 tonnes, cargo vessels over 500 tonnes, and all types of passenger carriers. AIS transponders regularly emit information about the vessels' position, speed, and direction, giving us a (near real time) picture of the world's shipping traffic.[3] Archived information allows us to track the pirated ships' positions during their ordeals in Somalia. Most ships spent long periods at anchor close to coastal settlements. Some ships cruised slowly up and down hundreds of miles of coastline, dropping anchor in various locations. Other ships made excursions into the high seas as motherships or to pick up and deliver pirate action groups. They were not hassled by rival pirate groups or militias. No vessel was rehijacked for ransoming by another pirate group after being released by the original pirates. Yet, there are also large stretches of coastline where no pirated ship ever dropped anchor. Occasionally, some communities fought against pirates in their anchorage, a few even conducted long-range counter-piracy operations. So, on the one hand there were capable protectors who could secure pirates' 'property rights' over very long distances. On the other hand, some protectors chose counter-piracy over piracy.[4] What explains this choice?

Looking around the world, we observe the protectors' choice in many contexts. During the hiatus of Somali piracy after 2012, the Gulf of Guinea gained prominence in the International Maritime Bureau's piracy reports. Sea-jacking around the oil-rich Niger Delta is completely different in character from Somali piracy. If ships are taken, they are released as soon as their cargo of oil has been syphoned off. Abducted

investment in larger generators enabled communities to light their streets and markets at night. In Somaliland and Puntland, the light footprint of major cities is growing and intensifying, and new dots appear on the night-time lights map every year.

Somalia also remained integrated in regional trade networks during its long stint of statelessness.[10] Traders transported livestock from across the Horn of Africa to Somali ports for export. On their return journeys, they smuggled heavily taxed goods into Kenya and Ethiopia: a system sometimes described as a set of parallel conveyor belts.[11] Businesspeople built a competitive mobile telecommunications network to rival any in Africa. Somalis have mobile money, banking, and money transfer systems to facilitate domestic and international trade and handle transfers to and remittances from an estimated two million Somali diaspora members.[12] Expats have returned and built houses in their homeland. All this was largely accomplished without help from the central government. The state apparatus has been either entirely defunct or unable to project power beyond Mogadishu and a few nearby urban centres since 1991. In fact, on some measures standards of living have significantly improved since the fall of Siad Barre's predatory regime.[13] Scholars therefore see Somalia as a fascinating example of bottom-up design and the development of informal systems of regulation, jurisdiction, contract enforcement, and security provision in response to the prolonged absence of a central government.[14]

Who provides informal governance in Somalia? Throughout history, Somalis have heavily relied on kinship ties to structure social interactions: the patrilineal clan system. The clans' ancient, unwritten customary laws (*xeer*)—augmented by *Sharia* law as necessary—provide a widely accepted dispute settlement mechanism. *Xeer* strongly encourages conflict resolution through negotiation and consensus-building rather than settling disputes by force. To prevent disagreements between individuals or groups from escalating into damaging blood feuds, respected clan elders mediate between the conflict parties. The extent of the damage and culpability are established by negotiation. To settle a transgression, the perpetrator's *diya*-paying group pays a mutually agreed financial penalty to the victim and his *diya* group. *Diya* groups are kinship groups within the clan and the smallest political units in Somali society. *Diya* group members are jointly responsible for avenging injury against their members and share equally in any reparations or fines.[15] Initially, *xeer* was used to resolve unlawful killings, disputes over grazing or water rights, and cattle-theft, but it has proved highly adaptable. For example, *diya* groups provide informal car insurance for their members. After an accident, elders negotiate the amount of compensation due and *diya* members are phoned for their contributions to settle the case.[16] This joint financial responsibility creates a strong element of peer monitoring of individuals' actions. In addition, the elders can mobilize clan militias to enforce agreements and defend the clan's interests and territory.

Negotiations between elders are sometimes complex and drawn-out. *Xeer* can be contradictory or open to several interpretations—especially in new business areas. Overall, *xeer* works best within a clan. A clan's members share a single law, trust is high, and interactions are frequent and long term. The success of Somaliland in creating security and relatively inclusive and stable governance institutions is largely due to the dominance of a single clan—the Isaaq—in the territory.[17] Similarly, the Darod clan has created fairly stable government structures in Puntland. However, Somalia has three further major clan families: the Hawiye, the Dir, and the Rahanwein, as well as several minor clans and ethnic minority groups. *Xeer* and its interpretations are not harmonized across these groups. A long history of opportunism of locally powerful clans in disputes with minorities over access to valuable resources and political power often creates an atmosphere of suspicion and—occasionally—outright hostility. Bitter memories of discord and abuse can make cross-clan negotiations very difficult if not impossible. In southern Somalia, where multiple clans live side by side, intergroup conflict is so entrenched that it can only be suppressed by powerful warlords, violent Islamist movements, or foreign (usually African Union) troops.

To access the land, pirate groups had to make a deal with whichever clan, warlord, or Islamist movement controlled the relevant stretch of coast. Such deals went far beyond passive acceptance of a pirate presence. The local militia would have to protect the ships and the anchorage from opportunistic thieves or rival clans. Elders would have to strike deals with other clans (or Islamists) to facilitate safe passage for hijacked ships along the coast towards their anchorage. After release, vessels were highly vulnerable and needed *abaan*: passes of safe transit issued to those who had paid protection money.[18] Obtaining *abaan* was perhaps easier for cross-clan pirate groups where everyone stood to gain—but then the elders were needed to ensure a peaceful and fair distribution of the ransoms. Finally, the protectors had a joint interest in the smooth commercial resolution of hijacking incidents. Ship-owners' toleration of Somali piracy relied on ship, cargo, and crews remaining safe and pirates being honourable and reliable counterparties. If pirates had deliberately killed or maimed hostages, started firefights on board ships, and had damaged or run vessels aground, the navies' counter-piracy approach would have become much more robust. Elders thus had to check rogue behaviour and uphold norms ensuring the decent treatment of hostages. Although individual pirates might have benefitted from escalating violence, their clans were involved in a repeated game and a network of obligations which rewarded a minimal level of violence.

Considering that Somali piracy was an illegal business conducted in stateless territory it was surprisingly formalized. During counter-piracy operations, officers occasionally found handwritten contracts setting out the rewards promised to individual pirates, as well as codes of conduct. They also determined the profit shares for different types of contributors: investors, pirates, guards, and various landside supporters. Troublemakers would forfeit shares and face physical punishment.[19] 'If any of us shoots or kills another he will automatically be executed and his body thrown to the sharks', reported one pirate. Merely pointing a gun at another pirate would be punished with a 5 per cent reduction in the offender's profit share.[20] Pirates did not intentionally hurt hostages: anyone caught abusing captives was punished with a fine.[21] Another rule threatened that 'Anyone shooting a hostage will immediately be shot'.[22] Pirate captain Boyah even had a copy of the 'pirate handbook' printed.[23]

The legal scholar Gillian Hadfield finds that a wide range of innovative businesses use formal contracts to set out the mutual obligations of business partners, even if third-party enforcement institutions are weak or non-existent. Such contracts serve as 'scaffolds' aiding the informal enforcement of contracts. When rules and obligations have been formally agreed and are therefore common knowledge, it becomes possible to punish rule violations and non-compliance informally.[24] Indeed, there is evidence that the pirate contracts were enforced. Those who committed 'crimes' within the piracy business faced swift and draconian punishments. A ship's captain reported how people trying to take more than their ransom share 'had their hands slammed in doors as punishment'. This looks like a soft version of the *Sharia* sanction on theft (chopping off one hand), but it would explain why very few ransom drops degenerated into violent brawls and shoot-outs. A Puntland pirate interviewed by phone even referred to a 'court at Bedey' where piracy-related disputes could be resolved.[25] A significant governance effort was thus made to enforce rules to keep Somali piracy non-violent. What was in it for the protectors?

The Protector's Reward

The claim that Somali piracy was about protecting fishermen's livelihoods against illegal fishing and dumping is a persistent narrative.[26]

However, Somali piracy was always about making profit. Somali pirates rarely attacked foreign fishermen: even in the 1980s and 1990s they favoured cargo ships over trawlers.[27] Somalia's political elite—the noble clans—are pastoralists who care neither for seafood nor for marginal coastal communities. 'Speak not to me with a fish-eating mouth' is a common taunt and insult. Fish is not part of the traditional Somali diet: annual fish consumption is among the lowest in the world.[28] Although piracy had the side effect of driving away foreign trawlers, it had a devastating impact on local fisheries: pirates hired the best navigators, disrupted ice supplies, and drove away potential customers for fish and fish products. Fishermen fearful of entanglement with naval patrols lost access to the richest fishing grounds.[29]

To explain the protector's choice, we therefore examine the elite's financial incentives. Most of the proceeds of piracy were creamed off by the rich and powerful. If you pick a boy from a surging crowd on the beach clamouring to join your pirate gang, you offer a risk-adjusted, normal wage. We observe the same in drugs gangs: low-ranking crack dealers get such a poor salary that most of them live with their mums.[30] At first sight, the pirate contract looked attractive: a successful pirate could win his entire expected lifetime earnings in a single successful mission.[31] However, the pirates offered a 'no-win-no-fee' contract: the promised premium compensated the aspiring pirate for potentially wasting his time (in unsuccessful raids or in prison) and the family for the possible loss of the boy. In a country with low life expectancy, low per capita gross domestic product, and chronic underemployment, you could take your pick by offering just US$30,000 for a novice and up to US$75,000 for an experienced firearms expert.[32] In addition, the first pirate to board the target would earn himself a Landcruiser: the first head above the ship's railing was the one most likely to be shot at or coshed. Although jealous peers would whisper about the pirates' flash 'haram gaari' (illicit cars), many men went into piracy to create mustaq-bal (future) for their families and earn start-up capital for a business.[33] Similarly, money is money. Investors got a normal, risk-adjusted return. Yes, the winners would quadruple their capital on average. But many investors lost their stakes as skiffs were sunk in bad weather, by navies, or by their target's on-board security teams. Many attack teams came back empty-handed. The World Bank calculated that on average just 5.4 per cent of the ransom would be spent on personnel and 8.3 per cent compensating investors and creditors. The residual would go to those who facilitated piracy from the landside.[34]

The World Bank's 2013 report on Somali piracy and the joint World Bank/United Nations Office on Drugs and Crime 2013 report 'Pirate

Trails' explored and documented the various ways in which the elites benefitted from piracy. Pirates seeking shelter for a hijacked ship immediately had to stump up an 'anchorage fee'—reported to be between US$100,000 and US$300,000. Alternatively, they were charged a share of the final ransom of 10, 20, or 30 per cent. Administrative officials and regional politicians in Puntland's capital Garowe also received money to turn a blind eye to piracy.[35] The creation of the well-armed Puntland Maritime Police Force (PMPF) in 2010, with US$50 million donated by the United Arab Emirates, lent huge weight to officials' demands for protection payments. Indeed, the force was rarely deployed on counter-piracy operations, but devoted most of its time to hassling President Farole's opposition.[36] In central Somalia, Al Shabaab representatives demanded a 'non-interference fee' from pirates. Any piracy business within reach of an Al Shabaab militia unit was well advised to pay up. As one pirate explained: 'We are just the same people with different tasks and dreams. We like to party, we pay them a "protection fee" at checkpoints so it is a win-win for both parties.'[37]

Having secured elite support, pirates still had to hire guards from the local clan's militia. Guards themselves received the local wage, but those who arranged the contract hired them out at a substantial mark-up—and insisted that several dozen men were employed to guard each ship. The protectors also controlled traders' access to the ships. Consequently, food, fuel, and the locally popular drug *khat* were delivered with mark-ups of up to 300 per cent.[38] Low-paid guards on flat rates sometimes left the ships in debt if negotiations dragged on too long. Junior pirates' *khat* bills tore big holes into their pay packets. The discrepancy between the estimated pirate salaries in the two 2013 World Bank reports on Somali piracy (US$30,000 vs US$10,000) may be explained as the former being the gross salary and the latter the salary after the 'expenses' incurred during the negotiation.

After the ransom drop, pirates with a pocket full of cash were quickly approached by their family, their *diya* peers, and local elders. An exasperated pirate complained that he had no idea that 'his family was so big before he went into piracy . . . all of a sudden, he had all these dependents running after him to get money'.[39] The pirate organizers also provided inducements for local dignitaries and opinion-makers to keep the villagers on side. A before/after analysis of high-resolution satellite images of the 'pirate capital' Eyl and the similarly busy pirate anchorage at Hobyo revealed that neither town was transformed by pirate money, however. A few new or upgraded fortified compounds are consistent with some pirates (or elders) investing private gains locally, but the satellite pictures show little evidence of investment in public infrastructure.[40] Instead, pirates were famous for their lavish hospitality, which often included prostitutes and drug binges. Perhaps '*haram*' piracy money is best spent on '*haram*' activities.

Some pirate captains, organizers, and investors—often referred to as the pirate kingpins—became very powerful. Their primary skill was in leveraging their extensive social networks—family, political, and business connections—to create favourable conditions for piracy. Thus, they could share in the ransoms of others. Some reinvested their spoils into equipping new pirate action groups or stumped up the anchorage fees for others—to be repaid with interest. Some pirates diversified into different business areas. The infamous pirate organizer Mohamed 'Big Mouth' Afweyne eventually dominated the *khat* trade in coastal areas of Puntland and Galmuduq. The pirate captains Mohamed Garfanje and Isse Yulux emulated the southern Somali warlords and built up private militias.[41] These could be deployed to protect smuggling, gun running, and human trafficking—as well as their own piracy businesses. In 2013, the UN monitoring group reported that former pirates provided private protection for foreign fishing vessels engaged in illegal and unlicensed fishing off the coast of Somalia.[42]

Very few individuals became personally wealthy through piracy, however. In Somali society, there is a strong social obligation to share. Pirates had to pay off elders and businessmen. In turn, the protectors used the funds to employ clan members and help their family and friends. A Somali proverb says: 'if you have a hundred goats and your cousin has none, you are a poor man'. Spending money converts financial into political capital. Conspicuous acts of charity and lavish entertainment are better ways of enhancing one's social status than hoarding money. Pirate weddings where hundreds feasted for two days on camel meat and danced to a band flown in from Djibouti are the stuff of legend.[43] The lobster fisherman turned pirate captain, Abshir Boyah, was treated like a celebrity in Puntland's Garowe. When he was flush with cash, everyone wanted to shake his hand and the fawning police commander called him 'cousin'. But his admirers also bled him dry. Trying to cadge some cigarettes from an interviewer, Boyah explained: 'When someone who never had money suddenly gets money, it just goes...it's not like three people split a million bucks. It's more like three hundred.'[44]

The businessman turned pirate organizer Mohamed 'Big Mouth' Afweyne was said to have done rather better—investing his assets far away from his clansmen's grabbing hands: in India, Kenya, and Dubai.[45] But he laughed off the idea that pirates might have financial assets that could be seized and frozen by foreign law enforcers.[46] Clearly, he had invested a lot of money in his political connections. The pirate boss was appointed as a government counter-piracy officer by the Somali president himself—even before he had renounced his own business interests in piracy. UN officials were speechless with rage when the 'most wanted' pirate kingpin travelled around the world using a diplomatic passport. When political elites were pressured into arresting and charging pirates, junior pirates' long prison sentences contrasted starkly with the lenience (bordering on adulation) applied to those who ran the pirate networks.[47]

The Cost of Protecting Piracy

Although there were potentially large financial and social returns to protecting pirates and to controlling their access to local markets, befriending pirates also came at a significant cost. Most Somalis rejected and resisted piracy. Despite pirates' best efforts to portray themselves as informal coastguards or *mujaheddin* of the sea engaged in a holy war against infidels,[48] most Somalis consider the abduction of innocent merchant seamen to be *'haram'*—forbidden or wrong. An imprisoned teenage pirate lamented: 'My mum wants nothing to do with me. I brought my family irreparable shame and damage after I went astray. She never wanted me to go down this road.'[49] Locals who did not directly benefit from piracy suffered economic disadvantages. The influx of pirate dollars priced the poor out of local cafes and markets. Pretty girls no longer even looked at mere fishermen.

Harbouring pirates also created psychological costs. Many villagers feared that their homes and boats would come under direct attack by drones, foreign troops, or naval aircraft. Fishermen abandoned good fishing grounds rather than risk being blown out of the water by nervous armed guards who mistook their presence for a 'suspicious approach'.[50] Social tensions emerged, when traditionally revered elders were ignored or challenged by brash, cash-rich pirates. As a repentant pirate put it: 'Piracy brought in inflation and breakdown of social order in our communities. Pirates brought with them shameful practices like drugs, alcohol abuse and prostitution in areas they operated.'[51] Elites that traditionally govern by consensus and reciprocity had to overcome these considerable reservations by providing selective incentives to create winning coalitions for piracy.

An openly pro-pirate stance also interfered with regional politicians' ambitions of statehood and attracting international development aid. The impression that Puntland was in danger of 'becoming the pirate version of a narco-state' greatly diminished President Farole's standing in the international community.[52] Counter-piracy aid only became available when the president's clansmen at Eyl had 'chased' the pirates out of their anchorage. But as the pirates merely took their ships a bit further up or down the coast, the UN remained sceptical about the president's counter-piracy efforts. President Farole's repeated request for a tarmac road to Eyl was pointedly ignored.

There were also financial trade-offs in protecting pirates: the presence of drug-crazed bandits unnerves merchants. Dhows, ferries, and old cargo ships are no match for highly powered pirate skiffs. Some of them were pirated and used as motherships or raided to stock up on supplies. So, traders avoided pirate anchorages and harbours. But trade protection can be highly lucrative. A 2011 United Nations study of Al Shabaab funding revealed that the group made between US$35 million and US$50 million per year from controlling port facilities in southern Somalia. Traders arrived with sugar for smuggling into Kenya and left laden with charcoal. Al Shabaab charged them berthing fees, per sack import and export duties, and taxed the labourers carrying the goods.[53] With this kind of money at stake from vessels bringing goods into Somali ports, the protectors guarantee the traders' safety on the high seas. A good example of such an arrangement is the 'unusually swift conclusion' of the hijacking of the oil tanker *Aris 13* in March 2017. Its cargo was intended for an important businessman in Mogadishu. We can picture the clan elders resplendent in white robes, colourful scarves, and embroidered hats hastily converging in an air-conditioned hotel lobby to resolve the issue. Would the pirates release the ship forthwith? They did. 'After we came to know that the Somali traders hired the oil tanker, we released it without a ransom', the pirate captain explained sheepishly.[54] Nobody would have dared to offer him and his crew protection to conduct a ransom negotiation.

For areas far removed from trade routes, an alternative to protecting pirates may be to protect fisheries. However, protecting artisanal, subsistence fishing is neither profitable nor prestigious. Local fisheries protection was (just about) worthwhile where elites successfully mobilized aid funds to rehabilitate the fish-processing industry lost in the civil war. The real money, however, is in protecting foreign fishing vessels. As these agreements are illegal they tend to remain hidden—but foreign trawlers have been observed operating unhindered near Bosasso and Kismayo for years. We got a glimpse of the value of the fisheries protection business in 2016 when Puntland's president officially awarded a (legally questionable) fishing licence to a Chinese fishing company for US$10 million.[55] Soon afterwards, a fleet of South Korean and Thai trawlers arrived in Bosasso port to negotiate their own deals.[56]

If elites choose between protecting trade and fishing or piracy, a further consideration may be that pirate profits tend to be unpredictable in size and timing. Most elites prefer a reliable income stream to occasional large windfalls. Thus, if there is a choice to be made between protecting pirates and traders: pirates do make uneasy bedfellows.

A Rational Choice

Figure 3.1 shows where ships hijacked by Somali pirates were taken to conduct the ransom negotiation. The dataset is based on maritime crimes reported by skippers to the International Maritime Bureau (IMB). Incidents are classed as successful acts of piracy by the IMB if an unauthorized person boards a vessel with criminal intent. Rereading the skippers' short narratives of the incidents, it is notable that many of them are not classic 'hijack for ransom' incidents. For example, the only vessel reported as having been detained in Somaliland between 2005 and 2012 is *El Greco-2*. This fishing trawler and its sister ship have been repeatedly investigated for fraud and illegal, unlicensed fishing in several countries.[57] The authorities of Somaliland are not recognized as a sovereign government. Therefore, they do not have a legal right to detain fishing trawlers. However, Somalilanders' efforts to patrol their maritime resources are not equivalent to hijacking foreign merchant ships for ransom. Somaliland should therefore be considered piracy free—despite the incensed 'piracy report' posted by the captain of the *El Greco-2*. Similarly, the reported incidents in southern Somalia were either local traders, dhows, trawlers, or ships chartered by the World Food Programme (WFP) to deliver aid supplies. This was local shipping traffic with unresolved protection issues—for example, the WFP has a strict policy not to pay protection money. Only three foreign fishing trawlers were taken to shore in southern Somalia between 2005 and 2012—and were released after paying 'ransoms' of the same order of magnitude as official fines levied by legitimate states to punish illegal and unlicensed fishing. The map in Figure 3.1 therefore only considers classic hijack for ransom incidents that targeted international merchant ships. These cases are massed on the Puntland and Galmuduq coast. What explains this geography of piracy?

Away from the port cities, coastal communities everywhere in Somalia have the same problems of unemployment, poverty, and underdevelopment. Why did no coastal community in Somaliland choose to protect pirates? Some commentators stress that piracy would have undermined Somaliland's bid for independence.[58] However, the political decision was

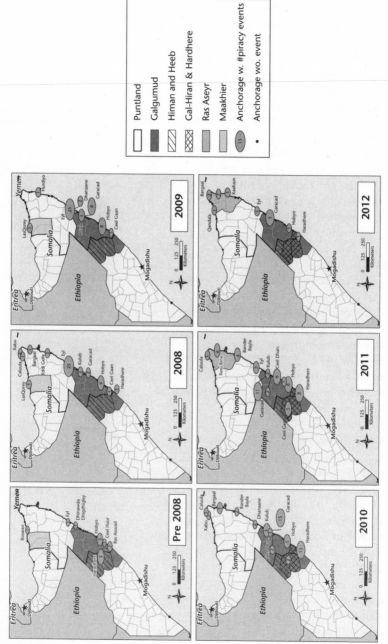

Figure 3.1. The geography of Somali piracy

Legend:

- Puntland
- Galgumud
- Himan and Heeb
- Gal-Hiran & Hardhere
- Ras Aseyr
- Maakhier
- Anchorage w. #piracy events
- Anchorage wo. event

underpinned by economic rationality: Somaliland's tax revenue largely accrued from customs duties. Unlike income taxes, levying and collecting import tariffs does not require much bureaucracy or political consultation. In 2011, twenty years after declaring independence, the Somaliland government still collected 46 per cent of its total revenues at Berbera port. Djibouti was a major competitor for Berbera. Fiscal sustainability dictated that Somaliland should shun piracy and embrace trade protection. Coastal communities were not given the choice to pursue the piracy option in their anchorages.

The elites controlling the southern ports of Kismayo and Mogadishu and the natural harbours at Merca and el Ma'an also refused to protect pirates. Although power was hotly contested, and different elites controlled the ports at different times, they all protected and taxed trade. In 2006, Islamic Courts Union militias ruling much of southern Somalia even mounted a punitive counter-piracy mission against pirates based in Hobyo and Harardhere in central Somalia. The invaders condemned piracy as *haram*, and summarily tried and executed a few pirates under *Sharia* law. However, the real, underlying message was that southern elites would not tolerate their traders being hassled by northern pirates. A few years later, the relationship between Islamists and pirates became more cooperative. When Al Shabaab invaded the pirate stronghold of Harardhere again in 2010, the pirates left their ships at anchor and simply paid their new protector. In addition, locals reported that pirates were directed to attack specific traders who were in arrears on their protection payments. This raised the value of the trade protection contract at no extra cost to the southern clans.[59]

The genuine pirate anchorages were all located in Puntland and Galmuduq. Yet Puntland's principal port—Bosasso—was piracy free from 2008. Before then, the port had a reputation as a convenient setting-off and resupply point for pirates. In 2007 the pirate captain Abshir Boyah took the hijacked *Golden Nori* towards Bosasso and escaped into the city with the ransom.[60] But soon thereafter, economic considerations turned the tide against piracy. Middle Eastern countries had restricted livestock exports from the Horn of Africa because of the presence of Rift Valley Fever in some herds. Bosasso did not have the necessary quarantine and documentation facilities for legal exports. With the lifting of the ban in 2009, the Puntland government suddenly stood to earn US$15–20 million in annual customs revenues. President Farole explained: 'The Puntland Port of Bossaso [*sic*] is our economic lifeline and our gateway to global trade networks.... Any threat to this vital economic lifeline is a threat against the security, stability and economy of Puntland State of Somalia, which also impacts the smooth flow of trade traffic across the whole region.'[61] So, the pirates were invited to leave—or at least conduct their business more discreetly.

Those who protected pirates had no comparable alternative income stream. It is difficult to appreciate how remote the coastal villages of Puntland and Galmuduq are when looking at a roadmap. The annotated travel time maps occasionally published by the WFP give a better impression. In 2011, you could hope to cover the 222 km from Garowe to Eyl in eleven hours—in a sturdy four-wheel drive. Driving from Galkayo to Hobyo? Plan around thirty hours to cover 253 km. The last pirate enterprise operating in 2012 was that of Isse Yulux at Caluula. From Bosasso the road distance is 437 km: you should allow thirty-one hours of driving time—if it's dry and the road is passable. There are no harbour facilities in the pirate havens. To load or unload goods, everything needs to be transferred to small boats and brought ashore on somebody's back—often in strong wind. Both licit and illicit trade therefore bypasses these places. Without ice, local fishermen could not get fresh fish to urban markets and any fish-processing and -canning plants built during the Siad Barre regime were long defunct. So, the choice was between subsistence fishing, herding—and piracy. It's not surprising that sea-scavenging and piracy have a long tradition along the Puntland coastline and the island of Socotra.

Until 2003, Somali pirate attacks against foreign merchant ships were rare and largely opportunistic. Most of the pirate activity was concentrated in northern Puntland and dominated by the Darod-Majerteen sub-clan. In 2004, the businessman Mohamed 'Big Mouth' Afweyne headhunted successful northern pirates to help create his own piracy venture in the central Somali Hobyo-Haardhere region—for his own benefit as well as that of his Hawiye-Suleiman sub-clan.[62] Like the first generation of Somali pirates, they usually held ships for a few months (until on-board supplies ran out) and released them for a few hundred thousand dollars. Although these ransoms represented a fortune in Somalia, ship-owners could easily raise them and the incidents were always resolved peacefully and swiftly. The ship-owners' financial risk could be mitigated by obtaining insurance. Information about this low-level pirate activity therefore rarely spread beyond the shipping community. When did piracy become frequent and serious enough to become perceived as a menace for international shipping?

Piracy escalated in the piracy-prone regions when clan elites needed a sudden injection of cash to pursue their political agendas. The first major pirate anchorage was Eyl, the ancestral sub-clan home of the Puntland presidential candidate Mohamed Farole. During his election campaign in 2008 and 2009, Eyl sheltered more than two dozen hijacked ships.

It was an open secret that piracy money smoothed Mr Farole's successful bid for the Puntland presidency.[63] Similarly, Mr Farole's competitor, General Iljakir, received protection money from Fuad Wasame Seed who held four ships hostage at Lasqoorey over the same period. Because there was now a political interest in maximizing ransoms, the time frames for negotiations expanded. Politicians provided protection and businessmen funded supplies. Ransoms spiralled as ship-owners (and nervous governments) overreacted to pirates' scare tactics and their new-found patience. Escalating ransoms attracted ever more hopefuls into the piracy business. Once in office, Mr Farole appointed General Iljakir as a minister and piracy ceased in both Eyl and Lasqoorey. Farole's and Iljakir's local supporters were compensated in other ways. Lasqoorey got a tuna-canning factory, but Eyl never got its road. Somehow, half-hearted development initiatives to rehabilitate Eyl's fishing sector never quite took hold either. Eventually, Mr Farole's clansmen were compensated with government positions or were offered work in the PMPF instead.

When the hijacked ships left Eyl, most of them were welcomed a little further south at Garacad. Further south, Hobyo and Harardhere emerged as major pirate centres. Several tiny anchorages on the north-eastern tip of Puntland also turned into pirate havens. Once again, political change was at the bottom of the piracy gold rush. International efforts to revive Somalia as a state proposed a 'federal Somalia'. Significant devolution of power and resources could be a promising solution to end clan infighting over central funds. The administrative regions which had been created under the Siad Barre regime were invited to amalgamate to form new federal states.[64] Anyone with a credible claim would be invited to attend the constitutional conference. So, the clans began to jockey for position: federal states would attract aid and federal funds; successful political entrepreneurs would gain power, status, and opportunities for patronage. Sub-clan groups who did not wish to join the larger federal units envisioned in the imprecisely worded transitional charter declared their own 'mini-states'. Their borders were hotly disputed as several aspiring 'states' laid claim to the same land. In addition, Al Shabaab—excluded from the constitutional process altogether and under pressure in the south—began to move northwards. This created a sudden and massive need for money to strengthen and upgrade local clan militias. Piracy served the purpose.

In the maps of Figure 3.1 we see that piracy emerged or intensified just before or as competing territorial claims were asserted. The busiest pirate anchorages were on the long stretch of coastline that was claimed by both Galmuduq and Puntland following the creation of Galmuduq state in 2006. Resource needs in the central Somali areas around Hobyo and Harardhere multiplied when new federal units and mini-states proliferated in the region. Disaffected sub-clans created the state of Himan-and-Heeb with its capital as Adado in 2008.[65] Himan-and-Heeb's territorial ambitions led to increased fundraising by elites supporting Galmuduq state. The year 2010 saw a further intensification of overlapping territorial claims with the registration of the state of Gal-Hiran-and-Harardhere. This state aimed to incorporate parts of Galgaduud and Hiran to the South. When Harardhere was taken over by Al Shabaab in 2010 even more resources were needed for self-defence or appeasement efforts further up the coast.

Similarly, the sub-clans in the Ras Asseyr region in northern Puntland established piracy businesses to fund a bid for power in the 2009 Puntland elections. Their candidates were unsuccessful and their region missed out on development funding. To add insult to injury, the Puntland government sold oil exploration licences for 'their' area to foreign corporations. So the local elites made a second attempt to grab power in 2010–12: once again they turned to piracy to fund a bid for a new 'mini-state'.

Not every aspiring politician invited or sponsored pirates. But those who didn't were not in a strong position to deny pirates access to their territory either. By 2010, some pirates had become so powerful that it would have been very risky to challenge them—in fact it was better to co-opt them.[66] The president of Himan-and-Heeb—an enterprising diaspora returnee from Minnesota—was asked why a well-known pirate boss was building a flash new compound in central Adado, right behind the police station. He shrugged. 'I'd take these guys on, but I can't right now because I don't have the resources . . . Besides, you can't just wipe out a whole line of work for thousands of young men. If you take something away, you must replace it with something else. Otherwise, more problems.'[67]

In summary, the geography of piracy in Somalia indicates that the protection of piracy was not the preferred income source for local elites. Whoever could make ends meet by protecting traders or trawlers instead of protecting pirates did so. Genuine high seas piracy was associated with poor communities who needed money and simply had no other fundraising options.

The Protector's Choice and Kidnap Insurance

We have considered the question when protectors—whose business model is extortion—shelter criminals preying on outsiders. As with any other business located in their territory, the protector can claim a significant proportion of the criminals' profits. Even if the outright protection payment is small, the protectors can ensure that the criminal businesses support and benefit key local interest groups. Yet, a cosy relationship with criminals also comes at a cost. First, it may be politically difficult to justify harbouring criminals—both to the local population and to foreign audiences. In Somalia, the informal coastguard and *jihad* narrative of piracy had some traction with local audiences, but most people were reluctant to condone hostage-taking and resented their country being associated with banditry. The UN and aid agencies always remained wary of political leaders beholden to piratical supporters. Second, preying on outsiders creates a risk of hostile intervention by the victims' own protectors. The protectors of Somali pirates had to deal with challenges from both local and international counter-piracy forces. Elites invested scarce military, financial, and political resources to reduce the risk of conflict, or mitigate its adverse effects on the local political economy. Third, protecting criminals can have a devastating impact on other potential sources of income. Finally, highly successful criminals may challenge the existing power structures and eventually turn the tables on their erstwhile protectors.

Analysing the protector's choice in a rational choice framework, we saw that most of the time, neither elites nor coastal communities thought that hijack for ransom piracy on the high seas was an attractive revenue source. Pirates only had a chance to obtain protection for ships plucked from the international shipping lanes in the remotest economic backwaters—and then only at times of high political tensions. With territory and power at stake, elites became myopic. Piracy offered a quick buck in a time of need. Once established, however, pirates entrenched themselves. As ransoms escalated, locals came to appreciate and eventually rely on the pirates' largesse. The pirate bosses soon had the families of the guards, navigators, cooks, traders, deck-hands, porters, and the parents of marriageable girls on their side. Copying the warlords of southern Somalia, shrewd pirates like Mohamed Garfanje and Isse Yulux built up private militias. When Garfanje's clan elders called on the pirate boss's personal militia to help defend their territory, they no longer had a genuine choice of whether to protect pirates.

The same rational choice framework can be applied to the protectors' choice around the world. In different contexts, the balance of costs and benefits varies. Regarding political costs: not every mafia has the ambition to govern territory by winning political office. For rebel movements, whose aim is territorial independence or even central power, a reputation for kidnap for ransom and piracy becomes a liability. Thus,

Mexico's drug cartels do not incur high political costs when sheltering kidnappers preying on outsiders, whereas Colombia's FARC rebels had to renounce kidnapping as a precondition for peace talks.[68] Regarding the risk of intervention: protectors who control large stretches of impenetrable jungle or wild mountain areas are less likely to face military challenges than those whose precise locations are known and whose territory is intrinsically valuable. Governments across the world undertake rescue operations and mount incursions only after careful cost–benefit analyses. Unless groups like Boko Haram and the Islamist rebels of Mali become seriously problematic for their central governments, they are usually left to govern the barren hinterland—even if they occasionally kidnap a foreign missionary or aid worker.

Many informal protectors refrain from kidnapping outsiders, because it interferes with more profitable business opportunities. Somalia's clans could offer protection to local traders, smugglers, traffickers, and foreign fishing trawlers. The case against piracy and kidnapping becomes even stronger when there are natural resources to be exploited or the area is attractive to tourists. We know that there are skilled hijackers and ample high-value targets around the Niger Delta, but pirates do not prosper there—their returns to kidnapping are pathetic. Gulf of Guinea pirates lack secure havens: they conduct their business hiding from both local protectors and state forces. The local protectors prefer to protect the oil companies—to the best of their abilities. Even if they cannot prevent occasional hijackings at sea, the protectors ensure that pirates only have a few days to conclude a ransom negotiation and face death if any ill should befall their hostages. In Colombia, the beautiful beach city of Cartagena is a well-established tourist destination: the local protectors prospered because they ensured the safety of holidaying rebels, *narcos*, and foreigners alike.

The final issue protectors must confront is their own survival in the presence of lucrative criminal businesses. Mafias, rebels, and traditional elites flourish when they can rake off profits from many small illicit businesses (e.g. prostitution, gambling, smuggling, loan-sharking, debt collecting) as well as legal businesses. But some crimes pay so well that criminals can challenge, co-opt, or even replace their original protectors. The declared political ambitions of revolutionary and Islamist movements sometimes seem strangely at odds with their criminal activities. The Taliban dealing in opiates and Abu Sayyaf hawking Muslim hostages has ruined the movements' local and international credibility. The question arises whether they are still political organizations or whether they are now primarily organized crime groups.[69] With kidnap for ransom, the risk of being put under pressure by one's erstwhile protégés may seem small. However, the case of Somali piracy shows that with multi-million-dollar ransoms, groups kidnapping outsiders can become dominant. Unless the protectors' overall profit dwarfs the best-case returns from kidnapping (as would be the case for drug cartels) protectors should think twice about inviting kidnappers. A welcome short-term funding boost can lead to the loss of power and influence in the long term.

Thus, although many areas of the world are governed informally, very few protectors choose to shelter and help kidnappers and pirates. If they do, they have a long-term interest in peaceful commercial resolutions. With good information on the choices faced by the protector, it is therefore not just possible to predict the risk of kidnap, but in many cases the risk can be reduced or eliminated by engaging constructively with the local elite. If this is not possible, the fact that the kidnappers are disciplined by local power brokers engaged in a repeated game makes the trade in hostages governable. Part II of the book examines how insurers do this.

Part II
Making Kidnapping Insurable

> In today's global business economy, serious threats to personal
> and corporate security are frequent. Incidents like kidnapping are
> difficult to predict and when they occur they require a swift,
> organized and expert response... [S]pecialist Kidnap & Ransom
> insurance...helps companies and individuals navigate through
> these dynamic, complex and constantly changing scenarios. We
> offer specialized knowledge and a wide range of insurance cover-
> ages to help clients manage their risk landscape. The financial
> impact of a crisis can be severe on any company or family...Kid-
> nap & Ransom insurance policy aims to take away this burden
> by reimbursing all associated costs incurred both during and after
> the event.
>
> XL Catlin Kidnap & Ransom

The advertisement above—taken from a kidnap insurer's website[1]—
describes the world's trickiest transaction and the emotional rollercoas-
ter of trading in human lives as a mere business risk. In the insurance
world, kidnapping is not portrayed as a matter of life and death, but as a
formidable yet manageable commercial problem.[2] The financial burden
can be 'taken away' by insurance, available from a wide range of suppliers. There is reasonable justification for this counter-intuitive assessment of kidnap for ransom. Very few insured people are kidnapped, and
if they are almost all of them come home alive.

When we read this advert through the lens of protection theory, we
begin to understand why. If one knows the local power dynamics,
kidnap risks are both predictable and manageable. Kidnap insurance
comes with detailed specialist advice on how to 'navigate [the] dynamic,
complex and constantly changing' security environment. The customers'
risk landscape is not a given, but it is 'managed' by professionals. In the
event of a kidnap, the insured rely on an 'organised and expert response'
to resolve the incident. Industry insiders have created a reliable and
robust protocol to order the trade in hostages. Yet, somehow the

existence of reliable arrangements to facilitate ransom payments and retrieve hostages does not lead the insured to take avoidable risks. Neither has it caused an escalation of abductions among those likely to have insurance.

This part of the book shows that insurers take a very hands-on role in managing the opportunities, behaviour, and the financial incentives of all participants in the hostage trade. Without this massive private governance effort, it would be impossible to create profitable insurance products for this fiendishly complex risk. Governance is provided on five different dimensions: (1) Managing opportunistic behaviour by the insured; (2) reducing kidnap risks by ordering the interaction between the insured and local elites; (3) encouraging ransom discipline; (4) facilitating a smooth trade in hostages; and (5) preventing opportunistic behaviour by insurers that might endanger the stability of the market.

Chapter 4 looks at kidnap insurance in detail: what exactly are you buying when you purchase a kidnap for ransom policy? Where can you buy it and under what conditions? I introduce the many agencies working alongside the specialist insurers to help the insured avoid being kidnapped and retrieve them safely and cheaply if a kidnap occurs. Kidnap prevention is very much Plan A in this business. Chapter 5 therefore studies the intriguing question of how an insured firm or individual can obtain protection from an extra-legal protector. How would such a protection contract be enforced? And how do you mask the arrangement from those who would consider it to be ethically or politically problematic that you are paying protection money?

Chapters 6 to 8 look at kidnap resolution. The first problem is setting a price. What is the 'right' price for a life? For the insurer it is the minimum price that safely returns the hostage. Furthermore, the ransom negotiators must avoid creating incentives for kidnappers to torture, mutilate, or murder hostages to drive up the ransom. Finally, the negotiation is conducted by the family or firm, rather than insurers or their agents. How can one control a highly stressful negotiation conducted by proxy? Chapter 6 focuses on the protocol designed to resolve these issues, while Chapter 7 analyses the transcript of a pirate negotiation to show how the theory is applied in the messy real world. Once the price is set, there is still the problem of effecting the transaction. How is the ransom paid to the right addressee without being intercepted by the authorities, rival gangs, or opportunistic passers-by? How does one avoid the messenger being kidnapped, and why would the hostage be released after payment? Chapter 8 describes and analyses the host of specialists and protocols designed to facilitate this tricky exchange.

Chapter 9 draws together all these threads by analysing the complex governance architecture ordering kidnap for ransom. It is a classic polycentric governance system as studied by the Nobel Prize-winning economist Elinor Ostrom.[3] Insurers do not directly manage their customers' risks or resolve hostage crises. This is the domain of highly specialized firms, that in turn subcontract or deal with other specialists, some of them in the economic underworld. The protocol is only stable because the market is highly concentrated. There are only three or four major providers of kidnap for ransom insurance in the world, and a total of around twenty counting the smaller providers. All of them are Lloyd's syndicates, operating in close physical proximity in the Lloyd's underwriting room at Lime Street in the City of London.[4] At the heart of kidnap for ransom insurance is a private members' club. This club governs the behaviour of its members for their mutual benefit—as well as the benefit of those wishing to travel, research, work, and invest in the many areas of the world that are informally governed.[5] Part III of the book shows that without such club governance the market for hostages becomes very problematic, as evidenced by the terrible fate of terrorist hostages.

4

What is Kidnap for Ransom Insurance?

[T]here was only one place to go for K&R insurance, and that is Lloyd's of London.

Jere van Dyk[6]

Buying Kidnap for Ransom Insurance

Kidnap for ransom insurance is a very strange product. Few people set out to buy kidnap insurance for themselves or their loved ones. Yet, kidnap for ransom cover is no longer a niche product for the ultra-rich. Many people exposed to kidnap risk are covered—but the insurance works much better if the insured are not aware of this. Most of the insured obtain kidnap cover through their employer—but as soon as they are told that they are insured, the insurance contract is invalidated. And, contrary to what an internet search for kidnap insurance appears to indicate, there is only one place where this insurance is underwritten: Lloyd's of London. A small group of syndicates in Lloyd's decide who and what is insurable and under what conditions. There are rigorous protocols for obtaining insurance and for resolving incidents, and, largely, everyone sticks to them. Let us look for an economic explanation for this peculiar insurance product.

Most people think about insurance primarily as a risk transfer mechanism. Insurance companies offer full or partial compensation for costly losses or accidents which are beyond the control of the insured in exchange for an insurance premium. People buy insurance if the expected benefits are higher than the premium. By pooling the risk among many, the insurer's risks become more predictable and less concentrated, so the insurance premium can be reduced. However, most risks are not fully exogenous: they are influenced by the behaviour of the insured. First, people who think that they are likely to experience a loss will be very interested in buying insurance cover. This is called adverse selection. Insurers always screen the risk profile of their customers before deciding on the terms of the insurance contract. In kidnap insurance this screening process is extremely rigorous, and many people and activities are denied cover or only obtain it on stringent conditions.

Second, once insurance has been obtained potential claimants might be less careful about limiting their risks. This is called moral hazard. It is especially prevalent if the insured event poses no physical risk—like washing a mobile phone or breaking a musical instrument. Becoming a victim of crime is unpleasant. Insurance for mugging, kidnap, and burglary is therefore akin to health insurance: nobody deliberately sets out to experience fear and pain. But when firms buy insurance for their employees, they could be tempted to reduce their effort to avoid the insured event. Insurers mostly manage moral hazard by rewarding clients for cautious behaviour. For example, non-smokers are offered more attractive terms for life cover than smokers. Insurers give discounts to careful drivers, houses with burglar alarms, and cars kept in garages. Insurers encourage us to engage in risk management by applying exclusions to our insurance (no hazardous sports). If we make a claim, we contribute to the cost of resolving the incident with an excess payment and expect our insurance premium to rise. Insurers thus always encourage and sometimes help the insured to make choices to reduce risks.[7] Kidnap for ransom cover is also designed to incentivize firms and their employees to take adequate measures to reduce kidnap risks.

Third, with some criminal risks it is possible to directly affect the profitability of the crime. For example, if a collector wants to insure a well-known, priceless Picasso, the insurer will do their best to encourage her to keep it safe. Certain precautions will be a precondition for insurance. Installing superior safety features lowers the insurance premium. In addition, it is in the interest of the insurer to keep a watchful eye on the art market in case thieves try to sell stolen paintings. If insurers can create robust institutions that bar stolen artworks from being traded in the open market, they can only be sold at knockdown prices in the black market—or hidden. For example, in 2017 two Van Gogh paintings were returned to their rightful owner fourteen years after the theft. They had never been sold, but were found 'wrapped in cotton sheets, stuffed in a box and hidden behind a wall in a toilet'.[8] If thieves have no ready market for their loot, it significantly reduces the attractiveness of targeting high-value art in the first place.[9]

Kidnap for ransom insurance is similar: if one can limit the profitability of kidnapping, then there will be fewer kidnaps. If one can facilitate a functioning market for private security and protection, then kidnaps could become very rare among the insured. If the full force of the law is brought to bear on kidnappers who kill, maltreat, or retain ransomed hostages, kidnappers have an incentive to conduct orderly resolutions. If firms and individuals trust in the resolution process, then more people will consider operating (and insuring their operations) in kidnap-prone locations. In fact, I argue that if insurers did not order this criminal market, kidnap for ransom would quickly become uninsurable.

Kidnap Insurance Without Governance Does Not Work

Kidnap for ransom insurance was first developed in 1932 as a niche product for the very rich following the abduction and death of Charles Lindbergh's young son. Initially, insurers did not get involved in the ransoming process, leaving the family or employer to negotiate and deliver the ransom. Over time it became clear that this laissez-faire insurance product was deeply flawed.[10]

If insurance is bought by families, moral hazard problems are probably minimal. The risk of bodily harm to the hostage and the psychological cost of bartering with dangerous criminals over a loved one's life can never be insured away. However, kidnap insurance can tempt some people to engage in fraud by conspiring in or staging a kidnap. Unless the insurer closely monitors the resolution process, this is difficult to pick up. Crisis responders interviewed for this project gave several examples of stopping negotiations when they realized that the 'so-called hostages were trying to fund a bender' by demanding a ransom from their parents or employer.

If insurance is sold to firms rather than families, the moral hazard problem is more acute. While firms have a strong incentive to protect their managers and engineers, it is arguably less important to invest heavily in the protection of low-skilled, locally hired staff. Insurers need to think hard about the terms on which local workers can be included in a multinational's kidnap cover. Firms in financial difficulties may also be tempted to make massive fraudulent claims by staging an insured event. For example, Lloyd's insurers became suspicious when one of their claims investigators was murdered in 2011, as he probed into an alleged pirate attack off the coast of Aden.[11] As more and more evidence emerged that the ship-owner could have been complicit in the attack, the insurers decided to deny the claim. As of 2017, the case was still to be resolved by the court.[12] It is therefore important to craft the insurance contract such that it does not create perverse incentives for the insured.

Insurance could also undermines ransom discipline. The gut instinct of stakeholders is to try and meet kidnapper demands to resolve the incident as swiftly as possible. However, kidnapper demands should not be thought of as a 'price'. Kidnappers generally expect a multi-round bargaining process. Their opening position is set above the level of their 'best-case' expectation. Quick agreement to pay that amount will probably lead kidnappers to revise it upwards. Unless stakeholders have good information about the kidnappers' actual ransom expectations and experience of haggling, it is very easy for cash-rich firms and families to inadvertently pay ransoms that are multiples of the kidnappers' actual targets.

This creates a second-round effect. News of high returns to kidnapping quickly spreads through criminal communities. As we will see in Chapter 7, Somali pirates shared information about ongoing negotiations to help drive up ransoms across the board. New entrants into kidnapping base their expectations on previously realized ransoms. Trying to revise inflated ransom expectations downward requires a lot of patience.[13] But exceeding kidnapper expectations in an attempt to shorten negotiation durations attracts further criminals into kidnapping. In this vicious circle, abductions and ransoms will escalate in tandem—putting ever more people at risk and causing losses for insurers.

Finally, it is vital to minimize the risk of hostage maltreatment, failed handovers, and murders. When there are risks to life and limb, people avoid kidnap hotspots.[14] Firms have a duty of care to their employees and withdraw from locations where kidnaps are frequent, violent, and lengthy. This in turn reduces the demand for insurance. Insurers therefore share information to create incentives for kidnappers to refrain from threatening or harming hostages but invest in a reputation for 'honest' trading instead. They also motivate extra-legal protectors to prevent opportunistic rookie criminals from kidnapping or from upsetting the market with wanton violence or murder.

Events in Argentina in the early 1970s illustrate what happens when kidnap insurance is sold, but insurers do not provide robust governance of the market. Several guerrilla groups targeted foreign firms, diplomats, and local VIPs to extract ransoms and political concessions. A major series of kidnappings started with the abduction of the Baltazar family in August 1970. They were ransomed for an unknown but clearly significant amount of money. The next kidnap was not far behind. In May 1971, the British manager of Swift meatpacking (and honorary consul of Rosario) was abducted and held for several weeks until ransomed by the factory owner for US$250,000. In September 1972, the manager of Phillips Argentina fetched US$500,000. In December 1972, the million-dollar mark was reached twice, with the release of senior staff members kidnapped from ITT and Vestry Meatpacking. In 1973, the Bank of Boston paid US$750,000, Coca-Cola and Amoco US$1 million, Kodak US$1.5 million, and British American Tobacco US$1.7 million. Then the Roberts Group offered US$2.3 million for its chief executive officer. Firestone raised US$3 million and Esso handed over US$14.2 million. In 1974 the family business Bunge and Born paid an incredible US$60 million plus US$1.2 million in clothing for the return of the business heirs Juan and Jorge Born. The US$5 million ransom paid by Mercedes Benz and the US$10 million paid by the Roberts Group to retrieve their unlucky chief executive officer for a second time (!) in 1975 seem almost tame in comparison.[15]

Others were not so lucky. Several intended targets were shot when they resisted capture. Chauffeurs and guards were routinely killed. Some hostages were tortured or murdered when the ransom process stalled, others when rescue attempts were made. Firms refusing to pay protection money to the guerrillas experienced targeted killings and abductions of family members. The upshot of these events was that foreign firms either closed their Argentinian operations altogether or at least moved their top executives and their families out of the country. The market for special risks insurance in Argentina contracted rapidly and was in danger of disappearing altogether. So how was that genie put back in its bottle? The rest of this chapter examines how insurers manage the risk of kidnap for ransom to prevent instability and chaos in the market for hostages.

Governing Kidnap for Ransom

As events in Argentina unfolded, two former special forces officers made an interesting proposal to special risks insurers at Lloyd's of London. What if insurers vetted the security measures implemented by their clients? Engaging in risk mitigation tailored specifically to local requirements should be made an integral part of obtaining insurance. This would directly address moral hazard and adverse selection. Expert advice on how to operate in complex security terrains would deflect kidnappers towards softer targets. Moreover, if insurers also took control of ransom negotiations, then commercial resolutions would be both more reliable and cheaper. Calm, experienced negotiators bring a welcome rational element into emotionally stressful situations. A measure of resistance in the ransom negotiations encourages opportunists to engage in 'express kidnappings' which end at the next cashpoint, rather than starting a lengthy negotiation. By pooling information about kidnappers' past behaviour, murderous and sadistic kidnappers can be punished, encouraging cooperative behaviour. If stakeholders know what the kidnappers' actual ransom expectations and time horizons are, they can structure their offers to meet that expectation rather than bartering over an unknown quantity.[16]

These revolutionary ideas created the professions of security and crisis response consultants and the company Control Risks.[17] Although the business model has been replicated many times since then, Control Risks remains the market leader in security consulting for kidnaps and for crisis response. Its competitors take the same hands-on approach to risk management. The system works—and kidnap for ransom insurance has become the default option for firms operating in crime-ridden, complex, and hostile territories. At least 75 per cent of Fortune 500 companies buy kidnap cover, even though all these firms could easily self-insure the cost of ransoms.[18] Major corporations and NGOs buy kidnap insurance not because they cannot afford ransoms, but because insurance is bundled with services to prevent kidnaps and resolve incidents safely. Moreover, kidnap insurance covers the legal costs of employers if staff (or their bereaved families) sue them for a breach of their duty of care after an incident. Kidnap insurance thus enables firms to operate in areas where law enforcement is weak or even non-existent. Total premium income for insurers was estimated to be more than US$500 million a year in 2011.[19] The following sections examine how this attractive and comprehensive insurance product can be profitably provided.

Who Provides Kidnap for Ransom Cover?

Any internet search returns dozens of different providers of kidnap insurance and the market looks highly competitive, but let us probe more deeply. Many of the companies selling kidnap for ransom insurance turn out to be brokerages rather than insurers. They make their money from commissions. Their employees are licensed Lloyd's brokers, who take the information provided by prospective clients to the underwriting room at Lloyd's.

The insurers marketing kidnap insurance fall into four different categories. The first group of insurers are (or have acquired) boutique kidnap for ransom specialists with a syndicate at Lloyd's.[20] The Lloyd's syndicates are formed by one or more Lloyd's members (which may be individuals or corporations). The members provide the syndicate's capital and accept insurance risks. Lloyd's syndicates are world famous for insuring unusual specialist business—such as satellites, racehorses, celebrities' smiles or legs, and musicians' fingers or vocal cords. There are around twenty syndicates in the Lloyd's market underwriting kidnap for ransom risks. Of these, three or four are the market leaders. They underwrite the large majority of kidnap risks; the others are followers with relatively limited exposure.

A second group of insurers market the products of various Lloyd's syndicates to their customers. Some major insurers act as 'coverholders' for one of the Lloyd's syndicates, meaning they are authorized to enter contracts on behalf of a specific syndicate. Other insurers sell the products of the market leaders to their customers for a commission. A third group of insurers uses brokerages or their own brokers to place the risk in the Lloyd's market. This means they can offer greater choice to their customers than the second group, which is tied to a specific Lloyd's syndicate. The final group of insurers issue their own kidnap for ransom products but reinsure them in the Lloyd's market. Kidnap risks are highly concentrated: if an incident occurs, it is potentially very expensive to resolve. Insurers who only have a small volume of such business prefer not to keep this risk on their own books. Through reinsurance the special risks insurers at Lloyd's can influence the terms on which kidnap insurance is offered in the wider market.[21]

Occasionally, the link between kidnap insurance and Lloyd's is deliberately opaque. For example, the insurer American International Group (AIG) offers a range of kidnap insurance products but does not mention Lloyd's anywhere on its website. Neither is there a Lloyd's syndicate underwriting kidnap insurance in AIG's name. It appears that from a public relations point of view AIG prefers to be 'all American'. However, Lloyd's syndicate 1414 'Ascot Underwriting Limited' says in its annual statement: 'The only related parties that have transacted with Syndicate 1414 are companies within the AIG group of companies . . . The ultimate parent company and controlling party of the Syndicate's main corporate member, ACNL, is American International Group Inc. ("AIG").'[22]

Thus, the market for kidnap insurance is highly concentrated. Three or four specialist insurers set the parameters for kidnap insurance. When one compares the products of different insurers, it is clear that there is a non-negotiable standard protocol—particularly for the resolution of kidnap for ransom.

Addressing Adverse Selection

Access to kidnap insurance is controlled by highly experienced brokers and underwriters. There are three types of kidnap for ransom products.

The norm for kidnap insurance is that those seeking insurance must provide in-depth information about the activities they wish to insure. Usually, clients approach a Lloyd's broker, who collects detailed information from the customer. Who is going where and for how long? What is the net worth of the company or the family seeking insurance? How much cover is being sought? What security measures are in place? Were there any threats or previous incidents? The Lloyd's brokers collate and present this information to a number of competing underwriters in the Lloyd's market. Traditionally, brokers approach the underwriters in person at their 'boxes'—the Lloyd's term for the desks occupied by the various insurance syndicates—to obtain a range of quotes for the customer. The underwriters decide whether they wish to insure the proposed activities—and if so how much to charge. The syndicates differ in risk appetite. If a syndicate is not interested in insuring a particular client or activity, the underwriters put off the applicant by quoting a ridiculously high insurance premium. But some risks are deemed uninsurable at any price. Jere van Dyk, kidnapped in 2008 while travelling in the tribal areas of Pakistan to interview insurgents, could not get kidnap insurance for love nor money when he wanted to return to Afghanistan and Pakistan to investigate the background of his own kidnapping. 'I . . . tried for weeks to get kidnap insurance . . . but no-one would insure me, a kidnap victim.' Quite right, given his risk-loving reputation and plans to interview jihadists and criminals in their own lairs. Realizing that he 'literally could not afford to get kidnapped again' he wisely curtailed his adventuring.[23] Non-availability of kidnap insurance for certain activities is not a market failure, but a sign that the market is operating well.

For permanent operations in crime-ridden or corrupt countries or travel in conflict environments, insurance cover is conditional on obtaining and implementing meticulous security advice from business risk consultancies. Security checks are made on actual and proposed business premises, staff accommodation, and transport to check that the company's protection arrangements are adequate. If not, the customers can greatly reduce the insurance premium by following advice on how to operate more safely in the specific security context. There is a good reason that in many countries the (relatively) rich live in gated communities and go jogging with bodyguards. The latter can be conveniently hired from the security response consultancy retained by their insurer. In complex and hostile territories, obtaining protection often involves striking implicit or explicit deals with local powerbrokers. Chapter 5 will discuss the many options in detail. For the highest-risk activities, insurers (or rather the security consultancies retained by them) become extremely prescriptive regarding risk mitigation. Large corporations and NGOs may have an in-house security management team instead of employing specialist security and risk consultancies. If so, their security management plans will be subject to intense scrutiny—especially if they have failed before.

Insurers thus invest serious resources into avoiding adverse selection. There is one exception: for individuals engaging in very low-risk activities, there are a few off-the-shelf policies. For example, gap year insurance might include limited kidnap for ransom cover. This kind of contract is only available from the largest kidnap insurance providers, who can absorb the occasional loss from a large premium income. The product makes sense on two levels. First, adverse selection is not much of a problem if insurance cover is sought for a beloved child. Insurers can assume that parents compel their kids to travel on the beaten path or pay for professionally organized 'adventure' activities that are lucrative for the local elite and hence worthy of extra-legal protection. This can be reinforced by the insurer by providing free advice on how to stay safe. Kidnaps of gap year students are rare, but if a kidnap occurs, insurers certainly do not want to leave nervous upper-middle-class parents to their own devices in a ransom negotiation. Remortgaging the Park Lane flat would probably bring young Freddie home—but it could also destabilize the local market for hostages. It is therefore in the interest of all market participants that these occasional kidnaps of well-off kids are resolved according to the tried and tested protocol.

Addressing Moral Hazard to Prevent Kidnaps

How do insurers prevent their customers from letting down their guard once the insurance contract has been obtained? Firms obtaining kidnap insurance are only allowed to share this information within a tiny circle of senior management. As soon as employees know that they are insured (or even what the insured amount is), the insurance contract is automatically invalidated. Insurers want at-risk employees to behave as if there was no insurance. Some employers therefore tell their staff specifically that they are not insured, or that it is company policy never to pay ransoms.

To reduce kidnap risks even further, the insurers mandate that at-risk employees receive anti-kidnap and awareness training. The insured's employees must complete a course to help them understand local dangers and appropriate risk mitigation strategies. Unless the employer can present certificates of completed training, individual staff members are not covered by the insurance. Training packages range from online courses recommending common-sense measures to avoid becoming an easy target to multi-day workshops for senior executives and security managers. There are also workshops on how to survive a kidnap. The training is country specific: what is excellent advice for hostages in one country may be a recipe for trouble in others. These courses are the 'bread–and-butter' business of crisis responders: if the security consultants do their work well, there is only an occasional need for crisis resolution. Providing tailored kidnap training may raise unhelpful questions about insurance or the firm's stance on ransoms—which conflicts with the secrecy clause. It is up to the course organizers to deflect any questions about kidnap insurance during these events.

Insurers rely heavily on the legal system to challenge negligence and fraud. Kidnap insurance is often conditional on implementing clearly specified guidelines on 'best management practice'. For example, there are detailed guidelines for ships transiting the Gulf of Aden and the Somali Basin to avoid hijack by Somali pirates. These guidelines are publicly available and were periodically revised in response to innovations by pirates. Over time, the insurers' expectations hardened from being alert and travelling fast, to travelling in convoy, to implementing ever more elaborate defensive measures to repel pirate attacks.[24] If an insurance claim is made, there is a rigorous *ex post* validation process to determine whether the insured complied with the conditions and exclusions applied to the insurance. If the loss adjusters decide that the customer acted negligently or recklessly—or even conspired in the kidnap—reimbursement is withheld as a sanction. If customers suspected of fraud want to obtain payment, they have to take the insurer to court. Most cases are eventually settled out of court, but with considerable delay: insurance fraud is definitely not a quick fix for a cash-flow problem. Similarly, the legal liability cover for companies being sued for breaches of duty of care is conditional on the employer having properly implemented the security consultancy's recommendations. With this strong conditionality and stringent *ex post* validation, there is little scope for moral hazard among the insured regarding getting kidnapped in the first place.

There is an interesting historical parallel here with guilds and knightly orders in the Middle Ages. Their statutes often made provisions to ransom their members, but wisely refused to grant an unconditional right to be ransomed from captivity. They would only assume financial responsibility if hostages were captured on an official mission of the organization, had demonstrably made every effort to avoid being captured, and had proven their courage in battle.[25]

Addressing Moral Hazard on Ransom Amounts

To contain stakeholders' instinctive weakness when faced with a strident and threatening ransom demand, insurers set a clear maximum ransom limit in the insurance contract. The maximum is set at the level that the firm or family would be able to raise themselves—hence the need for detailed financial information in the application form. Obviously, such a limit does not stop the insured from agreeing a higher ransom. However, a further contractual stipulation is that the insured must initially raise the ransom themselves. They are reimbursed by their insurer after the conclusion of the incident. The insurance contract cannot be used as collateral with a bank, making it difficult if not impossible to quickly raise a massive ransom.

The insured are allocated a crisis responder to contact in the event of a kidnap. If someone is abducted, crisis responders quickly dispatch an experienced consultant to advise the stakeholders on how to conduct the ransom negotiation. The consultant's brief is to ensure the 'timely and safe return of the hostage'. This service is free of charge to the insured. Response consultants take control of communications, ensuring that kidnappers only have one point of contact and do not open messy parallel negotiations. They organize a crisis management team and nominate a single communicator to conduct the negotiation.[26]

All decisions are made by the stakeholders in the perceived best interest of the hostage. However, the consultants have superior information and experience in conducting such negotiations and in general the stakeholders value and welcome their advice. Consultants brief the stakeholders on the kidnappers' most likely target settlement and the likely duration of the case. Ransoms vary significantly between geographical regions, so even if there is no specific information on the kidnappers, there is a likely target range. It is not in anyone's interest to inadvertently bid above this range and upset kidnapper expectations.

Hostages feel more secure when their abductors know they are valuable assets. But crisis responders struggle to contain ransoms when hostages whet their abductor's greed by telling them they are 'insured for a million' or 'my company is rich'. As already discussed, employees should not be aware that they are insured. Therefore, kidnap victims should direct their kidnappers to their families for a ransom rather than referring them to their (usually much richer) employer. This can be exploited by the crisis responders to lower the ransom expectations of kidnappers. Chapters 6 and 7 show how ransom negotiations are managed to ensure ransom discipline and prevent the escalation of violence against hostages. In a well-managed ransom negotiation, the actual maximum amount that could be raised by the stakeholders is irrelevant. For example, one crisis response company safely resolved more than 200 Nigerian kidnap cases in the period 2006–14. The median ransom was less than US$5,500 and 75 per cent of cases were resolved for less than US$12,800 per person. Even for foreign nationals the 75th percentile was below US$100,000. These figures are astonishingly low compared to the resources that companies operating in Nigeria that are aided by professional crisis responders could potentially mobilize. Clearly, many kidnappers do not realize who they are really talking to, which is exactly as it should be.

Ordering the Exchange

Once a price is agreed, a whole new set of problems arises. How does the ransom materialize in the destination country without being confiscated at customs or impounded by the police? Who takes it to the kidnapper? What is the best way of structuring the exchange, so that it is not interrupted or puts anyone at an unnecessary risk? How do you extract a sick or weak hostage from 'tiger country' without becoming a target yourself? By mule, by car, or by helicopter? Again, there are specialists who can deliver satisfactory answers to these questions—and these answers vary considerably from case to case. As individual insurers are unlikely to regularly experience multiple cases in the same area, it is not usually worth permanently employing or retaining local specialists. Instead, the specialists are engaged by the crisis response companies as needed. The crisis responders exercise tight quality control over these service providers, by informally sharing information about their past performance and recommending the top specialists to each other. It is also usual for the clients to obtain cash-in-transit insurance for the ransom drop (generally this is included in the kidnap for ransom cover). This is a highly bespoke product and the insurance premium will reflect the insurer's faith in the method and the specialists selected for the job.

A Market for Private Governance

As we consider kidnap for ransom insurance in detail, we see many different governance specialists at work. The obvious ones are the brokers, underwriters, and loss adjusters, supported by security consultants and crisis responders. But we should also include the legal and extra-legal protection specialists who can reduce the probability of a customer being kidnapped: private military security companies, warlords, traditional elites, rebels, and mafiosi. The specialists for making payments and retrieving hostages from the kidnappers are employed on an ad-hoc basis—but are nonetheless essential for the functioning of the system. Loose ends are tidied up by law firms and—if absolutely necessary—in court. Each of these agencies or individuals competently solves an important governance problem—and everyone is paid for doing so. Private governance works because the system is incentive compatible: governance functions are reliably fulfilled where it is profitable or prestigious to do so.

It is in the private interest of insurers to select exposures that match their risk appetite and set an appropriate risk premium. The syndicate's 'book of business' must be commensurate with the members' strategic objectives and reliably cover losses and expenses. The Lloyd's syndicates therefore pay good money to employ high-quality underwriters, experienced at spotting dangerous projects and crafting a balanced portfolio of exposures. Underwriting at Lloyd's is sometimes described as a boy-to-man profession: outstanding underwriters often spend several decades at Lloyd's, occasionally moving between different syndicates. But if underwriters misjudge risks and their loss ratios become problematic for their syndicate, they quickly find themselves on the job market.

Brokers earn significant commissions in the Lloyd's market, because they fulfil important governance functions. Brokers screen applications, elicit truthful information from the clients, cross-check it where necessary, discuss the security measure to be taken, and then present a concise information package to various syndicates to get quotes. Brokers facilitate competition in the Lloyd's market, but also prevent wasteful duplication of efforts. Although kidnap insurance is a bespoke product, the brokers obtain directly comparable quotes by presenting the same information to several syndicates. Yet, the brokers also know the underwriters' specialist fields and risk preferences, so they only approach those most likely to want to insure particular risks.

It is definitely in the individual insurer's commercial interest that kidnaps occur rarely among their customers—as long as the overall risk is sufficiently high to create demand for insurance. It is therefore worth pointing the insured towards high-quality security consultancies. These in turn employ experienced security consultants and dedicated researchers to collect detailed information about current kidnap dynamics and changes in the local power relationships. Most of the security consultants are former elite military officers who have many years of experience of operating in the most complex and hostile terrains. Their focus is on conflict avoidance. The best security measures deflect criminals by visibly hardening the target, rather than repelling attacks.[27] As the customer pays the bill for the security measures, there is considerable pressure on the consultants to provide value for money rather than design completely safe but ruinously expensive fortifications. We will see in Chapter 5 that often the most cost-effective way of doing so is to help the client to engage positively with local elites to obtain support for conducting business in their territory.

If a kidnap occurs, an experienced, highly skilled crisis response consultant will help and encourage the stakeholders to barter the ransom down while retaining the confidence and support of the customer. Hostage stakeholders often get frustrated when ransom demands and offers converge at a snail's pace. As one ship-owner whose tanker was taken by Somali pirates complained: 'How can I tell my crew that I kept them in Somalia for another fortnight just to shave US$100,000 off the ransom?' Plus, the ship was out of commission, the cargo was deteriorating, and the entire senior management team was preoccupied with the crisis. An extra US$100,000 would have been no problem for the ship-owner—or in all fairness, his insurer. However, by jumping the gun and paying a little extra to conclude a bit earlier, impatient hostage stakeholders can easily shift the 'target ransom' for concurrent and future cases upwards. Professional negotiators thus not only have to manage and discipline the kidnappers, but also counsel the stakeholders to hold the line. We will look at one such negotiation in Chapter 7: it perfectly demonstrates how negotiators earn their money.

The various professionals working as messengers, mediators, or ransom couriers and those who retrieve the liberated hostages from the kidnappers' territory fulfil delicate and crucial tasks in the system and are handsomely rewarded for their dangerous missions. And of course, the fees charged by lawyers when contesting questionable cases in the commercial courts are the stuff of legend. High-quality private governance providers can often name their price. The system creates strong incentives for the experts to deliver the promised service and to innovate in response to or (ideally) in anticipation of emerging challenges. Throughout my research I have been amazed by the creativity and problem-solving skills of the various market participants. Every problem that repeatedly results in the failure of a potentially lucrative trade is eventually resolved—for a sizeable fee. If something works well and is cost-effective, it soon becomes the industry standard.

Innovation and quick diffusion of best practice is facilitated by a highly competitive market for private governance. Reputations are the key to career advancement. Most crisis response consultants I spoke to immediately volunteered how many cases they had resolved and whether they had 'lost' any hostages. They often proudly report that they have settled a case for a small percentage (perhaps 2 or 5 per cent) of the original ransom demand. Tough cases are allocated to the best consultants, so knowing who faced which opposition also conveys important information. When I meet previous interviewees again, they update me on their vital statistics straightaway. Crisis responders are also very aware of how parallel cases were resolved. Even if individual consultants would like to keep their less successful cases under wraps, the underwriters obtain all the relevant information from settling the claims: ransom, duration, and anything that happened to the hostages. The names of those who repeatedly mess up negotiations and drive up prices are common knowledge—and mud.

There is a highly competitive market for experts. Only a few consultancies employ crisis consultants on permanent contracts. For the syndicates that are less active in kidnap insurance, incidents are too rare to keep a permanent staff of regional experts. Many consultants are therefore employed for specific cases based on their local or regional expertise and language skills. Premium ransom settlements, violent negotiations, deaths, unhelpful media coverage, and unnecessarily long case durations result in a loss of reputation. Even outstanding consultants may occasionally lose control of a negotiation and pay a premium ransom—or worse, lose a hostage. But repeated failures are career limiting: reputable crisis responders do not retain or hire inept consultants. I interviewed a few people who had been drafted in to assist ship-owners in negotiating with Somali pirates, when there was a brief unanticipated shortage of experienced negotiators. Those who failed to perform were derided, marginalized, and eventually faded from the scene. Their erstwhile peers are still furious with them for letting ransoms escalate.

Quality control operates at the syndicate level, too: only a few syndicates have long-term contractual relationships with a consultancy. If a consultancy does not deliver, it can be replaced by one that does. If a consultancy builds a reputation for the quality of its services in a specific region, it might become the 'named responder' for cases in that region for several syndicates. The market for expertise is therefore highly competitive. Those who succeed are held in high esteem within their community and advance in their careers.

A Complex Private Governance Architecture

We should be amazed that the world's trickiest trade is insurable. Insurers can approximately predict the volume and prices in the market for hostages—as long as they successfully manage kidnap opportunities and the price of hostages. This chapter has analysed the many problems inherent in ordering the market for hostages: adverse selection, moral hazard, and the problem of ordering transactions at the ragged intersection of the legal and underground economies. As we traced the history of kidnap for ransom insurance, we saw that insurers did not reason through all these economic problems at the outset. Instead, they offered a product that seemed sensible at the time. When ransoms spiralled out of control, kidnaps took off and losses mounted. Some insurers exited the market: the survivors innovated. They were offered ever-better business solutions by experts with relevant experience in negotiating and facilitating complex transactions. Each layer of expertise, every standard practice, and every enforcement mechanism in the system was added to remedy a problem that threatened to wipe out the industry.

Insurers now carefully manage the risk profile of their customers and prevent the insured from relaxing their vigilance. They have created effective institutions that monitor and control ransom negotiations to avoid overpaying kidnappers. They supply kidnap insurance in a reasonably competitive setting where all market participants subscribe to a common protocol. Although the syndicates compete vigorously for market share they also know how to cooperate in the interest of the overall market. The small and tight-knit community of underwriters in the Lloyd's market, security consultants, and crisis response experts facilitates vital information sharing between competing firms—reliably, cheaply, and very discreetly. As with other complex and secretive business transactions, it is better for insiders to develop private governance solutions and only take recourse to the legal system in exceptional circumstances.[28]

Almost all aspects of governance in kidnap for ransom insurance are delivered by private sector agencies. Unless we look for the hand of special risk insurers in this system, it is easy to miss it among the various consultancies, lawyers, and the curiously old-fashioned members club of Lloyd's with its syndicates, underwriters, and brokers. On the opposition side there are kidnappers, mafias, insurgents, and various local informal governance providers. Private governance solutions to complex economic problems often feature multiple governance providers, each specializing in solving a particular class of problem. They develop stable relationships to govern any areas of overlap and structure their interactions through norms and rules. There is free entry and exit: governance providers innovate and compete for market share. These features of spontaneous, private order systems are summarized in the term 'polycentric governance'.[29] In Chapters 5–8 we will look at each of the governance challenges in turn. Chapter 9 will pull all the threads together, showing that the observed market structure is indeed the best (if not the only) way of ordering this difficult market.

5

Crafting an Effective Protection Contract

I was working in Somalia and had hired a local security team for protection. One day my own bodyguards kidnapped me. They stopped the car in the middle of nowhere and explained there were 'unforeseen additional expenses'. We would only drive on if I made an immediate extra payment of a thousand dollars. I was on a tight budget and certainly did not have that kind of money on me. They proposed a solution: I had a satellite phone and could call my girlfriend at home and persuade her to withdraw the cash. If she made a hawala transfer to a stranger in Minnesota, the money would be passed on to 'the right people'.[1] Of course, my girlfriend was perturbed and highly sceptical, but thankfully she agreed— eventually. Twenty-five minutes after she reported her mission accomplished, the bodyguard's phone rang out, too. The money had arrived: backs were slapped, and our journey continued amid laughter and smiles. But I was really annoyed in the evening, when they celebrated by ordering the most expensive dishes on the menu for dinner—and expected me to pay for it!

Interview, April 2013

Contracting at the Legal/Extra-legal Interface

Part I of this book developed the idea that kidnapping is disequilibrium behaviour. In equilibrium, people pay the local protector not to get kidnapped. They know how much and whom to pay and successfully make their payments. In return, the protector refrains from kidnapping those who have paid and prevents other kidnappers from operating in the territory. But how exactly are such agreements implemented? The farmer who has paid *la vacuna* ('the vaccine') in Colombia, or *lala salama* ('sleep peacefully') in the Democratic Republic of the Congo, the shop owner in Palermo who gave the *pizzo*, and the researcher who obtained *abaan* to interview Somali pirates are powerless if the protector reneges. The researcher's story above illustrates the many temptations for the protectors to wrangle a little bit more money out of their customers at every opportunity. Similarly, in a weak or rogue state, paying your taxes and observing the law does not necessarily prevent police officers from randomly stopping you and threatening you with an arrest. This can usually be avoided by paying an on-the-spot fine for some obscure transgression.[2] It is probably not worth reporting the incident to the commanding officer, unless you really want to spend a night in a dank police cell while your case is 'investigated'. In the protection contract, the power rests with the protector. The 'customer' cannot enforce it—yet in many cases extra-legal protection works well enough for firms to make significant sunk cost investments.

To examine how firms and insured individuals can prevent their protectors from behaving opportunistically, we use the concept of a 'relational contract'. These are informal agreements and unwritten codes of conduct that—although unenforceable—powerfully affect individual behaviour.[3] A successful relational contract is self-enforcing: cooperation is sustained by the value of future relationships—either with the same partner or (through reputation building) with different partners over time. A good protection contract is designed to ensure that it is in the self-interest of the protectors to uphold their end of the bargain. The value of the future income stream from protection exceeds the benefit from kidnapping and extracting a ransom.

In the legal economy, people enter relational contracts when formal contracting is impossible or prohibitively expensive. For example, it may be impracticable to specify the exact terms of a contract *ex ante*— or it may not be feasible for a third party to verify whether the terms of the contract have been breached. This makes a formal contract unenforceable. Even if a formal contract is theoretically possible, it is worthless if there is no one to enforce it. By contrast, relational contracts are self-enforcing and can be based on outcomes that are only observable to the contracting parties and adapt as new information becomes available.

Co-authoring papers with colleagues is an excellent example of a relational contract. As we develop the initial idea, we don't know where it will lead: an intellectual breakthrough, a marginal contribution, or the filing cabinet. We roughly divide the work—there are social norms regarding what constitutes a fair division of labour. But then family emergencies, lucrative consultancies, sports injuries, and job changes intervene. We either reallocate the work or put the project on the back burner. If the results are so-la-la, is it still worth writing the paper? There is scope for opportunism: if one party is desperate to publish, the other can free-ride. The relational contract is successful if both parties value their reputations sufficiently highly to continue the cooperation. A so-la-la paper and a second-rate co-author may be dispensable—but disappointed students and colleagues talk. If you let people down or put your name on someone else's paper, your future co-authoring options contract.

Many relationships within and between firms are ordered by relational contracts. Common examples are supply relationships, networks, strategic alliances, performance-related pay, promotions, and quid pro quo arrangements between colleagues. The problems that make formal contracting impossible are that actions (e.g. effort) are unobservable, or outcomes cannot be externally verified. In a protection relationship, I don't know how hard the protector worked to keep me safe—I only observe whether there is a kidnap. If there is, I don't know whether this occurred because of my employee's carelessness, through lack of protector vigilance, or with the connivance of the protector. After a failed ransom drop, it is probably impossible to prove whether a police officer appeared by chance, or whether and how the ransom was 'lost'. Scholarly work on the theory of the firm investigates under what conditions relational contracts become self-enforcing. The most critical factor is the value of continuing the relationship for both parties. But it may also matter whether the counterparties are an upstream and a downstream enterprise, or whether the contracting happens within a (vertically integrated) firm.[4]

This chapter discusses different ways of making protection contracts with extra-legal groups self-enforcing. Contracts and payment structures must be carefully designed to keep opportunism in check. We will see that many interactions have prisoners' dilemma characteristics: although both parties would benefit from cooperating, each side is better off breaking the agreement in a one-off transaction. Only the expectation of future payments to a reputable protector constrains the temptation to extract additional payments today. Thus, if one side perceives the interaction to be a one-off interaction, relational contracts tend to fail. Yet, every family hopes and prays that a kidnap is a one-off event, rather than the start of a beautiful relationship with a kidnapping gang. Many protection contracts are for short-term business. If at most a week's or a month's protection is required, the protector may prefer to renegotiate the price or break the contract. How do tourists, business travellers, NGOs bringing disaster relief, researchers, and journalists obtain protection? Firms which make significant sunk cost investments for extractive or productive activities have longer time horizons—but the temptation for the protector to renege is also greater: multinationals can afford big ransoms and assets can be looted or expropriated. A further complication is that often there are multiple protectors to satisfy. The state can threaten to withdraw licences or nationalize the enterprise—but separate local protection contracts may be needed to guarantee the safety of the workforce, supply chains, and export routes.

If there are multiple protectors, who designs the contract that keeps them from each other's throats as well as protecting the staff from kidnap and the assets from sabotage? Companies do not look good if army units or paramilitaries terrorize, shoot, or disappear local opposition leaders to protect their installations.[5] There is a further potential problem: what if the protector or kidnapping gang is an insurgent or proscribed terrorist group? You will have to pay them if you want to stay safe in their territory. The host government wants to sell you a mining licence, but categorically states that you cannot fund the insurgency. The UN and your own government forbid you from funding terrorism. The press will have a field day if they find out that you do. How can you design a protection contract that is both effective and plausibly deniable?

We know that oil, gold, and diamonds are extracted from conflict areas and rebel-held territory. People travel and do business in areas where there is no police presence, or where the police can conduct their own extortion operations. Most of them do so safely. Most of them also have kidnap insurance. As a condition of their kidnap insurance, they were given safety advice. Let us consider the advert of a security consultancy through the lens of protection theory:

> [Our] hostile environment protection service provides the best possible security solution when operating in hostile and complex territories. [We] will conduct a detailed risk assessment as well as, develop a protection strategy tailored to the perceived threat. Our security consultants and staffs will not only manage your security plan and advise on risk management issues; we will also provide holistic professional advice, deploy intelligent strategy [sic] that will help sustain maximum security so that our clients can focus on their business without safety worries.[6]

An 'intelligent strategy that will help sustain maximum security' in 'hostile' territories will require some level of engagement with the local power brokers. This is something that few Western firms have much experience in. However, insurers retain the services of experienced security consultants with in-depth country knowledge to advise their customers how to avoid kidnap, threat extortion, and sabotage. I argue that these various specialists order transactions between legal entities and extra-legal protectors. Operating for private profit, they provide governance services to facilitate mutually beneficial exchange and investment in weakly governed areas. Because they advise many customers over long periods of time, they can make even one-off relational contracts self-enforcing.

This chapter discusses seven distinct ways of making self-enforcing protection contracts with cleptocrats, criminals, rebels, and even terrorist groups. This generally requires promising a steady income stream to whichever armed group controls the relevant territory. The obvious solution—openly making protection payments—is rarely acceptable. The host government usually objects to people funding the enemies of the state and to a home audience doing so looks corrupt. If the counterparty is a designated terrorist organization, a whole host of UN resolutions forbids anyone from making financial concessions. And yet—as Part I argued—there is no way of combining operations in rebel-controlled territory with a duty of care towards one's employees and a complete refusal to make payments to the informal protector. Some of the strategies discussed in this chapter are therefore surreptitious—but most are carefully designed to be hidden in plain view.

If it is impossible to outsource protection to the informal protector (option 1), option 2 is to bring the protector inside the firm as a co-owner or by employing his people on the staff. A third option is to buy goods and services from local firms who in turn pay the protector. In some cases, entire business operations have been outsourced to the informal protectors, but this fourth option rarely makes business sense. Option 5 is to contract with a private security company, which in turn subcontracts with the informal protector. A sixth option is to satisfy the informal protector's demands through a corporate social responsibility programme. The seventh and final option is to accept occasional kidnaps and pay ransoms. In different areas of the world and over time, firms adopt different approaches to obtain security—and sometimes several strategies in parallel. This chapter argues that these choices are rational economic adaptations to distinct and often shifting local and international security environments.

Outsourcing Protection as an Economic Decision

Let us consider security (or 'protection') as an input to the production process of a (downstream) firm. Protection can be outsourced to one or more (upstream) security providers. Alternatively, the firm can (try to) self-protect.[7] The firm aims to minimize the total cost of security, which consists of production and organization costs. The production of security requires guards, weapons, and physical security measures. The organization costs include arranging tasks, coordinating activities, and adapting to contingencies. In addition, the firm must manage the risk of opportunistic behaviour by the supplier, such as undersupplying protection or renegotiating the price.

In terms of production costs, whichever (armed) group currently controls the territory will be the most effective and cost-efficient provider of protection.[8] In the extortion business, the protector's foot soldiers simply refrain from hassling paying customers and the 'Don' prohibits criminal and illicit enterprises operating under his protection from targeting his protégées. The Don just needs to deal with impostors, opportunists, and rivals. All other security providers have massively higher production costs: they face threats from the incumbent, every resident criminal, local pressure groups, and the Don's rivals.

In some cases, the cost difference between the local protector and security produced within the firm or bought on the spot market is so great that the only alternative to paying off the incumbent—however politically unpalatable—is to shelve the project. For example, the proposed TAPI gas pipeline from Turkmenistan to Pakistan and India will pass through the Afghan provinces of Herat, Helmand, and Kandahar, parts of which are under Taliban control. Even with 7,000 Afghan troops promised to guard the 773 km-long pipeline and its construction, one thing is clear: 'The Taliban...will need to be included in security discussions should the pipeline have any hope of remaining secure'.[9] Indeed, the Taliban signalled that they would like to make a deal: 'The Islamic Emirate not only backs all national projects which are in the interest of the people...[but] are also committed to safeguarding them...The Islamic Emirate directs all its *mujahideen* to help in the security of all national projects that are in the higher interest of Islam and the country.'[10] Drafting this protection agreement will be a very interesting political exercise.

Sometimes competition between different security providers is feasible at the award stage of a contract. However, once the chosen protector makes contract-specific investments the contractual relationship can be transformed into a bilateral monopoly.[11] For example, the UN missions UNOSOM I, Unified Task Force (UNITAF), and UNOSOM II in Somalia rented trucks, houses, security guards, and armed cars (so-called 'technicals') from local strongmen. The munificence of the 'UN cash cow' enabled the service providers to build up their own militias and turn themselves into powerful warlords—who then fought each other for territory, resources, and the next UN contract. Although the UN missions were intended to save Somali civilians from the warlords, on the ground their forces had no option but to buy services from and thereby strengthen their declared enemies.[12] But the monopoly was bilateral: once the UN forces withdrew and the funds dried up, the warlords' patronage and power collapsed too. Protectors must limit their opportunism to retain their customers. To people specialized in the production of violence, confiscated productive assets are worth very little indeed.

If there are large cost differentials between the local and an outside protector, how can the downstream firm incentivize the upstream protection enterprise to exert high effort? The firm might offer a bonus if there are no incidents of kidnap, sabotage, and threat extortion over the month. The supplier chooses how much effort to devote to protection, but even with maximum vigilance incidents will occasionally occur. If there is an incident, the downstream firm could withhold the payment and threaten to buy protection from a different supplier. However, if the protector is well-entrenched, alternative suppliers are likely to be much more expensive and provide lower-quality protection. Any outsider faces opposition from the local protector, now turned kidnapper and saboteur. It is likely that people will die. The downstream firm's threats to change supplier may therefore not be credible. Anticipating this, the protector may choose to exert low effort or secretly tolerate or engage in kidnapping, earning income from both protection and criminal activities. Yet, there is a limit to the protector's opportunism: too high a protection fee and too much insecurity and the firm will choose to withdraw from the territory governed by the opportunistic protector.[13] The withdrawal of a large firm has negative impacts on local suppliers, contractors, and workers. This reduces the value of other protection contracts, too. If the protector (who is after all a local monopolist) provides security to multiple large firms and their supply chains, the temptation to renege on individual contracts recedes.

Opportunism in the protection relationship is not entirely one-sided. The firm has a strong incentive to understate its profitability and thereby lower the protector's expectations or perhaps evade paying protection money altogether. A tourist may plead ignorance of local customs and lack of cash, while a contractor could try to circumvent the roadblock. The relationship between the protector and the protected therefore has clear prisoners' dilemma characteristics. Let us assume that a firm seeks protection for a profitable business opportunity in the protector's territory, but the profits are private knowledge. If the firm truthfully states its profits and the protector faithfully provides security, both make a good return from the protection relationship. However, the protector is tempted to cheat: he could take both the protection payment and profit from a kidnap. The firm's profit is reduced when paying the ransom, but also by their workers' reaction to greater insecurity. Similarly, the firm is tempted to cheat: it could reduce the protection payment by understating its profits. The protector suffers both a financial loss and a reputational damage—especially if the deception comes to light. If both parties cheat (the protector kidnaps occasionally and the protégée underpays), they can limit the damage their counterparty can inflict on them. The protector augments the reduced protection fee with the occasional ransom, while the firm invests most of the savings from the reduced protection payment into additional security measures or higher compensation for its workers. Both parties are worse off than if they had successfully cooperated. If the mutual toleration of each other's dishonesty also breaks down, the firm must self-protect at a high cost and the protector exerts effort to disrupt the business. If self-protection is prohibitively costly, the firm will withdraw from the protector's territory unless it is likely that a cooperative protection relationship can be resumed. Complete withdrawal ends the game and results in a zero payoff for both sides.[14]

In a one-shot game both sides will cheat. Although both parties know that payoff is maximized if both sides deal honestly, each side is better off reneging on the contract, regardless of what the counterparty chooses to do. A cooperative equilibrium can only be reached and sustained if both parties have a sufficiently long time horizon and value the gains from future cooperation more than the one-off gains from cheating. Similarly, if protectors have a large portfolio of customers they have an incentive to guard their reputation: if they cheat one customer, then others might renege or withdraw too.

This analysis abstracts from an important further problem: uncertainty. In practice, neither party can correctly observe or cheaply verify the other's actions. The protector will find it very difficult to ascertain the profitability of the foreign subsidiary of a multinational company. The complex financial architecture of multinational companies allows profits to be declared anywhere. Similarly, the security provider's effort is not fully observable: opportunistic criminals and impostors can make perfect protection prohibitively costly. Even a highly vigilant protector will occasionally fail. A kidnap is therefore not proof that the provider undersupplied security or was complicit in a kidnapping. This uncertainty makes it problematic and costly to monitor performance and punish infractions. In the conflict scenario, the protector does not know the cost of self-protection and the firm may wonder how long a warlord can sustain a conflict without the next cash injection.

The protection contract must therefore be carefully designed to reveal truthful information as well as create the time horizon or horizontal diversification to make it self-enforcing. The rest of the chapter looks at various approaches which have been developed in different contexts. The key to understanding which solutions are appropriate in different circumstances are transaction costs: firms look for contracts which minimize the production, organization, and enforcement costs of security. We observe both relational outsourcing and relational employment contracts. Occasionally there are mergers between firms and their security providers, which bring the transactions inside the firm.

We also observe that many protection contracts are arranged and enforced by third parties. Often this is because the deal must be done surreptitiously. One needs specialist knowledge to identify the correct counterparty among impostors and informers, negotiate in secret, and craft a self-enforcing agreement with an extra-legal and perhaps proscribed group. Any agreement must be plausibly deniable for the customer. There is the potential of huge reputational damage if a large foreign firm buys security from an illicit supplier and this becomes public knowledge. It is therefore often worth subcontracting the negotiation and enforcement of the protection contract to a security specialist. Security consultancies have two further advantages. First, if they can act on behalf of several firms, they have more leverage over rogue protectors. Second, they usually have an armed response capacity that makes their threat of punishing defections credible.

When firms engage reputable security consultancies or private military security companies to help them negotiate complex and hostile terrain, they enter a formal contract. It is up to the security specialists to negotiate the local, relational contract and craft a package of sensible safety measures and payments to incentivize the protectors to refrain from kidnapping. Ideally, the ultimate customer remains blissfully ignorant of the details. As outsiders, we only observe that people and companies peacefully travel and conduct legitimate business in areas we know to be rebel-controlled or in open conflict. Business or other activities which require protection must be very valuable to remain profitable after all the transaction costs of obtaining effective protection are considered. It is therefore not surprising that in most informally governed territories many benefits from trade and foreign direct investment remain unexploited. Often only mining and oil companies have a presence. These are diversified companies with large profit margins that can afford to obtain security for their staff. The rest of the chapter explores the seven different ways of making a protection contract self-enforcing.

Option 1: Direct Outsourcing of Protection

In the classic protection contract, the protector extorts a fee from every person in the territory who produces a surplus—but leaves enough surplus to encourage individual effort in production. Usually, the protection fee extorts a proportion of profits. For example, militias in the Democratic Republic of the Congo sometimes charge local farmers to access their fields.[15] It is in the interest of the militia that the farmers plant valuable, nutritious crops rather than the subsistence choice: cassava. The militia therefore can neither take away the money needed for seed and fertilizer, nor confiscate all the profit from planting higher-value crops. If there are roving bandits nearby, the local militia must guard the fields. The short-term gain from beating up a farmer and stealing her crop, or from abandoning land to a rival gang, would be dwarfed by the loss from reduced effort or crop substitution by other farmers in the community. Rebels would also gain little from driving foreign mining operations from their territory. Yes, the protector could expropriate the sunk cost investment in buildings and machinery. But running a sophisticated mining operation for example, extracting gold-rich ore from great depths, refining it to the point where it becomes transportable, and obtaining all the human capital, spare parts, and consumables necessary to do so is far beyond the capability of the average rebel outfit. Where both sides gain from continued production, the protection contract can become self-enforcing.

Where there are multiple protectors, firms may have to pay multiple taxes: both formal and informal. Mogadishu's largest market—the Bakara—operated throughout the Somali civil war and was rarely disrupted by fighting. Largely this was due to traders being pragmatic about paying off whichever groups had the military capacity to threaten their business interests. In 2017, five years after the federal government took office, Bakara traders still paid double taxes. Based just a three-kilometre walk away from the centre of government in Villa Somalia, an anonymous trader reported: 'All the big shops you see in Bakara have to pay a tax to Al Shabaab or they risk facing consequences... I have been paying it myself. It's for my own security. If I don't pay they can assassinate you. I am only protecting myself and my business.'[16] The better the informal protector is at preventing government officials from collecting taxes, the higher the proportion of the total tax burden that goes into informal channels.

If the protector operates in the shadows, the main difference for local enterprises will be that the payments are non-traceable and perhaps disguised. In the Bakara market, the Al Shabaab representative 'would call directly to ascertain... adherence to paying the protection fee'.[17]

If he gets a special deal on camel meat or a gun, no one will be any the wiser. Similarly, the Sicilian mafia sends 'Uncle Pino' to pick up an envelope with the monthly protection fee in cash. Another Sicilian entrepreneur reported that when he took over a business, he found a monthly payment of €1,000 for maintenance services in the account. He knew not to expect any workmen: 'They [the mafia] made me a bill of €1,000 per month for routine maintenance ... it was the "vigilance"'.[18]

For outsiders, the direct outsourcing model is more difficult. They must find out who to pay for protection, how to pay, and how much. It can work, if the market for private protection operates openly. When I conducted my research on Somali piracy I jokingly suggested to a security consultant that we could conduct some fieldwork together. I would have felt safe with him—he is a capable marksman and experienced close protection specialist. However, he said that this would not be a good idea: it would be considered a provocation and I would be much better off with a local solution. His advice was to inform Puntland government officials of my travel plans in advance. 'The person who turns up at the airport is the right one. Take him. They sort it out amongst themselves beforehand.'[19] As the intrepid researcher's tale in the introduction to this chapter showed, the system broadly worked, even if the price was sometimes subject to renegotiation. It worked, because this was the best travel advice money could buy. The local protector was not challenged and therefore provided security at minimal cost. It would probably have been sufficient to announce our 'friendship' at a lavish public dinner—at my expense, of course. Alternatively, I could travel with his charming cousin or with a whole troupe of (otherwise unemployable) retainers. While my protection contract would have been a one-off, dealing honestly with me meant that future travellers would also receive the same advice. Everyone wins.

The roadblock model operates on a similar basis: the protectors reveal themselves. It can be the army, the police, or a rebel outfit that decides to extract a payment from travellers to smooth the rest of the journey. The fee is set according to ability to pay—the farm labourer pays a different price from the trucking company and the tourist. But even the VIP does not pay an extortionate amount and kidnaps are rare: it is in the protector's interest that people use the road. Although tourists look like an attractive target for extracting a big fee at first sight, they are also easily diverted. Government travel advice often specifically states that tourists should only travel by air—depriving the protector of an important long-term income source. The bundling of information about the protector's behaviour and the large cost of reneging makes the series of short, one-off protection contracts self-enforcing.

It gets more difficult when the protector operates in the shadows, however. From a protection theory point of view, the German company Mannesmann acted as a responsible employer in Colombia. The company won a contract to build an oil pipeline through territory controlled by the insurgent National Liberation Front (ELN) in the 1980s. After suffering several attacks and kidnappings, Mannesmann (through local partners) allegedly arranged for the ELN to guarantee the security of the workforce and the completed parts of the pipeline.[20] The pipeline would always be vulnerable, so insurgents had a long-term interest in the completion of the project: it would need protection forever. The relational contract was self-enforcing. However, the sudden influx of money transformed a failing rag-tag rebel outfit into a formidable fighting force. The Colombian government sent in troops to battle the ELN. The German 'superspy' Werner Mauss, who had helped Mannesmann negotiate ransoms for kidnapped employees and was rumoured to have arranged the protection contract, was arrested and charged.[21] The company's rational response to a security threat became a public scandal. The reputational cost of the protection contract quickly outweighed its benefit. Protection contracts with extra-legal organizations must be carefully designed to avoid detection by outsiders. Often, this makes direct relational outsourcing impossible and more complex options must be explored.

The stream of expected future benefits does not make all relational protection contracts self-enforcing. Disputed territory is particularly problematic, because the protector's time horizons can suddenly contract to the point where the short-term gain of reneging is preferred. One-off engagements which do not leave a valuable, long-term asset for the extra-legal protector are similarly problematic. The UN's experience trying to deliver aid to war-torn Somalia in 1992 is instructive. The local guards charged with protecting the quays, trucks, stores, and the distribution routes kept coming back to UN officials for additional protection payments, while looting the goods behind their backs.[22] The only way to resume deliveries to the hungry was to boost the military capacity and mandate of the UN humanitarian mission 'Restore Hope' in Somalia (April 1992—March 1993). In August 1992, UNOSOM I's mandate and strength were enlarged to enable it to protect humanitarian convoys and distribution centres throughout Somalia. In December 1992, the UN Security Council authorized member states to form UNITAF to establish a safe environment for the delivery of humanitarian assistance. UNITAF worked 'to secure major population centres and ensure that humanitarian assistance was delivered and distributed'.[23]

The presence of armed troops made relational outsourcing possible again: a well-armed customer can punish the cheating protector for reneging. For example, the Italian contingent participating in UNITAF was charged with safeguarding the airport. This was an essential supply route for the UN mission. However, the airport area was controlled by forces loyal to General Aideed, leader of one of the warring factions.[24] The commander of the Italian army units, General Loi, elegantly solved the problem by outsourcing the protection contract to General Aideed.[25] This facilitated aid deliveries with minimal risk to all parties involved. The Italian troops remained safely behind the wire—only venturing out on pre-agreed routes. There was just one hostile event in which three Italian soldiers were killed by an angry mob while on patrol (apparently due to a communication failure). As US helicopter gunships rushed to the aid of their embattled allies this 'mistake' was also very costly for the protector.[26] The balance of power made the relational contract self-enforcing. The contract only broke down when the US leadership put their foot down: paying General Aideed for protection meant 'taking sides' in the civil war.[27] Yet, without protection money being paid the conflict escalated: the formerly warring protectors immediately united against the 'occupiers'. Soon there was no longer a way of continuing either a humanitarian or a peace-keeping mission in Somalia with a body count that US voters were willing to support.

Private military security companies can also enforce protection contracts by force—and therefore they only need to do it in exceptional circumstances. A former mercenary was offended when a publisher criticized his memoirs as: 'not exciting enough, we need more stories of you in a hail of bullets'. He sighed: 'You see, if there had been whistling bullets, I would not have done my job properly.' Erik Prince, the founder of the security company Blackwater extols his company's excellent working relationships with local warlords. Blackwater's so-called 'in country assets . . . were men with nasty reputations but an appreciation for getting things done'. When the US armed forces prepared for the invasion of Afghanistan, Blackwater was 'able to set the CIA up with the most useful men in the region'.[28] Clearly, it is good to know who the local warlord is and strike a deal—while being 'careful to maintain the highest ethics while dealing with these contacts', of course. With a well-equipped mercenary force, able to inflict grievous punishment on attackers, the protection contract becomes self-enforcing—for both sides. As Blackwater's example shows: security companies do not look good either, if their gunmen cut a swathe through the local population with a hail of whistling bullets.[29]

Thus, both long-term and short-term protection contracts can be designed to be self-enforcing. The price depends on the balance of power in the relationship—and perhaps on additional services rendered by the protector. For example, in 2015 the Italian-Argentinian company SICIM was investigated for paying protection money to Marxist rebels in Colombia to facilitate the building of the Bicentennial Pipeline. The problem was not so much the extortion payments (by then tolerated as unavoidable), but the evidence that the protector deliberately hassled other oil companies in the region to give SICIM a competitive advantage.[30]

Option 2: The Coase–Williamson Solutions

The economists Ronald Coase and Oliver Williamson examined how businesses are shaped by transactions costs.[31] The cost of negotiating, drawing up, monitoring, and enforcing agreements between two enterprises can be high—especially when there is uncertainty, when information cannot be easily shared or verified, or when enforcement is unreliable. Coase noted that often transactions costs can be significantly reduced by vertical integration. In some cases, it is better for the upstream and downstream firm to merge rather than trying to write and enforce an incomplete contract between two separate entities.[32] How could this be done and what would it achieve in a protection context? If the national government must expend additional effort to become an effective protector in the region in which an enterprise wants to locate, both sides gain from vertical integration. This is usually done by creating a joint venture in which the government (or, in cleptocracies, the president's family) has a significant stake. The foreign parent company gains, because the host government now has a direct interest in protecting its asset and the income stream it produces. The government gains, because it can monitor—and thereby prevent—the foreign enterprise from paying the local rebel outfit for (cheaper) security. The government can also monitor profitability and is interested in maximizing its profit share. So, rather than sending a handful of scared conscripts into rebel territory, the government ensures that the joint venture company gets value for money. A well-equipped security team of battle-hardened veterans makes insurgents and criminals think twice about attacking the facility.

Deterrence is always better than getting involved in firefights. The foreign company's shareholders will raise objections if the security detail regularly commits human rights violations to protect their assets. In the late 1990s, British Petroleum (BP) was continuously in the news over the 'dirty war' Colombian soldiers and allied militias waged on rebels and their suspected civilian sympathizers.[33] Headlines such as 'BP hands tarred in pipeline dirty war'[34] and 'BP at war'[35] wreaked havoc with the company's reputation. In contemporary joint ventures in rebel territory (for example gold-mining operations in Mali), foreign companies invest heavily in training and equipment to ensure that their local security personnel are competent, well-briefed on human rights, and formidable enough to deflect would-be attackers to softer targets.

It is probably inevitable that the local protector also gains something from the presence of the foreign enterprise. If not, there is a risk that insurgents engage in a scorched earth strategy: no firm may be better for them than a foreign presence from which only the government benefits. The Coasean solution may be to bring the protector's clients and proté-gées into the firm, too. An interviewee put it beautifully succinctly: 'If there is a Don, I hire his peasants. He will make sure they earn their money.' The 'peasants' do not need to have a direct security role. In many contexts, it is better if they don't. It is perfectly reasonable that the company and its expatriate staff employ local cleaners, gardeners, drivers, and secretaries. They will be vetted (probably by an experienced security consultancy) beforehand and will have a reputation for being 'reliable'. If there is a problem with the implicit (protection) contract, the formal (employment) contract can be immediately revoked.

However, not all mergers or relational employment contracts are self-enforcing: as soon as time horizons contract or future pay-offs are heavily discounted, the temptation to renegotiate the contract arises. An unstable government can threaten to nationalize foreign enterprises or levy additional taxes. For example, Zimbabwe's indigenization law of 2008 requires companies to hand over 51 per cent of their shares to black Zimbabweans. The policy was designed to generate patronage opportunities for the struggling president—but instead many foreign firms avoided compliance by making 'alternative arrangements' with the government: clearly a euphemism for bigger protection payments.[36] At the individual level, drivers who only have two weeks left on their contracts could betray the manager's route to work or make an unauthorized detour resulting in a kidnap. The cleaner or gardener could accidentally forget to lock the gate. For firms which are only in a country for short periods and those who are about to withdraw, relational employment is not an effective way to obtain protection.

Option 3: 'Reputable' Providers

For short-term operations, business meetings, conferences, and tourism, relational contracts are problematic: self-enforcement relies on the shadow of the future. However, with a sufficient overall business volume over long time periods it is possible to incentivize the protector to protect. If the protectors can derive a steady income stream from being reliable, they will guard their reputation. As in the roadblock scenario, if we permit the protectors to collect a (small) fee from every trade or visit, they will not beat up, rob, or kidnap individuals: opportunism is punished by a heavy contraction of the protector's business volume thereafter. This system relies on good communication: there needs to be excellent information flow between all those who need protection over time.

Such a reputational solution was famously adopted by the Maghribi traders in the eleventh century. To trade with their business contacts across the Mediterranean, merchants employed agents—who could easily disappear with goods or withhold some money. To make the contracts self-enforcing, the merchants created a sophisticated multilateral information transmission system. They wrote each other letters exposing agents who cheated (or seemed less than fully reliable). Many of these historic documents were preserved in the Jewish *geniza* in Old Cairo. Any agent who was tempted to cheat his principal knew that he probably would not be employed by the traders' coalition again—and if so, on a much-reduced commission. The importance of maintaining a good reputation made the relational contract self-enforcing.[37] A recent reappraisal of the letters by Lisa Bernstein shows that the system functioned so well because of a few highly prolific letter writers. Rather than information being transmitted (rarely and chaotically) between the nodes in the system, Old Cairo was the information hub. Here, complaints were collated, and information was quickly dispatched across the entire network.[38]

Information about how reliable a protector is spreads quickly among locals. It is difficult (and expensive) for foreign visitors to collect and evaluate this dispersed local information. As a visitor—do I need to worry about gang violence in a city? Is the shocking homicide rate relevant to what goes on inside the trade fair or conference centre? Where should I stay? Can I take the underground or a taxi? I am happy to hire a chauffeured limousine—but a pink stretched Cadillac would make me very conspicuous. Is there a company that people recommend? For tourists, the first point of call is the government's travel advice. If there is no explicit travel warning, one chooses depending on one's degree of risk aversion. If I choose a package holiday or book a trip with a reputable tour operator, then it is up to the travel company to work out a sensible route and the protection arrangements on the ground. Otherwise, old-fashioned travellers buy a guidebook to obtain information on where to go, stay, eat, and party. Others get the information from the concierge, fellow travellers, and the internet. Troubled areas are given a wide berth—often long after any problem has been resolved. So, the revenue-maximizing protector may well decide to play it safe and send small-time criminals packing. I remember my voluble host in central Naples: 'Don't worry, you are entirely safe here. Look—I dropped my money there. Nobody will take it. This is *Mafia* territory.' To the 'consumer' of mafia protection it is not relevant how exactly it works. Maybe the mafia owned the hotel. More likely, my host paid the *pizzo*. I had a lovely time.

The government's foreign travel advice ('only essential travel') is often not fine-grained enough for the business community. How do I make my 'essential travel' safe? Do I need to repatriate my workforce yet? Companies need a super-communicator who collects, interprets, and disseminates relevant information—if necessary on a daily, street-by-street, or even house-by-house basis. Once again, we arrive at the doorstep of the security consultancies retained by the insurers. Insurance comes with professional security advice—sometimes called proactive loss prevention.[39] It is the consultant's business to know the reliable, reputable service providers and hotels. You will be fine at the Caliph's Beard hotel. Use the International Backside Taxi Company and say hi to Hamdi for me. These are the four places Westerners eat out in Djibo. The consultants can help to vet the staff and find you appropriate premises. A safe house in Bamako? No problem, here is the address. A safe house in Timbuktu? Sorry, not possible at the moment.

Companies operating in complex and hostile territory also subscribe to security alert services. Based on remote monitoring and local sources, firms receive timely advice on emerging trouble spots and even detailed plans to target specific events to kidnap foreigners. 'Information indicates that a group of known terrorists are moving southwards through Burkina Faso in the Gayeri-Yamba area, 186 miles east of Ouagadougou. The group is heading toward Fada Ngourma but could split or detour toward the capital....In Eastern Burkina Faso, keep a low profile or evacuate over the Tabaski festival period (1–3 September).'[40] In 2015, foreign investors in Mali received security advice that the Radisson Blu in Bamako was a likely target: it was attacked a few weeks later leaving twenty people dead.[41] Thus, security consultancies can pause, redirect, or stop very lucrative income streams as soon as a protector loses control or turns rogue. This bundling of information and its timely dissemination sustains the reputational equilibrium.

The other beauty of this arrangement is that firms and their staff do not engage in corrupt behaviour—and neither do the consultants. The best advice is based on performance, rather than on detailed knowledge of why exactly Moussa's taxis never runs into trouble at roadblocks and Oumar's garden restaurant is so peaceful. It's a safe house. What else do I need to know? We like staying at the Caliph's Beard hotel. Yes, it's a bit more expensive than the one down the road. But it's nice and all our friends stay here as well. The security guards are snoozing most of the afternoon, but we never have any trouble.

This happy state of affairs is upset when new rebel groups form and try to claim territory. In recent years, hotels and restaurants popular with expats and local VIPs have increasingly been targeted by rising Islamist rebel groups. The Al Shabaab group, for example, attacked the Dayah Hotel in central Mogadishu in January 2017, killing twenty-eight and injuring forty-three people.[42] This was not an isolated incident, but was preceded by attacks on the SYL, Nasa Hablod, and Ambassador Hotels in 2016, and the Central, the Makka-al-Mukarama, and the Posh Hotel in 2015. In Mali's capital Bamako, the Radisson Blu was targeted in 2015 and Le Campement Kangaba in 2017. Islamist militants have also targeted hotels and restaurants in the Egyptian tourist resort of Hurghada, as well as Libya (Tripoli), Tunisia (Sousse), and Burkina Faso (Ouagadougou). Many analysts stress the *jihadi* terrorism angle (killing Westerners for propaganda purposes), but there is a clear economic purpose here. A reduction in tourism revenues weakens the government's fiscal position.[43] Moreover, other hotels will be less likely to blow off the extortion attempts of rebel groups that have just proved their ability to launch a devastating attack on a well-guarded hotel two blocks away. Until a new equilibrium with a dominant protector emerges, the situation will remain volatile.

Option 4: Wholesale Outsourcing

When protection arrangements become unreliable as roving bandits contest territory and menace traders and producers, many economic activities become unprofitable. Affected firms initially evacuate their foreign staff and eventually close their operations. If a rebel group manages to take over a mine or plantation, there is no need for a protection contract. If the output is competitively priced, it can be acquired on the spot market (unless the press draws attention to the situation, such as the campaigns against 'blood oil' and 'blood diamonds'). But civil wars and state failure also usually create dire humanitarian emergencies, which the international community wants to alleviate. How can aid agencies reach the at-risk or starving populations in complex and hostile territories? In some areas, any white face, laden truck, and Landcruiser is a conspicuous target. Famines and water shortages which force (ethnic minority) people to migrate can be usefully incorporated into a war-fighting strategy. In this case, foreign-managed and -monitored aid deliveries are not welcome at all.

After the withdrawal of the second UN mission to Somalia (UNOSOM II) in early March 1995, international efforts to help stabilize and create new governance structures in Somalia, as well as deliver disaster relief, were run from neighbouring Kenya.[44] Even World Food Programme aid shipments were so vulnerable to attack that the international naval counter-piracy force was tasked with providing escort services for the ancient aid freighters chugging along the coast between Mombasa and Mogadishu. But what happened to the aid once it was unloaded at the quay? The most difficult part of the journey still lay ahead. The obvious answer was to subcontract aid distribution altogether. Other developmental initiatives, opinion polls, collection of local weather and price data, and the monitoring of these activities were also sub-contracted to local firms. It would be up to them to fulfil the contract to the best of their abilities.

Designing a self-enforcing contract where nothing is verifiable is impossible. Some enterprising Kenyans spotted a brilliant opportunity for making money from the dicey security situation in Somalia: acting as pirates in foreign documentary programmes. Their fixer offered an attractive safari package for journalists keen to interview pirates, but rather than engaging in the messy business of organizing protection in Somalia, he led them to his accomplices. They were an excellent substitute for real pirates: cheaper, safer, and just as scary.[45] A contract is only self-enforcing if the customer can verify the outcome or at least monitor effort. Local interlocutors hired to conduct a survey in rural south central Somalia were unaware that their satellite phone was traced by the employer. When they submitted the completed forms, they were confronted with evidence that their data were collected from the comfort of a hotel in the regional capital. The next group of interlocutors made sure that (at least) the phone completed the set itinerary, and their data were accepted.

Remote sensing and local human intelligence can help to verify that journeys were completed, goods delivered, and aid distributed to the intended population. In difficult security situations, the customer tolerates that a proportion of the cargo is handed over at every checkpoint, taken in ambushes, and lost in the melee at distribution points. One expects that extra money will be required for 'permits'.[46] Nobody knows how much of the loss or additional expense was unavoidable. Still, relational outsourcing contracts in which little was independently verifiable are sometimes deemed to be successful. One rather suspects that in many cases both sides are aware of opportunism and perhaps willing participants in the deception. It may be the best one can do in an impossibly difficult security situation.[47]

Option 5: Private Military Security

In the corporate world, declaring failing contracts a success is not a sustainable business strategy. If a company is continuously approached for additional bribes and extortion payments, employees are kidnapped, and production is impaired by acts of sabotage it can hire an international private military security company (PMSC). The company now has a formal, legally enforceable protection contract. There are still some relational aspects to the contract: the PMSC may not be able to prevent all attacks (especially on low-level employees) and may want to renegotiate its terms occasionally as the security situation develops. However, whereas in the country one must make the protection contract with the local protector, multinationals have the choice of many security companies competing globally for contracts. Competition strongly reduces the incentives for opportunistic behaviour.

Elite soldiers and special forces officers turned mercenaries come at a price. Hiring two close protection specialists to guard the CEO on a week-long business trip is one thing. Guarding an industrial complex, its supply and export routes (whether an air-strip or a pipeline), key staff, and their families around the clock is another. To make protection affordable, Western PMSCs will—wherever possible—employ cheaper local personnel for routine guard duties and subcontract some services altogether. There are more than 1,500 private security contractors in Nigeria alone—and contracts often end up 'in the hands of the very groups responsible for the attacks on oil facilities'. You may have thought 'you were employing,...a genuine, bona fide contractor, and yet he is probably a militant or a warlord'.[48] As discussed in option 1, private security companies have a huge advantage in enforcing a relational protection contract. If the local protector turns poacher, a military security company can quickly respond by laying off local guards and bolstering its own forces—perhaps by bringing in mercenaries from another province or a neighbouring country. The possibility of employing a trigger strategy which reduces the protector's income for several periods makes the local protector less likely to renege.

In disputed territory, a private security company hiring the Don's 'peasants' gains an additional advantage over a civilian enterprise.

Hostage-taking is a classic way of enforcing relational contracts.[49] If a mafia wishes to be paid for illicit goods in advance, the buyer is reassured if the supplier's favourite child stays with them until the arrival of the shipment. The honest supplier has no qualms about sending the young lad or lady on a holiday. Willingness to volunteer a hostage is a classic economic signal to help the receiver of a message distinguish the honest from a dishonest sender. If a compound guarded by both foreign and local private security guards is attacked, it is inevitable that the local guards will suffer heavy losses. They can get shot by either side. This implicit threat may suffice to make the relational contract self-enforcing, especially if the protector volunteers a close relative to command the guards.

The firm's reputation on the other hand is not a hostage, if the protection contract is brokered through a PMSC. If the press picks up a problem, the company is not at fault. PMSCs can be replaced when their reputation becomes toxic—or they change their name.[50] If countries do not allow foreign companies to bring in foreign mercenaries, but hire out armed forces or veterans for profit, companies have little or no control over how the security is provided. In 2012, the Nigerian arm of Shell was questioned about tens of millions of dollars of opaque security expenditure in the Niger Delta and human rights abuses committed by armed police deployed by the Nigerian government to guard Shell installations.[51] As a first line of defence, the company responded that 'any allegations of corruption should be addressed to the Nigerian authorities'.[52] Shell managers are doing their best to fix the problems: 'In our discussions with the security authorities we have highlighted the UN Code of Conduct for Law Enforcement Officials and the Guidelines on Use of Firearms.' But unfortunately, there is little to be done: 'there is a challenge in engaging this group as they operate solely under the command and control of the Nigerian government or security headquarters'.[53]

Yet, brutal suppression of local discontent rarely achieves meaningful security. Large installations and particularly pipelines always remain vulnerable to acts of sabotage and theft. In extreme cases, such as Nigeria's Forcados pipeline, repair costs can make pipelines too costly to operate.[54] In such cases it might be wise to engage the 'local community' in protection.

Option 6: Corporate Social Responsibility

The more closely local security arrangements are monitored for bribes and extortion payments, the less scope there is for a relational contract with armed groups. If mercenaries or the host government's troops are not formidable enough to deter attacks, or firms worry about human rights violations committed in their name, they need local security arrangements that remain below the radar. A corporate social responsibility programme may be the way forward. The optics are excellent: the company is 'giving back' to the local community. In exchange for providing much-needed public services, the company gains social legitimacy for its presence in the area. The community's wish list is usually tightly proscribed: healthcare, education, agricultural development, poverty alleviation, and infrastructure. A community might get a new school, hospital, well, aqueduct, sewer, or a paved road—but nothing that would directly increase the arsenal or fighting capacity of rebel groups.

Yet, locals know why foreign companies are pouring resources into their communities. Effectively, companies are 'buying a stable working environment through the provision of development goods'.[55] The community's requests are often preceded by violent protests, kidnapping, theft, and sabotage. When the community's demands are met, this enhances the reputation of the rebels. When the Colombian ELN rebels reached a multi-million-dollar development deal with Mannesmann, the company was apparently issued with bumper stickers for their cars and trucks. These served as a signal to villagers that the company was protected by the ELN, as well as advertising the ELN's role in bringing much-needed social investment into the area.[56] Oil and gas companies are spending hundreds of millions of US dollars every year on corporate social responsibility programmes in developing countries.

Even when companies do their best to interact with civil leaders, it is difficult to exclude the leakage of benefits to the protector. Insurgents often have 'deep roots' in local communities and are directly involved in key areas of governance. In a 2017 study of former rebel-held areas in Côte d'Ivoire, former Force Nouvelle (FN) commanders continued to run armed networks. High-ranking former rebels 'were involved in the administration of . . . local policing, land governance, education, healthcare, and infrastructure. FN rule thereby created a thick web of formal and informal affiliations, patron-client ties, and personal friendships that intertwined community members with rebel governance structures.'[57] Time and time again observers point out the disappointingly small benefits for the wider community, because company social investment funds are used to solve short-term security problems. One oil company built three town halls in one African town to win the support of three community chiefs who stood to profit personally from the construction contracts.[58]

Corporate social responsibility programmes could be purely philanthropic rather than pragmatic conduits for protection payments, but this is unlikely to work in conflict-ridden territory. Armed groups are quickly drawn to any undefended area where largesse is distributed. In 2005, intercommunity violence erupted in the Niger Delta town of Rumuekpe. 'Armed gangs waged pitched battles over access to oil money, which Shell distributed to whichever gang controlled access to its infrastructure ... the place ... becomes a contest ground for warring factions. Who takes over the community has the attention of the company.'[59] British Petroleum (BP) in Colombia once implemented a hugely expensive 'military ring' to protect communities in its direct vicinity from paramilitary incursions. Such a strategy is not economically sustainable, even though this one may have helped to repair BP's tarnished reputation after Colombian soldiers engaged in large-scale human rights abuses to protect BP facilities.[60] Overall, it is probably best to ensure that a capable protector benefits from the continued presence of the company in the area.

In terms of creating a self-enforcing protection contract that looks like a social development programme, large, one-off infrastructure investments are risky—unless they come with a juicy maintenance contract. A constant flow of employment opportunities, scholarships, small credits, etc. channelled through 'community leaders' is better suited to keeping the local warlord or rebel commander on side—and the flow can be redirected to more capable protectors if local conditions change. Ultimately, however, a company's bargaining power derives from having a credible threat of halting production in response to a deteriorating security situation. Foreign investors and particularly oil majors are known to evacuate key staff, halt production, and stop repairing pipelines until security threats diminish.[61] If the protectors need a regular flow of employment contracts and cash to underpin their own standing in the community, a well-diversified company is in a strong bargaining position.

Option 7: Paying Ransoms

When the local power brokers are known to be affiliated with proscribed terrorist organizations, it is often too risky to make even an implicit protection contract. In the 2017 famine in Somalia, many aid organizations were reluctant to bring aid to alleviate suffering in Al Shabaab territory. Even if they could resolve their security problems on the ground, they feared they would fall foul of counter-terrorism finance laws—and perhaps be shut down.[62] If governments do not give credible assurances that they will turn a 'blind eye' to whatever local compromises are necessary to prevent kidnapping, tolerating it may be a solution.

Aid workers are commonly advised to prioritize their survival in a hostage situation: to offer minimal resistance to their kidnappers, remain calm during the abduction, cooperate, and never, ever try to escape. It is up to their employer to negotiate their release.[63]

Once kidnapped, firms and NGOs are not expected to abandon their employees. NGOs tend to avoid making monetary concessions but can change their local practices to make their continued presence more desirable to the protector. If a ransom payment is required, the people who receive the ransom cannot be part of a terrorist organization. In Somalia, one cannot make a deal with Al Shabaab, but one could ransom hostages from 'the pirates'. Negotiators were amused when a Somali negotiator explained that he represented the 'commercial arm' of Al Shabaab, but they had to explain that this was not sufficiently removed from the parent organization to have a payment authorized. In Colombia, one could not pay the FARC, but one could ransom hostages from Venezuelan criminal gangs just across the border. 'If it's criminal, it's legal', was the laconic summary of a UK bureaucrat regarding making ransom payments. A secondary market for hostages ensures that people end up with whoever is best placed to extract a sizeable ransom.

Although private entities and their insurers cannot legally make concessions to terrorists, governments can choose to do so. If an individual's or company's government is known to pay ransoms to terrorists, then the hostage will stay with the terrorists—or will be passed to them by whoever carried out the kidnap. With budget constraints relaxed and a nation on tenterhooks over the fate of a hostage, ransoms often escalate—a topic we will return to in Chapter 10. The combination of (sizeable) ransoms and protection money extracted via plausibly unconnected third parties (such as elders, religious institutions or community leaders) ensures that even the most violent terrorist organizations often tolerate a foreign presence in 'their' territory. Firms and NGOs react pragmatically: nationals from countries which adhere to the UN ransom ban are now rarely deployed in areas where hostages might end up in the hands of proscribed organizations. Responsible employers know that Italian, French, Swiss, and German employees are likely to be ransomed, while their US, UK, and Canadian colleagues would likely be tortured and killed. Nations like France and China, with their extensive economic interests in Africa, would find it very costly to implement the UN ban on paying ransoms to terrorists.[64]

Another context in which ransoming is the dominant form of paying off organized crime is piracy. With vast sea areas to patrol, both military and informal protection are highly costly and likely to be unreliable. For example, in the Gulf of Guinea pirates regularly abduct oil workers for ransoms. However, the companies' land-based protectors ensure that pirates cannot hide hostages for extended periods and know they would be punished if they abused or killed the hostages. With short negotiations, safe returns, and ransoms in the low five-figure range, tolerating the occasional hijacking is more cost-effective than paying someone to patrol vast sea areas or putting armed guards on every single vessel.

Orderly ransoming can thus incentivize armed groups to accept a foreign presence. This is not exactly a protection contract, but an implicit understanding that the criminals or rebels will only strike occasionally and will not use excessive violence against hostages. Oil and mineral extraction, aid deliveries, development activities, and trade can continue and hostages (of the right nationalities) will be reasonably treated.

Choosing from a Menu of Options

All profitable economic activities require protection. Where states are strong, taxpayers obtain the necessary security for safe travel, agriculture, extractive and productive industries, and trade. Where there are gaps in state provision, firms and individuals may bolster their security by employing private guards. The cost of operating safely is then only partially defrayed by the state. Even in developed countries burly bouncers outside shops, clubs, and bars, gated communities, and celebrities surrounded by bodyguards are an increasingly common sight. In mafia-controlled or rebel-held territory such private security solutions are the norm. Conducting business requires the extra-legal groups' consent or toleration—usually in addition to satisfying the financial demands of the legitimate government. Disappointed protectors who derive no net benefit from individuals, firms, and NGOs in their territory tend to attack. Some strike indiscriminately with massacres or suicide bombings, others focus their attention on specific individuals, firms, or vital infrastructure. But usually the aim is a financial settlement: geese laying golden eggs are rarely shooed away.

This chapter has discussed seven options of making a mutually beneficial arrangements: (1) a direct protection contract with the informal protector, (2) bringing the protector inside the firm, (3) using 'reputable providers' directly or indirectly linked to the protector, (4) outsourcing the entire operation to the informal protector, (5) employing a PMSC to subcontract with the informal protector, (6) a corporate social responsibility programme that benefits the informal protector, and (7) occasional, low-violence kidnapping. These options are not mutually exclusive. For example, an informal protector can derive benefit from hiring out security guards, taking protection payments from the firm's local suppliers, and from controlling access to maintenance contracts, medical care, or scholarships provided by a firm.

The menu of options also opens the possibility of satisfying several protectors at once. In Chapter 2, we saw the sudden spikes in violence and kidnapping when oil fields were developed in Colombia—but this always settled down after a few years. If one armed group takes care of protecting (i.e. not attacking) the pipeline, another protects local contractors, and a third group guards the facility itself, everyone may earn enough not to upset the status quo—or at least settle disagreements at some distance from the company's premises. The company with the frightened group of teenage soldiers dispatched into tiger country by their corrupt government kept them safe by giving them guard duties inside the compound (alongside some foreign mercenaries just to make sure), while the real protector's men were charged with perimeter security.

Usually, these tricky details are worked out by professional security consultants. The specialists have a detailed knowledge of who is who in the local security landscape, how to start a conversation with the key players (rather than plausible-looking impostors), and how much to offer them. And if they don't know—they know how to find out. They conduct security audits to eliminate weak points in the security arrangements that could be exploited by opportunists. Their greatest strength derives from being able to shape the contracts and the behaviour of multiple firms. It is easier and cheaper to create self-enforcing protection contracts between many firms and one protector. If a protector is not vigilant or starts to exploit one customer, all others can be diverted. A trigger strategy deployed across protection contracts (e.g. all foreign firms vacate expatriate staff from a region) creates genuine pain for a rogue protector.

Their second advantage is that risk consultancy and private military security are closely linked: firms insured by Lloyd's and advised by the insurer's security consultants can credibly threaten to self-protect at very short notice. The security management and crisis response firms retained by Lloyd's kidnap for ransom insurers also have in-house private military security capabilities. Hiscox, the market leader, retains the services of Control Risks. The company provides customers with a complete package of 'strategic consultancy, expert analysis and in-depth investigations through to handling sensitive political issues and providing practical on the ground protection and support'.[65] Travellers retains Constellis, which again provides risk and crisis management services, as well as protective security. Even the smaller crisis responders and risk management consultancies such as Neil Young Associates (working for AIG), S-RM (working for XL Catlin), Ackermann (with Chubb), and Unity Resources Group (Tokio Marine/HCC) provide short-term close protection services in-house. However, for long-term and large-scale contracts they refer their customers to trusted partners in the private military security industry. Knowing that Plan B can be implemented within twenty-four hours, protectors will think twice about engaging in opportunistic behaviour.

Therefore, many firms operate surprisingly safely in the most challenging security environments. It is very rare that deteriorating security situations lead to the permanent abandonment of profitable mines, oil wells, and gas fields. Reconstruction efforts in former war zones do not need to wait until new or transitional governments are in a position to provide reliable law and order. Instead, highly experienced firms order the exchange at the rugged intersection between the legal and the informal/extra-legal economy—using a mixture of carrots and sticks. They fail occasionally—but the risk is low and dispersed enough to make the problem insurable, in particular because there is a robust protocol to contain ransom payments. This will be the topic of Chapters 6 and 7.

6

The Price of a Life

Why don't we just pay them a million? We spill more than that in a day.

Question put to a crisis response consultant by the director of an oil firm

And business is booming: While in 2003 [Al Qaeda] received around $200,000 per hostage, now they are netting up to $10 million.

New York Times, 29 July 2014

Insuring Somali piracy became unprofitable when ransoms went above US$3 million.

Interview with crisis responder, November 2017

The Importance of Ransom Discipline

Private insurers only provide commercially viable products. Insurance only works when kidnaps are relatively rare as well as quick and cheap to resolve. This requires ransom discipline. Ransoms are inherently unstable—as the quotes above indicate. If kidnappers think that hostages could be worth a lot more than they have hitherto been paid, they start to probe more deeply. Gangs innovate to create more pressure on distraught families and stressed employers: long detentions, threats, torture, and perhaps murder. Occasionally, cruel kidnappers succeed in shocking people into making further concessions. But every record ransom resets expectations and creates hopes for a new record down the line. When rumours of multi-million-dollar ransoms start to circulate in disadvantaged communities, kidnapping (or hijacking) looks like an attractive business for anyone with an ounce of criminal entrepreneurialism. Kidnapping becomes uninsurable when premium ransom payments set off a vicious cycle of more kidnappings, longer detentions, and escalating kidnapper expectations.

Most parents' gut reaction to a kidnapping is that they would raise 'whatever they can' to end their child's ordeal in the hands of criminals or terrorists—whether it's their own, their friends', or taxpayers' money. This plays into the hands of the kidnappers. Insurers ask a very different question: 'how much is necessary to bring the hostage back safely?' Driving ransoms down makes kidnap insurable—but it also helps the victims. Paying a minimal ransom lowers the financial and emotional disruption when hostages return to pick up the pieces of their former lives. Prevaricating and settling for a miserly ransom reduces the probability of being targeted again. The shocking first response of the oil millionaire John Paul Getty to his abducted grandson's desperate plea for help was: 'If I pay one penny now, I will have 14 kidnapped grandchildren.'[1] He spoke like a true businessman: even if he was a disappointing grandfather for young Paul Getty, he kept the rest of his family safe. Moreover, ransom discipline has broad social benefits. First, it stabilizes criminals' expectations at a level that is affordable for both insured and uninsured kidnap victims. Rich stakeholders do not put poorer hostages at risk. Second, negotiations can converge fast if there is a stable 'going rate'. Third, if kidnappers are earning a 'normal' return (i.e. they cover their costs), there is little incentive for new gangs to enter the market for hostages. This stabilizes kidnapping and raises the probability of a good outcome: nervous rookies often harm their hostages—a topic we revisit in Chapter 10. Fourth, paying ransoms raises important ethical questions. If you pay criminals or terrorist organizations, some of the money will likely be used to harm innocent third parties.[2] Paying kidnappers a normal economic return alleviates this concern to some extent. If kidnappers just cover their costs, ransoms cannot be used to fund additional crime or terror.

It is extremely interesting to see how this tension between the stakeholders' gut reaction to the kidnapper's manifold provocations and the broader social interest in ransom discipline is managed in practice. Crisis responders cannot dictate how stakeholders behave, they can only advise and influence. How do response consultants convince families that what is good for the insurers is best for their loved one, too? This chapter explains the economic reasoning behind price formation in the market for hostages. What is the 'right' price for a life? And, more importantly, how do you agree a price that your criminal counterparty is happy to stick with? No one can enforce the agreement if the kidnappers change their mind. Chapter 7 takes us step by step through the ransom negotiation for a hijacked ship, which perfectly illustrates how these complex economic problems are solved in the real world.

Price Formation in an Anarchic Bargaining Situation

Bargaining over the price of a hostage is a highly unusual bartering situation. There is a single seller and no close substitute for the hostage. There is a circle of prospective buyers, who place different monetary values on the hostage. The potential buyers may barter jointly or separately, cooperatively or competitively.[3] There are no clear rules or norms to structure the negotiation. Who calls whom and when, whether to accept the call, and the topic of conversation are important aspects of signalling power, intentions, and preferences. Asking and offer prices can be revised upwards or downwards at any point in the negotiation. The physical and mental state of the hostage is hidden from the buyers—and can be manipulated by the seller. No agreement is binding or enforceable. Even without the problem of establishing trust and a cooperative bargaining protocol, price setting is fiendishly complicated. The buyer's and seller's reservation prices are private knowledge. Price targets may shift over time, for example if there are police operations nearby, or the hostage's health deteriorates. Finding a price that reflects each party's valuation of the hostage and appropriately apportions buyer and seller surplus requires a lengthy and possibly violent negotiation. It is the role of crisis responders to bring stability, predictability, and discipline into this trade.

First, one needs to establish whether the hostage is alive and under the control of the person demanding the ransom. If so—what is the 'right' price for a human life? An economist would immediately point out that a hostage trade could succeed at a (potentially wide) range of prices: any price that is at or above the reservation price of the kidnappers and affordable for the victim's stakeholders is potentially the 'right' price. The kidnappers' reservation price is usually based on 'covering costs'. Costs depend on how the hostage was acquired, the length of detention, and how many people expect a share of the ransom.[4] The maximum price that could be obtained for a hostage depends on who is raising the ransom, under what legal rules and law enforcement conditions, and over what time frame.

If there is a range of affordable prices that would satisfy the kidnapper, a process of bartering establishes how the difference between the reservation prices will be split between the bargaining parties. On the one hand, the kidnappers are in a strong bargaining situation: the hostage is highly valued by their family and friends. Kidnappers can try to coerce the family to reveal their valuation by threatening or mutilating the hostage. On the other hand, scoping out the maximum price requires time—and holding hostages is costly and potentially dangerous. Inflicting violence risks killing the hostage and the family calling the police to attempt a rescue. Well-treated hostages are excellent human shields.

Ultimately, all transaction partners want the trade to succeed. Even badly conducted negotiations can result in an agreement—albeit often at the cost of long durations, hostage maltreatment, and ransoms that encourage the criminals to carry out further kidnaps. Skilled negotiators know how to structure negotiations, exert pressure, and send credible signals to the opposition to influence the bargaining process in their own favour. It is therefore not unusual for kidnappers to employ experienced negotiators.[5] This makes it advisable for the stakeholders to get professional help, too. The crisis response consultants retained by insurers have the ethos, information, and experience to safely retrieve hostages in a timely manner—without putting others at risk.

Kidnappers only release hostages when they have convinced themselves that the cost of holding out exceeds the benefit from prolonging the negotiation. Offering to meet the kidnappers' first demand only works if kidnappers are already desperate to get rid of the hostage. But if they are desperate to conclude, they will also release without or for a minimal ransom. If kidnappers are under no time pressure to release and their demands are met, they can revise their expectations upward. So, stakeholders must structure their offers carefully to achieve price convergence. There is no convenient shortcut: when kidnappers are experienced and patient, hostage crisis resolution takes time.

If stakeholders understand this and barter patiently, they reduce the risk for their hostage, as well as the risk of being targeted again. While a 'time is money' approach looks individually rational, it is not necessarily successful. Even if it works, paying an outsize ransom imposes costs on future hostages and—of course—the special risk insurers. This creates the impression of a principal–agent problem for crisis responders. If stakeholders believe that the advice they receive is not in the best interest of the hostage but in the best interest of the insurer, they will disregard it. Crisis responders must steer the negotiation through this minefield of (unspoken) suspicion and mistrust. Let us see how they do it.

Prove That You Have a Live Hostage!

Negotiations should only be opened after the kidnappers have provided proof of life and proof of possession of the hostage. Otherwise the 'phantom kidnap' business model can succeed. Here criminals demand a ransom during a period when a person cannot be contacted, e.g. while trekking up Kilimanjaro or on a romantic date. Being observed entering a cinema creates a two-hour window of opportunity for criminal entrepreneurs. If worried stakeholders quickly pay to end the 'ordeal', the supposed 'hostage' innocently returns to find their family and fortune in disarray. If a kidnap has occurred, all manner of opportunists may try to extract some benefit from the situation. Witnesses or those who hear about an abduction may attempt to insert themselves into the negotiation. Some pretend to be the kidnappers or speak on behalf of the kidnappers; others offer information or mediation services. Unless those demanding a ransom can prove that they have access to the hostage, such offers should be treated with caution. In piracy cases, ship-owners prefer to negotiate ransoms through the ships' on-board telephone system. If the negotiator is on the bridge and can put the captain on the phone, stakeholders know they are in business.

Hostage stakeholders must find out whether they are negotiating over a live hostage or a body. The kidnapping itself is the most dangerous moment, but it is worth checking throughout the negotiation that the hostage is still alive.[6] Proof of life can be provided in many ways—direct telephone conversations with the victim being preferred. Kidnappers may use phone calls to raise the pressure on stakeholders by asking the victim to convey tales of hardship and fear. Well-prepared families and employers agree code-words with potential victims to ascertain whether lives are at stake. A code-word for 'I am generally treated well' takes the edge off the most harrowing begging phone call. Because of this and as calls may be traceable, some kidnappers prefer stakeholders to provide a question that only the hostage can answer.[7] In the past, kidnappers often sent a photo of the hostage holding a current newspaper—but the credibility of such a snap is compromised by the power of computer software for manipulating images. Instead, video evidence with the hostage referring to current news events is sometimes provided. Here, stakeholders need to be cautious if the 'current event' was predictable and the message is couched in very general terms, such as the 'death of Bin Laden'.

Asking for frequent proof of life throughout the negotiation may upset kidnappers and slow down the negotiation. However, it is important to do so just before the ransom drop. The preferred routine for ransom drops in Somalia was that pirates would line up the crew on deck, so the crew of the aircraft delivering the ransom could count them on the first flypast. If satisfied, they would drop the ransom during a second loop. This norm fixes the importance of hostage safety firmly in the kidnappers' minds. It also promotes honesty in negotiations where repeat business is expected or where there are multiple hostages.

Who is Negotiating?

Prices for hostages are highly variable. They crucially depend on who demands the ransom and where. We observe massive differences in ransom levels between countries.[8] 'Market norms' also vary by region within countries. For example, kidnapping in the Niger Delta is mostly resolved cheaply, quickly, and non-violently, whereas in northern Nigeria Boko Haram conducts lengthy negotiations and occasionally achieves high ransoms. Within a region, more patient and sophisticated kidnappers achieve higher ransoms on average. Over time, ransom patterns can shift as kidnappers learn and change targets and tactics.[9] Victim status is similarly important. In Colombia, ransoms for farmers are four or five orders of magnitude below that for executives of multi-national companies.[10]

In equilibrium, kidnappers expect to earn a risk-adjusted, normal return. There are a multitude of kidnap business models ranging from purely opportunistic 'lightning' and 'express kidnaps', via 'miracle fishing', to targeted kidnaps of key personnel. Hijacking ships for ransom is even more expensive. Costs vary significantly depending on whether the kidnap or hijack was planned, whether the planning required extensive surveillance or bribery, and the number of people and weapons involved in the kidnap. Add to this the cost of guarding and feeding the hostage over the period of detention, which depends on the country's price and wage level.

An opportunist who picks up a tipsy tourist only has a few hours before the hostage becomes a liability. If he wants more than the victim's phone and wallet, he needs a friend or two to help. They will share in any profits, of course. Should they take the hostage to a cash-point straight away—or call the family to extract a ransom? Unless the family is very rich and panics, such 'quickie' kidnaps tend to be resolved for low ransoms.[11] Risk-adjusted earnings in low-level criminal activities are generally meagre.[12] If the kidnappers want more money, they could take the hostage to a gang that knows what to do. But will the gangsters pay the rookies—or beat them up and take the hostage away? A secondary market for hostages requires reliable governance—such as a mafia that enforces contracts in the criminal underworld. This increases the number of people who expect payment—and mafias have the power to take big shares.

Some kidnappers develop an entire infrastructure to support their operations—but this is expensive. Even the remotest jungle camp needs a guard—24/7. The guards need weapons, wages, food, and probably some stimulant to pass the time. The supplies must be bought from someone, perhaps on credit. This widens the circle of expectant benefi-ciaries. For example, Somali pirates had to pay the investors who financed the attack groups, traders who provided food, water, fuel, and recreational drugs on credit, local communities who sheltered the pir-ates, clan militias guarding the ships, and regional politicians who controlled the counter-piracy police.[13] Such a complex ransoming infra-structure drives up the kidnappers' or hijackers' reservation price: large ransoms are now required to break even.

The rise in 'quickie' kidnaps in Latin America in recent years illustrates that often the best approach is to go for the quick buck.[14] In 2016, Control Risk analysts advised that ransom negotiations in Venezuela had contracted during the economic crisis: 'Urban criminals tend to be unwilling to hold their victims for extended periods...kidnappers who are living hand to mouth in poor neighbourhoods will be wary of entering into protracted negotiations. During this time, they may forgo other sources of income while they use up their own scant sup-plies, feeding and maintaining their victim.'[15] Yet, opportunists operat-ing in the territory of sophisticated criminal gangs may try to free-ride on the reputation of more established gangs. To drive a hard and suc-cessful bargain, stakeholders need to find out who really controls the hostage. Even if nothing is known about the identity of the kidnapper, opportunists and small-time criminals will eventually betray themselves by their impatience to strike a deal.

The maximum price to be obtained for a hostage depends on who is paying the ransom. If a government negotiates on behalf of its citizens it is very difficult to demonstrate a credible, hard budget constraint. Budgets are even more flexible if a third-party government tries to curry favour with a (potential) ally by effecting the release of a hostage as a diplomatic 'gift'. The massive inflation in ransoms obtained by ISIL/Daesh, Abu Sayyaf, and Al Qaeda in recent years testifies to that.[16] In addition, governments could also fulfil political demands, such as policy changes and prisoner releases. We return to the problem of government-led negotiations in Chapter 10. Most firms and NGOs have lower maximum budgets than the hostage's government—and any political concession would be at a local level. Employers' budgets for hostages depends on which level of the firm takes responsibility: the multinational parent company, a subsidiary, or a local contractor. The employer's stance on ransoms also depends on whether the firm is worried about setting a precedent and attracting further criminal attention. Some firms and NGOs take a hard line and never negotiate financial settlements. This pushes the negotiation one level further down: to the family. Very few families can match the financial clout of firms or governments—and political concessions dwindle to a one-page newspaper advert outlining the kidnappers' political agenda. If kidnappers suspect that the hostage is insured they expect a substantial financial settlement, whoever conducts the negotiation. Insurers must therefore stay invisible, even though they have a commercial stake in the outcome.

Thus, all sides' ransom expectations are conditioned by who they think their counterparty is. Insurers employ highly specialized crisis response consultants to find out as much as possible about the opposition and advise stakeholders on the best way to conduct the negotiation. Response consultants try to ascertain who holds the hostage and what their likely ransom expectations are. They streamline the negotiation process to speed up price setting by influencing and managing kidnapper expectations.

Setting Up

Having ascertained that there is a hostage situation and that the stakeholders are talking to those holding the hostage, the response consultant ensures that there is a single point of contact. Parallel negotiations reduce the probability of a clean, swift, and cheap resolution. The negotiation should be 'fronted' by either the family or the employer. Most kidnap victims are domestic citizens. Foreign nationals are a tiny minority of kidnap victims, between 2 and 6 per cent depending on the region.[17] It is in the interest of foreign companies and NGOs not to be seen to take full financial responsibility for their local staff and that of their contractors—otherwise they will become preferred targets. Whatever happens behind the scenes, it is best if kidnappers think they are only talking to the family. With key local or expatriate staff this is less plausible, and a company representative will probably front the negotiation—especially if several employees are kidnapped together. However, it is better to do this from the dusty back room of a local subsidiary with a tiny balance sheet rather than from the glitzy head office in London, Tokyo, or Washington. Appearances matter. For hijacked ships, the identity of the owner is often opaque enough for a tycoon to hide behind a struggling shell company. Many small shipping companies operate on the edge of profitability—pirates need to understand that they were unlucky once again. However, disaster strikes when someone blows that cover.

The case of the crew of the Danish-owned MV *Leopard* illustrates this well. Somali pirates abducted the *Leopard's* crew—two Danish and four Philippine seamen—in January 2011. They had damaged the ship in the attack and had to leave it drifting. Shipcraft, the company which owned the *Leopard*, revealed (predictably) that it was on the brink of bankruptcy and would not be able to pay a sizeable ransom.[18] As there was neither a ship nor cargo at stake, pirates' expectations should have been shaped by the parallel negotiation for the seven-member crew of the Danish yacht *ING*. The *ING* was hijacked in February 2011 and the hostages returned just over six months later for US$3 million.[19] The first ransom demand for the *Leopard* crew was US$10 million, the second US$6 million—indicating the pirates' willingness to compromise. Unfortunately, the tabloid *Extra Bladet* and the *TV2* channel then exposed that the owner of the ship was a multi-millionaire, living a 'lavish lifestyle' while his crew languished in hell. The pirates were only too pleased to provide pictures and videos of the frightened, emaciated, desperate sailors. The media campaign triggered an outpouring of public rage against their 'callous' employer.[20] The pirates immediately revised their ransom demand from US$6 million to US$15 million. As the campaign on behalf of the abandoned mariners gained momentum, the pirates re-evaluated their expectations again, taking a new punt with a US$35 million ransom demand. Dislodging the pirates from this unrealistic position took a very long time. The case was resolved after 839 days for an unbelievable US$6.9 million raised from several sources.[21] After their release, the Danish hostages sued the tabloid newspaper and TV channel.[22] They had been beaten, humiliated, and smeared with goat blood by the pirates to create maximum media impact. However well-intentioned the media campaign might have been, it prolonged and compounded their ordeal in Somalia.[23]

From a kidnapper's point of view the circle of concerned parties cannot be too large. Hostages are often asked to provide a list of wealthy and influential contacts. Beyond the immediate circle of employer, family, and friends, there may be pressure groups, newspapers, philanthropists, fundraisers, and charities. Everyone is very welcome to contribute to the ransom—or lobby others to be more generous. If stakeholders can motivate politicians to engage on behalf of a hostage, so much the better. Once the hostage is centre stage, the threat of police intervention recedes and the negotiation time frame extends. Sophisticated kidnappers therefore do their best to mobilize everyone with a conceivable interest in the hostage situation to take an active role in lobbying, negotiating, and funding a ransom. Conversely, the crisis responders do their very best to avoid this. If employers fund and negotiate the ransom, the family (or families) must be kept informed and on side to avoid a media leak. A negotiating family must present a united front. In northern Europe, this might not be too difficult—but negotiators on South American cases routinely deal with around fifty opinionated family members. And then the mistress appears on the scene. For multiple kidnaps, we can multiply the actors. It just takes one person to lose confidence in the handling of the negotiation and phone a newspaper for everything to fall apart.

In some situations, it is therefore best to prevent the media from reporting about ongoing negotiations altogether. If high-profile hostages suddenly drop off the media radar, the explanation is usually an injunction. After the release of the Chandler couple, taken off their yacht by Somali pirates, newspapers explained: 'A news blackout was ... imposed on the media, prohibiting references to the couple's wellbeing or speculation surrounding their release for fear of compromising their safety and jeopardising the rescue effort.'[24] In some cases, regulators even impose a 'double injunction': newspapers can neither report on the case nor discuss the injunction. We should therefore not be surprised that terrorist groups often use social media to broadcast the plight of their hostages.

Opportunistic kidnappers and those acquiring hostages from them often turn to the internet to form their ransom expectations. As a thought experiment: view an aspirational social media profile through the eyes of a kidnapper sitting in an internet café in an impoverished slum. A new(-ish) car! Look at our house and stylish buy-to-let holiday flat. Isn't the garden looking splendid this year? Here we are with family and friends at a glamorous wedding. Who cares if it's a rented tuxedo? Here's a sneaky selfie with the mayor/MP/chancellor of the university. Exotic (bucket and spade) holidays. Toddlers in (bargain rail) designer dresses clutching the latest electronic gadgets. Bling (costume) jewellery. An open-top (hire) car at the beach ... And then think how you might get across the message that these are the standard trappings of middle-class life in your country; financed with a credit card and a mortgage. You—or your family—need to convince the kidnapper that you are not a VIP and, unfortunately, he has not hit the jackpot. If you would rather not have that conversation, you could revise your family's Facebook page. Alternatively, if you are insured for kidnap and are reported missing, the link might just magically disappear.

Kidnappers prefer a direct line to the ultimate decision maker—and crisis responders want to avoid that at all costs. It takes the wind out of the sails of a kidnapper putting a gun to the hostage's head when the contact person must tell him that she will take the new demand to the 'boss' or the 'board'. That she will get back after due deliberation and could the kidnappers please keep the hostage safe in the meantime. Who would trust themselves to make a considered decision when hearing a beloved nephew, child, or spouse sob and beg for their lives? Giving in makes matters worse, as we will see later. It is better for the person on the phone not to be able to make snap decisions. As with police officers negotiating in barricade situations, the standard protocol is that the 'voice' or 'communicator' is only a conduit of information. By now we are not at all surprised to find that highly experienced specialists are available to execute this delicate role. But crisis responders will not insist on this. When pretending that the ransom is raised by a struggling business or a family in disarray, it is sometimes better if the communicator's performance is not too polished.

Perhaps the most important task in setting up the negotiation is to settle who makes the decisions and how different interest groups are going to be represented or included. The members of the crisis committee must be available to meet at short notice throughout the negotiation. Companies usually make decisions about ransoms at senior management level. The wider family must at least be kept informed. Law enforcement may insist on officers being present or being regularly briefed during the negotiation. If the firm obtained kidnap insurance, working through a kidnap scenario is a standard component of the training encouraged by the insurer. Thus, companies operating in kidnap hotspots usually know in advance who will deal with the kidnap, what the parameters of the negotiation are, and—in theory—how to conduct a successful negotiation.

If a sophisticated gang conducts a ransom negotiation, it is not unusual for there to be a considerable gap between the disappearance of the hostage(s) or the ship's Mayday call and the first contact from the kidnappers. Creating fear and uncertainty is part of the psychological arsenal of kidnappers. The crisis response consultants counteract this by using the time productively. They set up the crisis response infrastructure, brief and reassure the stakeholders, coach the communicator, and put in place an appropriate media strategy. Until someone calls, they scour the small ads in the local newspaper: is anyone selling a puppy for a million? If so, the contact details may well lead to the missing person's kidnappers.

The Bidding Starts

Let us assume that there is a genuine hostage situation, that the hostage is alive, and that the communicator is talking to the right person. There is a ransom demand of US$1 million. What would be a sensible counter-offer? Let us look at this from the kidnapper's point of view, who is trying to sell a unique good of unknown value. It is tempting to think of the kidnapper's price-setting strategy as a Dutch auction: the price of the good is progressively reduced until a buyer comes forward. However, this is anarchic bargaining, there are no rules. The opening demand is not a binding price, but a figure beyond the kidnapper's best-case assumption of what the hostage might be worth. A counter-offer to pay this amount will reset the kidnapper's expectation. Nothing stops kidnappers from probing beyond the initial demand: the pirates of the MV *Leopard* went from US$10 million to US$15 million to US$35 million. Whatever the stakeholders' ability to pay, the opening offer should be well below the opening demand, to avoid confusion and unleashing greed.

From the point of view of the stakeholders, the opening offer must turn the hostage into an asset that will be protected. A refusal to nego-tiate could spell the death of the hostage. The initial offer should be both high enough and low enough to tempt opportunistic kidnappers to release immediately. Opportunists may try to negotiate a ransom while driving the victim around a city in a stolen vehicle. They are pressed for time. A well-judged cash offer can end the situation in a few hours.[25] If stakeholders prevaricate, Plan B is the 'lightning kidnap' or 'millionaire's ride'. This ends at a cashpoint soon after midnight, when the victim has withdrawn the maximum daily cash limit twice. Scary—but cheap.

If the initial offer is quicker and higher than expected, it suggests that the victim could be seriously wealthy. Opportunists may re-evaluate their options. They could traffic and sell a 'VIP' hostage to someone with higher criminal capital or acquire mafia protection to hold out a little longer. We can consider kidnapping to be a contestable market—open to anyone with an opportunity and a weapon or sufficient physical strength to abduct someone. Hiding, guarding, and feeding a hostage over an extended period is more complex. Conducting a ransom negoti-ation, picking up a ransom, and releasing a hostage without detection is a highly skilled criminal activity. In mature kidnapping markets, victims may be explicitly offered the choice of going 'express or regular'. The question implies that there are ransoming specialists—and places where hostages can be safely traded and kept. The local mafia provides extra-legal governance for the hostage market and everyone can rely on receiving a fair payoff.

The advantage of employing professional crisis response consultants is that they know what the appropriate first response to a given ransom demand would be in the specific circumstances. Perhaps cases in a particular region can be swiftly settled for a three- or four-figure sum.

With certain gangs, a four-figure first offer reliably produces convergence at a five-figure ransom within a few days. When the counterparty is an experienced or well-supported kidnapper (or pirate enterprise), a general indication that the stakeholders are looking towards a 'commercial resolution' can be enough to safeguard the hostage. The crisis responder's tradecraft is in pitching the first offer in the right ballpark. Nervous, unsupported stakeholders tend to offer too much too quickly, setting the scene for an extended negotiation and an unnecessarily high ransom. Occasionally, an unexpectedly generous ransom offer produces a swift release, but one should reserve judgement on whether this was a successful strategy for a few months. Usually, a 'soft', well-off family or employer will be targeted again as soon as the first ransom has been frittered away.

Negotiations and Signalling Theory

When analysing strategic interactions, it is useful to analyse what happens in the end game to develop a sensible strategy for the entire exchange. So, why does a ransom negotiation end? Kidnappers release hostages when the cost of holding them exceeds the expected benefits from doing so. The cost of prolonging a negotiation can become prohibitively high if the police or rival criminals are homing in on the kidnappers' lair, if the kidnappers' peers or elders disapprove of the situation, or if the hostage falls ill. In this case, the amount of money offered up to that point is largely irrelevant to the decision to release. But even if the kidnappers feel perfectly secure, there is a financial cost–benefit analysis to be made: how much extra money can they squeeze out of the family if they hold on for x additional days? Will that cover the costs of doing so? Holding a hostage costs money: for food, for guards, for local support. If there is a net cost to holding on, it's time to release. Even a kidnapper operating from an impenetrable fortress will eventually respond to the economic incentives of marginal costs and benefits. But in this case, it is crucial that the criminals believe that they have extracted everything of value from the stakeholders. So, how do you convince the kidnappers that you have offered them all you can, that there is simply no more to give?

The sociologist Diego Gambetta's work on how criminals communicate asks a similar question. How do people convince their counterparty that they possess an unobservable quality, if it is in their interest to misrepresent their situation? Diego Gambetta gives an intriguing answer: by making a costly sacrifice. He cites the case of the Roman soldier Caius Mucius. Having been caught in an assassination attempt, Mucius had to convince the Etruscan king that he would not betray his co-conspirators however badly he was tortured. He did so by roasting his own right hand in the fire directly in front of the king. We still know this brave man by his honorific Mucius Scaevola, the left-handed. Good signals convey truthful information, because people who do not have the unobservable quality only send them at great personal cost. Anyone can claim that they won't confess under torture. Few can provide proof of their tolerance of pain in the way Mucius Scaevola did. His striking performance convinced the king and he avoided the potentially fatal torture. Indeed, the signals of the criminal underworld often involve self-harm—for example the facial tattoos of some US gangs or self-amputations of digits as performed by Japanese yakuza. By sending such costly signals, the senders provide evidence that they have the hidden quality (e.g. courage, loyalty, self-control) and are completely committed to their organization or cause.[26]

In the ransom negotiation, the stakeholders must send a credible signal that they have exhausted their resources. Saying 'whatever you threaten to do, we can do nothing more for our son' is the psychological equivalent of roasting your own hand in the fire. But if you have already promised all you have, you have no other choice. There simply is nothing more to give whatever the opposition threatens to do. If the message is patiently repeated, kidnappers eventually come to believe that they have extracted all there is. A study of thousands of Spanish travellers captured by and ransomed from the Barbary pirates between 1575 and 1692 confirms that longer detentions are associated with lower ransoms. Each year's delay lowered ransoms by an average of 8 per cent. Interestingly, pirates were unable to distinguish between families who delayed for strategic reasons and those who lived far from port cities and were slow to raise ransoms because of this geographic disadvantage.[27] As long as you send the costly signal, it does not necessarily have to be truthful.

To test whether the family is telling the truth, there is usually a series of threats to escalate the psychological costs of saying 'there is no more' to the kidnappers. Will you still send the same signal if there is a threat of torture? A mock execution? Body parts in the post? One negotiator sat with a distraught family as they received a gory photograph: the very moment their loved one's finger was cut off with a knife had been captured on camera, with blood spattered everywhere. The negotiator kept calm: 'If they have cut it off—why haven't they sent us the finger?' Moreover, if you raise your offer in response to a finger having been cut off, you are rewarding torture and creating perverse incentives.

The family trusted him, kept firm, and soon welcomed their lost relative home—with both hands intact. A copy of the photo and a knife with a carefully cut out finger-shape found its way into the crisis responder's teaching collection: 'You can always get a pint of blood from somewhere, but of course, in a photo ketchup will do just as well.'

The negotiator was confident in his assessment, because he had very carefully observed and analysed the signals sent by the kidnapper, too. If one wants to pay the minimum price to ensure the safe return of the hostage, one needs to ascertain how patient the opposition is. Are we dealing with a sophisticated criminal who has all the time in the world here? Does the family really have to liquidate all their assets to meet the kidnapper's reservation price? Should the house go on the market—or can this be resolved in a couple of days for a few thousand dollars? The kidnapper tried to send the following message with that photo: 'I am negotiating from an impregnable stronghold and I can do whatever I like with impunity. Even if it takes you six months to sell your house, I can wait. In the meantime, I enjoy torturing people and if sepsis sets in I can deal with that, too. Either way.' But as the kidnapper had sent mixed messages throughout the negotiation, his 'torture' photo was not a credible signal. The negotiator (correctly) concluded the opposite of the intended message: here was a kidnapper running out of time. Years of negotiating experience had taught him that it was best to ignore the threat. He was right.

So, as we develop our bargaining strategy we bear two things in mind. First, if we are dealing with a time-poor kidnapper, we don't have to pay very much to achieve a release. And we don't want to either: kidnappers should not earn supernormal profits. Second, if we are dealing with sophisticated, patient kidnappers, the task is to convince them that they have done the best they could—whether that is strictly true or not.

'There is a Pace, a Rhythm to These Things'

Criminal gangs maximize their profits from kidnapping by retaining the hostage until the return from prolonging the negotiation exceeds the cost of doing so. What is the additional return from an extra day of negotiation? Imagine that the counter-party is a family that honestly strives to mobilize every penny to save the hostage. If the period of captivity is just a few hours, only ready cash and valuables are available. Over a period of days, money can be withdrawn from savings accounts, collected from friends and family, and financial assets can be sold. Selling a car takes more time, selling a house or flat even longer. How much this raises depends on the size of the mortgage. Then there are a few pieces of family jewellery, the furniture, and clothes: items of largely sentimental value. Eventually the family will run out of assets. However hard the kidnapper pushes, the additional drips and drabs will not cover the cost of holding the hostage. It is time to release. The process of scoping how much money can be raised is often called 'wringing the towel dry'. The initial 'squeezes' produce big pay-offs, but over time the returns get smaller and smaller—even if the squeezes get more vicious.

How should this knowledge inform the stakeholders' tactics? Any ransom that meets or exceeds the kidnapper's reservation price is potentially the right price. The ransom that maximizes the return to crime by liquidating every single asset the stakeholders can mobilize is one extreme. Even so, convincing the kidnappers that this is the maximum requires going through the towel-wringing process. Aiming to just meet the kidnappers' reservation price is another option. As already described, it requires staying firm when the psychological warfare begins. If you cannot avoid the threats, the tearful begging, the fear, and the uncertainty either way—which price would you rather pay?

An even more extreme position would be to frustrate the kidnappers and offer less than the kidnappers' costs. Previous settlements shape kidnappers' ransom expectations.[28] Where high ransoms are expected, kidnaps and negotiations are executed, financed, and supported by larger groups. Their members invest significant resources of money, goods, social capital, and time to share in the eventual ransom. A criminal who is offered a few thousand dollars instead of the expected US$1 million usually prefers to probe harder and delay the day of reckoning, when he must break the news to his gang's creditors and supporters. The experience of Colonel Steed in Nairobi, who patiently resolves the fate of Somali piracy victims from poor countries who were abandoned by their employers, illustrates the problem. Pirates who obtained credit in expectation of multi-million-dollar settlements risk their lives when waving a meagre fistful of Somali shillings at their financiers. Disappointing kidnappers is also very risky for hostages. As the hope of a substantial payment recedes, feeding a hostage becomes an act of charity, rather than good business sense.[29]

Crisis responders therefore encourage and enable stakeholders to meet the kidnappers' minimal ransom expectation—the one that gives a normal economic return. This price achieves the safe return of the victim without destabilizing the local criminal market. Paying more raises the attractiveness of kidnapping and increases the risk of abduction for everyone. Subsequent and concurrent comparable victims are tested at the new price as well. In Chapter 7, we will see how Somali pirates learned about the value of ships over time, leading to the explosion of ransom expectations—and ever more probing. This was detrimental to insurers, ship-owners, and crews. Negotiations that used to last a few weeks, extended beyond six months, then twelve months, then eighteen months. If everyone had held a firm line on ransoms, the piracy problem might never have escalated to the point where navies and ship-owners spent billions of dollars on counter-piracy measures.[30]

Figure 6.1 sketches a stylized model of a perfectly managed ransom negotiation. The ransom amount is on the y-axis and time on the x-axis. The kidnap occurs at time zero. The dashed curve shows how the kidnappers' ransom demand develops over time. The first actual demand (indicated by the dashed vertical line) comes after a period of silence, suggesting that kidnappers are not in a rush to conclude. Similarly, the stakeholders do not counter immediately. The development of their offers over time is represented by the dotted curve. The first low offer (the first dotted vertical line) tests whether the kidnappers are truly patient. After receiving the first offer, sophisticated kidnappers signal that they are not time-poor opportunists by delaying their response. Hostage bargaining does not follow the protocols we commonly assume in game theory: turn-taking is optional. There may be a second, third, or fourth offer before a lower demand is issued. Patience is expressed by sticking firmly with a price in subsequent conversations or by maintaining complete 'silence'. A refusal to engage is a powerful bargaining strategy that can be used by both sides.

The dashed demand and the dotted offer curves are only implied by the amounts that are demanded and offered at each point of communication. As the two curves start to converge, communication usually gets more frequent. This is when the 'squeezes' get tough. Experienced crisis responders almost welcome the dire threats of violence at this stage: they indicate that the final phase of the negotiation has been entered: 'They are beginning to believe us.'

It is of the utmost importance never to respond to a threat by raising the ransom offer. A good hostage negotiator will always prepare and rehearse two scripts with the communicator: one for a cooperative conversation and a second one for the threats scenario. If any threat to hostage safety is made, the cooperative script is immediately substituted, even if an increased offer had already been planned for this call. Instead, the conversation is deliberately derailed into unproductive side discussions, wasting the kidnapper's time and resources. 'We can never reward a threat', urge the negotiators. Use the silence: 'We cannot be seen to make an offer or any concession that could be linked to a previous threat.' If a squeeze succeeds, 'we will start a trajectory of escalating threats, abuse, torture, and murder every time.'[31] Unfortunately, we know this pattern from negotiations with terrorist kidnappers—a topic discussed in Chapter 10. In a well-run negotiation, however, it soon becomes clear to the kidnappers that making threats is costly and counterproductive. Indeed, when the squeezes prove unproductive, the tone of the negotiation changes. We are finally on the path to a settlement.

So, what is the optimal counter-offer when the initial demand is US$1 million? The answer (and the shape of the offer curve beyond) depends on the location, the time, and the opposition. If I know that all previous cases in an area have settled for around US$10,000 in an average of five days, an initial offer of US$5,000 might be a good start. During the subsequent negotiation, more money will be 'found'—though in decreasing increments according to the curve. Additional funds peter out in the region of US$10,000. In a region where the precedents are in the region of US$100,000, a paltry initial offer of US$5,000 could be perceived as an insult and put the hostage's life at risk. Crisis responders have the vital local knowledge about the kidnappers' likely target to start the negotiation at the right point. This safeguards the hostage and contains kidnapper expectations. With the second and third offers, stakeholders signal their 'curve' and the likely convergence point. When kidnappers get the message, they start the squeezes. If stakeholders hold firm, the bargaining converges. If stakeholders reveal that there may be some untapped resources somewhere, the process restarts: at a higher level.

There is an (unfortunate) element of theatricality in a well-managed ransom negotiation. Even though the outcome is predictable, there are

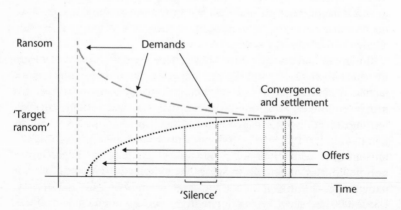

Figure 6.1. Stylized model of a ransom negotiation

no shortcuts to achieving it. The price will only stick if the kidnappers believe that they have extracted the maximum ransom. They will only believe this when they have tested it with periods of silence, by raising concern about hostage welfare, by threats, and perhaps even by mutilating a hostage. In Somali piracy, negotiators on both sides kept a running tally of the common ruses and replies of their counterparties. Ship-owners could be warned: 'we usually receive a message about food running out around this time'. The communicator would be briefed to answer that the welfare of the hostages was solely the pirates' responsibility. However predictable these exchanges were, there were no shortcuts. Pirates had time to probe until they were convinced that they could not do better. 'There is a pace, a rhythm to these things.'

Principal–Agent Dynamics?

A major threat to a successful ransom negotiation is the perception of principal–agent problems between the hostage stakeholders and the crisis responder. The set-up is extremely unpromising. The crisis response consultant is paid by the insurer to advise the stakeholders how to safely retrieve the hostage. Crisis responders are adamant that their primary concern is for the victim and that they work solely for the stakeholders. The incentive structure of their profession rewards clean and cheap resolutions within a reasonable time frame. But—could stakeholders trade off time against money in the interest of their loved one (even if it is to the detriment of everyone else)? Looking at the 'curve' naively, it looks like an extra week achieves a laughably small 'reduction' in the ransom demand. Why should the stakeholders listen to the insurer's agent, when the ultimate principal has such a clear stake in maintaining ransom discipline? And is the agent's own objective really aligned with either of his principals' interests?

Kidnappers have an arsenal of tactics to try and convince stakeholders to reveal their assets. So far, we have focused on threats and shock tactics. A family that has exhausted its financial means must remain firm, even if an ear arrives in the post. (If it does, it is worth doing a DNA test: most belong to unrelated locals—'there are usually plenty of stiffs lying around in these places'.) But a family that is told to hold out at a ransom level below their ability to pay (and well within the insurance ransom limit) is vulnerable. Imagine that a family has indicated through patient negotiation that they will settle at around US$30,000, starting at US$18,000 and slowly increasing in decreasing increments. The negotiations are stuck at US$28,983. This odd figure looks like stakeholders are collecting everything they have: nice round numbers look artificial. The crisis responder advises that the next offer should (appear to be) funded by a yard sale next Saturday. If that is still not enough, the wife will tearfully pawn her wedding band—a popular deal-clincher that makes perfect sense in Diego Gambetta's framework of costly signals. In fact, the insurance would cover ransoms up to US$100,000. What if the kidnapper's communicator offers an immediate release for US$50,000? Or a third-party mediator appears, promising to settle everything for a cash fee of US$20,000—on top of the US$29,000? It is very tempting to trust the siren call; to embrace the hope of closure and moving on.

The consultant knows the ruse. Being patient now is not about 'reducing' the ransom demand from its current (unenforceable) level, but about making the agreement stick. He knows that a massive increment at this stage destroys the carefully created cover story of a middle-class family keeping up with the Joneses purely by the power of their credit cards and hire purchases (statements available on request). Agreeing a substantial rise in the ransom will reset the game, not end it. The consultant therefore advises the family to whet the kidnapper's appetite for a quick settlement instead. 'Yes, next Saturday there will be more money, somebody said we can sell the dining table and chairs for US$200. Our kind neighbour has offered to run a lemonade stall, too … We are almost confident we can make US$800. Please keep Uncle Fred safe until then.' And then: 'I have the US$28,983 in small notes right here in a holdall in my office. I never knew how much that amount of money weighs. I hope nobody breaks in and steals it.'

Who will cave in first? The responder knows that the kidnapper cannot make a profit from holding a hostage for a further five days for US$800. But a family may well ask: what if the consultant is just trying to spin out the negotiation? Is the agent working in his own interest rather than in the interest of either of his principals? He is paid US$2,000 per day. Here we are talking about a release next weekend. US$10,000 for him—or US$20,000 for the plausible-sounding mediator and it's all over today? Shall we take the chance that it's a genuine offer? Even if it doesn't quite work, there is still plenty of room until we hit the US$100,000 threshold. Or is this about the insurer, who wants to settle this case at US$30,000 rather than at the limit? Who is the real principal here? Negotiating this tricky terrain of suspicion with stressed and fearful stakeholders may be the most delicate aspect of guiding a ransom negotiation to a successful conclusion.

Stakeholders are the ultimate decision makers; the consultant only advises. He influences the stakeholders by setting out the pros and cons of different options: 'I make the options—they make the call. That's how it works.'[32] Research in neuroscience, social psychology, and experimental economics shows that high-credibility sources have significant power to influence decisions, particularly when people make risky choices.[33] Consultants working for reputable crisis responders are highly trained and have a wealth of experience. Some have been involved in more than a hundred cases and all have access to their firms' previous case files. They are calm under pressure and know the kidnappers' tactics. Many immediately recognize when a negotiation enters a new phase from subtle shifts in the tone of conversation. If they are convinced that the kidnappers are using a ploy rather than making a genuine offer, they will do their best to persuade the stakeholders to hold firm.

In a price theorist's model of a ransom negotiation, the stakeholders' offers would lie on a smooth curve converging at the target ransom level. If stakeholders decide against the better judgement of consultants and a negotiation derails, the consultants pick up the pieces, regroup, and move on. Most likely, the negotiation will proceed on a higher curve than before and convergence will be achieved on terms that are more advantageous for the kidnapper. Even the most charismatic and experienced consultants are unable to exert perfect control at every point in every negotiation, but an outstanding consultant can bring the negotiation back on track after a deviation. Arguably, an early deviation from the curve could even be helpful. It would illustrate how easy it is to destabilize kidnappers' expectations, making stakeholders more careful later. Moreover, if kidnappers can plot a perfectly smooth logarithmic curve through the offers, they might suspect that stakeholders have highly professional support.

Finalizing the Deal

After the final set of threats, everyone's mind turns to agreeing the price and organizing the ransom drop and hostage release. The tone of the conversation shifts. It becomes more respectful and cooperative, setting the scene for the stakeholders' leap of faith of paying money with no guarantee that the seller will dispatch the goods. The kidnappers are often asked to promise that the hostages (and their families or firms) will not be targeted again. The future protection relationship is thereby made explicit. Meanwhile, the kidnapper fears that the exchange will be interrupted by law enforcement to release the hostage without payment and decides how best to avoid detection during the handover. We will look at the details in Chapter 8, which discusses how the crisis responders manage the exchange. On the criminal side, the communicator may use the improved atmosphere to try and haggle out a side-payment for himself or extract a few more minor concessions to expedite the release.

There is a tendency to soften in the last stages of bargaining, but it's best to keep firm. Unfortunately, not every hostage situation ends shortly after the ransom drop. In the dreaded 'double cross' the kidnappers come back with a further demand after the receipt of the ransom—acknowledging the 'first tranche' or 'down payment'. Alternatively, only some of a group of hostages might be released. Somali pirates occasionally kept some crew members behind.[34] If there is any hint that there are further, hitherto untapped resources, a new negotiation begins. Crisis response consultants encourage stakeholders not to send mixed messages during the negotiation process and rarely encounter the double cross. If they do, their reaction depends on the situation, but often the hostage is released without further payment when this final 'squeeze' is fruitless.

The Right Price Returns the Hostage *and* Stabilizes the Market

This chapter showed how complicated it is to set a price for a hostage that will be accepted and honoured by the criminal counterparty. Both a price theorist and a family naively monetizing their assets will produce an offer curve with decreasing marginal returns for the kidnapper: the first by design, the second by necessity. Once the reservation price is met, the decreasing increments eventually fail to cover the kidnappers' holding costs and convince them to release the hostage. The art and craft of hostage negotiation does not lie in creating *a* curve, but in knowing *the* curve that produces swift convergence at the kidnapper's reservation price—and in helping the stakeholders stick to it through threats and temptations.

We saw how crisis response consultants guide the hostage stakeholders through the minefield of the anarchic bargaining process. There is little opportunity to think through the implication of every minute decision and utterance—and of what is left unsaid and undone. A mistake can result in fear, pain, or even death. Most stakeholders are only too relieved to learn that there is a protocol that has been proven to work. They are keen to discuss the options and rehearse the responses with highly professional, calm, and experienced experts. Perhaps they even delegate the role of communicator to a professional.

But—exhausted from weeks of heartache and worry—they will also question and perhaps challenge the experts when their advice seems counter-intuitive or disappointing. We saw that despite the problematic principal–agent set-up, consultants' objectives are very closely aligned with those of the stakeholders; especially if stakeholders have some other-regarding preferences. But even if the problem is largely one of perception, it nonetheless must be astutely managed.

Equally importantly, consultants impose discipline on the kidnappers. They consistently reward cooperation, ignore threats, and punish maltreatment. Although each negotiation is a unique, one-off interaction, crisis responders interact repeatedly with the same or similar criminal organizations. In kidnap hotspots reputations are built, and norms and protocols can be established. The full force of the law (or the extra-legal protector) is deployed against those who transgress against the norm of treating hostages decently. Eventually, kidnappers come to understand that they are better off treating their victims 'well': their 'treatment [of the hostage] would act as a presentation card for future victims...no-one's going to negotiate with someone who has a track record of blowing his victims' brains out'.[35] If everyone accepts that there is a 'going rate' for hostages and plans accordingly, negotiations can converge rapidly. The large majority of kidnappings are resolved in under a week.[36] Thus, in practice most kidnappers do not go through the full process of scoping their victims' ability to pay. Stakeholders do not liquidate every single possession to retrieve their loved ones.

There is a level of kidnapping that—if well ordered—broadly works for everyone. In this 'Goldilocks' state, firms can take advantage of business opportunities, insurers make a profit, kidnappers get a limited payoff, and hostages return unharmed in a reasonable time frame.[37] Even the host government benefits from taxable economic activities in its territory without having to expend resources on tackling organized crime. However, this 'not too hot, not too cold' Goldilocks state is not necessarily stable. Ransoming gets complicated and negotiations extend when price expectations are upset. Chapter 7 examines the themes developed in this chapter in the context of a pirate ransom negotiation during a period of rapid ransom inflation. The further, equally important questions of how to organize the ransom drop and retrieve the hostage are left for Chapter 8.

7

The Case of the *CEC Future*

> A: Tell him fuck you, fuck you, and fuck your white ass mother-
> fucking boss...
> S: ok, you take care Ismail.
> A: Just watch me what I do, just watch me and tell your boss the
> same thing. Tell him fuck you, too, you motherfucking white
> bastard.
> S: I will tell him that, ok and I will speak to you later, ok.
>
> FBI transcript of the CEC Future negotiation, kindly made
> available by Per Gullestrup, former CEO of Clipper Shipping

Listening in on a Pirate Negotiation

Ransom negotiations are generally conducted in secret. Occasionally, someone will talk about a negotiation afterwards. You will get one side's recollection and usually it will be 'off the record'. Many negotiations are recorded, which would give us more insight: the conversation would not be filtered or edited by a participant's memory. An insider may play you a few audio clips—without breaching client confidentiality of course. This will give you an excellent impression of how difficult it is to establish and conduct a conversation over a crackling high frequency radio. You will struggle to understand the heavily accented, ungrammatical communicator. What was he trying to say there? Some tapes are transcribed for evaluation by law enforcement or for training purposes, but neither the police nor the crisis responders release this sensitive information.

We are therefore extremely fortunate that Clipper Shipping made a very different decision. Clipper invited a television crew to observe their efforts to retrieve their ship, the *CEC Future*, from Somali pirates. The tense negotiation was broadcast as a documentary on Danish television afterwards.[1] In addition, the ship-owners had the recordings of the negotiation transcribed and made it available to the police, journalists, and researchers. The pirates' negotiator, an American Somali who somehow ended as a translator for the pirates, decided to tell his side of the story, too. Eventually, the material became the basis for the TV documentary *Stolen Seas* and (with more artistic licence) the film *A Hijacking*.[2] Even more details emerged when the pirate negotiator was tried for piracy offences in the US.[3]

The film's focus on the suffering of the crew and families, the boredom and fear on board, and the suspense of waiting for the next threat or offer in the boardroom. I mostly abstract from this and use the material to illustrate the many theoretical problems a ransom negotiation must resolve in a very practical context. What is a ship and crew 'worth'? How do you end up paying the price that you want to pay? How do perceptions of a principal–agent problem arise and how are they resolved? Who negotiates and who makes decisions? How does power shift in the negotiation? How does confrontation turn into cooperation? These are interesting problems and—uniquely—I had the opportunity to discuss them with Per Gullestrup (the former CEO at Clipper Group who oversaw the negotiation), the pirate negotiator, and the crisis response consultant. So, in addition to the script, we have information about the perceptions and motivations of all the main actors in the case. The final stroke of good luck is that the hijack occurred at a very important juncture in Somali piracy: the beginning of the ransom inflation which eventually triggered the world's largest counter-piracy task force. What can the *CEC Future* tell us about why insurers were unable to prevent the escalation of pirate ransoms in Somalia?

Somali Piracy

'Sea-scavenging', 'informal taxation' of traders, and piracy have a long history in Somalia. Following the fall of the Siad Barre regime in 1991, formal governance broke down. Somalia's fish-rich territorial waters were no longer policed and there was no recognized authority to issue fishing licences. Foreign trawlers therefore made deals to obtain informal 'protection' from local elites instead. But the boundaries of the Somali clans' areas of influence are permeable and fluid. Trawler crews kept being approached by armed local fishermen demanding payment with menaces—and refusing to recognize other groups' handwritten 'fishing licences'. Eventually, trawler crews armed themselves and fought off the rag-tag boarding parties. The frustrated 'coastguards' realized that unarmed merchant shipping and aid vessels were much softer targets.[4]

Put yourself in the shoes of an aspiring pirate for a moment. Imagine you and some good friends know how to get alongside a promising target, scramble up to deck level, and subdue any crew resistance. But what are you going to do when you are on the bridge? I would probably feel a bit like a dog that managed to stop a bus: elated, but at a complete loss regarding how to proceed. Indeed, most maritime crimes are incidents of petty robbery at sea. The International Maritime Bureau's annual piracy reports mostly describe how unarmed thieves shimmied up an anchor cable and fled with a few items of limited value—often just a bit of rope, paint, or tools. Armed thieves occasionally target crew possessions or the ship's safe. More money can be made by abducting crew members for ransoming—a common tactic in the Gulf of Guinea. Very, very few pirates hijack entire ships.[5] The highest returns to piracy are made by criminals who can unload and sell on the cargo, repaint the ship, and sell it with forged papers. Such incidents of piracy occasionally occurred in the Strait of Malacca—but very rarely: it takes an excellent infrastructure controlled by corrupt harbour-masters to pull this off. This combination is very rare; it certainly was not available in Somalia.

Somalia's criminal entrepreneurs came up with a different option—hijacking ship, cargo, and crew for ransom. Taking the whole caboodle had several advantages over just abducting the crew. The ships had food and water on board and could safely convey everyone back to Somalia—so pirates only had to fund supplies for one-way missions. Once on board, pirates and any additional guards could live in comparative luxury and rifle crew possessions at their leisure. Comings and goings on a ship can be closely monitored—it is easier to defend a ship from marauding rivals than most land bases. Negotiations could be conducted using the ship's telephone system: no need to rely on Somalia's telecommunications infrastructure. And having a ship out of action and the worried cargo-owners, families, and crewing agents on the phone would surely focus the ship-owner's minds on finding a swift solution.

But how much to ask for? Somali pirates had little idea what the ships were worth to their owners. In 2005 and 2006 pirates hijacked a few slow, older cargo ships alongside the usual fishing trawlers. They were ransomed for between US$20,000 and US$300,000, mostly at the lower end of that range.[6] With thousands of ships insuring their transit through the Gulf of Aden and the Somali Basin, a handful of such incidents per year troubled neither the shipping nor the insurance sector. The crew generally came home just as on-board supplies ran short. In 2007, a sea change occurred. The owners of the *Danica White*, a small cargo ship with five Danish crew members on board, reportedly paid the full US$1.5 million ransom demand to retrieve their ship after

133

eighty-three days. This set pirates' minds whirring. So, the next group of pirates demanded a US$1 million ransom for the Japanese tanker *Golden Nori* and left satisfied after a six-week negotiation. In early 2008, a new record was reached with US$2 million for the French luxury yacht *Le Ponant*. Fewer and fewer merchant ship-owners settled below the million-dollar mark. The Spanish government re-educated pirates about the value of fishing trawlers with a lightning quick US$1.2 million ransom for the *Playa di Bakio*. Poor young men started to dream dreams of avarice, and shrewd businessmen developed an infrastructure that could support negotiations beyond the limits of on-board supplies. The scene is set for the arrival of the *CEC Future*.

The *CEC Future* hijack

The MV *CEC Future* was owned by Clipper Group and contained cargo belonging to McDermott International. The vessel was attacked by a pirate gang far off the coast of Somalia on 7 November 2008. Although the crew was on high alert and all recommended passive safety features were installed, the pirates overcame the ship's defences. They shot a rocket-propelled grenade across the bow and when they aimed the next grenade at the bridge the captain conceded. The pirates boarded and directed the vessel to their stronghold Eyl in Puntland. Here the pirates inveigled (or recruited) Ali Mohamed Ali, a returnee from the US with excellent English and some previous experience of mediating in piracy cases, as their translator (or negotiator).[7] Mr Ali conveyed the pirates' first ransom demand of US$7 million to the ship-owner on 10 November. We do not have a transcript of this call.

The first record we have is from mid-afternoon of the 10 November. By then Clipper's incident management team was assembled and advised by a highly experienced consultant. The company had also engaged a professional communicator, Mr S, to handle the negotiation and the contacts with the crew. Contact was established using the ship's on-board communication system. The first recorded conversation is between Mr S and the captain. Then Mr Ali, the pirate's communicator is introduced. If Mr Ali expected an immediate counter-offer to the pirates' demand he was disappointed. He is told to 'be patient', that there will be 'hopefully a good solution', and that Mr S would be calling the ship when Clipper had an answer to the pirates' demand. Clipper is sending a clear message that they will not be pushed around. Clipper next makes contact more than two days later—on the evening of 13 November at 18.00. By this time, the pirates have allowed the crew members to phone home; presumably in the hope of raising the pressure on Clipper. Mr S announces that tomorrow at the same time there will be an offer in response to the pirates' demand. Mr Ali tries to call Mr S twice during the following afternoon on the pretext that there may be something wrong with the ship's telephone system. Yet Mr S phones the ship as promised at 17.55 and conveys the first offer: US$400,000. Mr Ali says he will take it back to the pirates. He requests that the offer is sent by fax.

The Parties' Aims and Objectives

At the start of the bidding process, Clipper expected to pay a ransom in the region of US$1.2 million. The figure was based on previous ransoms for comparable ships. The ship's value was closer to US$12 million—and the company had the mandatory insurance for the total constructive loss of the hull. Cargo, crew, and loss of hire insurance would have been obtained in addition to this. The target of US$1.2 million indicates that the management team wanted to get the crew home safely as fast as possible—but without causing problems for others. Clipper had no intention of bartering down pirate expectations to the detriment of their crew. At the same time, Clipper was determined not to contribute to ransom inflation: they would pay no more than the 'going rate'. Unfortunately, Clipper was 'overtaken by other ship-owners', as Per Gullestrup put it. Ship-owners and crisis responders constantly monitored and shared information about the state of concurrent negotiations and ransoms for each release. The moving average of ransoms was rising inexorably. The owners of a ship comparable to the *CEC Future* were just ahead of Clipper in their negotiation: they would be setting the 'benchmark' for the *CEC Future*. Clipper's bargaining strategy had to adapt to a moving target.

The pirates were on a steep learning curve—both at sea and on land. At sea, the naval coalition patrolling in the Gulf of Aden was joined by ever more nations, raising the risk of attacks being interrupted. However, there was limited legal follow-through on these interruptions and pirates largely shrugged off the naval 'catch and release' operations.[8] For the few on whom the navies had collected enough evidence for arrest and trial, the huge expanse of the Somali Basin provided a good alternative. The open seas are simply too big to patrol. For pirates with the spirit to venture far from home shores, there were rich pickings. The brigands innovated by tying their attack skiffs to motherships and used the winds and currents of their old trade routes to drift far into the ocean.[9] Official advice about keeping a minimum distance from the Somali coast created informal shipping lanes just outside the designated 'danger zone'. Rather than sitting in the middle of the ocean in a tiny skiff, waiting for a target to appear on the horizon, pirates knew where to look for prey.[10] It was a shameful waste of time for a dashing young pirate to sit in the anchorage. They were bored to death—only the odd bunch of *khat* made it bearable. This locally popular drug was supplied on (interest-free) credit but with a huge mark-up by shrewd traders. Many pirates found that as negotiations dragged on, their *khat* bill made massive dents in their pay-out. They had to stay on board to stake their claim on the ransom. They were very keen to conclude. The money would help them launch their next attack—perhaps as captain next time? Let's please finish this well before the next monsoon season sets in.[11]

But perhaps a much bigger ransom could be obtained with a mixture of patient negotiating and wild threats? Rather than risking their lives at sea again, some pirates wanted to maximize the return on what they had already got. Senior pirates and investors usually expected a profit share. Nobody really knew what these ships were worth to their owners. As long as the on-board supplies set an effective time limit on the negotiation, it would be difficult to find out. Local businessmen (some of them former pirates) therefore decided to provide the financial and social capital to stretch out the negotiations.[12] The ransoms would have to be shared among more people. This might not make strict financial sense for a criminal entrepreneur, but sharing resources greatly enhances status in Somalia. So, let's just sit tight for a little longer and see what happens? As we will see later, the pirates on the *CEC Future* were split regarding the best negotiation strategy.

There is one more party to consider: Mr Ali, also known as Ali Mohamed Ali, Ishmael Ali, or just Ali or Ismail. He is an American Somali, who returned to his country of birth and looked to make a living there. A pleasant, well-spoken, and caring single father with a young son in a land of famously limited opportunities. But he is both bilingual and bicultural—he knows how business is done in Somalia and the West. After successfully mediating on behalf of a German couple taken from their yacht in June 2008, Mr Ali thought he might turn himself into a local piracy expert. Foreign sociologists and journalists dominated the international discourse on Somali piracy—where was the genuine Somali voice? Some acquaintances invited the Somalilander to Eyl, the 'pirate capital'.[13] Once on board the *CEC Future* he was asked to work as a translator and eventually came to feel like a hostage himself. He says he negotiated his own release by brokering a deal for the *CEC Future*. Not quite—asserted the US government: Ali was a professional negotiator, lured by the promise of significant pay-out. Looking at the transcript, Ali did not consider himself as a pirate. He strongly objected to any suggestion of it throughout the negotiation. Ultimately, the jury at his trial failed to convict him.[14] Let us therefore assume that the pirate's agent had his own interests: he wanted to conclude the negotiation as fast as possible and get back home. His principals suspected this and monitored him as closely as they could. All official offers had to be sent by fax. Although the pirates could not monitor Mr Ali's conversations, they could check the numbers and confirm the company logo on the fax.

Let us see how the stylized model of price formation in an anarchic bargaining scenario with asymmetric information fares with the additional complications of a shifting ransom target and the pirate agent's potential conflict of interest with his principals.

On and off the Curve

The next important conversation took place on the following day, 15 November. Mr Ali roundly rejects the offer of US$400,000, explaining that 'you have to understand that these people are not amateurs ... some of them just (inaudible) fourth time'. At interview Mr Ali recollected that the pirates interpreted Clipper's relatively swift opening offer of US$400,000 as extremely encouraging and tried to push for a ransom as high as US$7 million. Then Mr S indicates that Clipper is looking to settle for a ransom 'below 2 million'. Mr S clarifies the following day that what he meant was that the pirates should come down to a demand below US$2 million before Clipper would move again. Mr S explains that the financial crisis in Europe makes a settlement above US$2 million impossible. However, the pirates get the message that Clipper's current target figure is US$2 million. They counter with a demand of US$5 million.

Over the next days there are several long phone calls, talking about the pirates' high costs of keeping the *CEC Future* in the Eyl anchorage, ways of delivering the ransom, and the captain's reports about conditions on board. On 18 November Clipper raises its offer to US$700,000. The additional US$300,000 follows the negotiation protocol rule of decreasing increments. However, it comes very quickly after the first offer. The pirates view the swift and generous increase as a sign of weakness and Clipper's ability to pay top dollar. In terms of signalling 'a curve', pirates would extrapolate from this second offer to expect a ransom above two million after four to six weeks. Mr Ali tells Mr S that the pirates are in no rush to conclude the negotiation.

137

In the next few conversations the communications are at cross purposes: Mr S wants Mr Ali to come down to a demand below US$2 million, but Mr Ali is looking for a sensible next demand to ensure final convergence at or above US$2 million. And the pirates refuse to make a lower counter-demand. On 22 November, the captain starts to complain about conditions and supplies on board. His concerns are more vehemently expressed on 27 November: fuel, food, and water are low. The stalemate continues until the pirates come down to US$4.9 million on 30 November. Clipper counters immediately with a proportional increase of 1/50th to US$714,000. The management team has learned its lesson: the pirates are in no rush to conclude. Although the phone calls continue there is no movement, much to the frustration of the crew. On 3 December, Mr S confirms Clipper's intention to stick with US$714,000—so the pirates give them 'the silent treatment': calls cease.

The silence is expected and Clipper patiently waits for the pirates to make the next move. Mr Ali calls Mr S from his private phone on 11 December, on 12 December Mr S calls the ship. This time there are threats: destroying the navigation equipment, taking the crew off the ship, capsizing the ship. Some of the threats are conveyed by the captain, who receives whispered instructions. The pirates demand an improved offer—or else. Sticking to the protocol of never, ever responding positively to a threat, Clipper does not react and the silence resumes. On 20 December two crew members are reported sick. On 21 December there is concern about a third crew member's health. The Clipper team does not panic. Instead, Mr S tells the pirates that because of the Christmas and New Year holidays things are unlikely to move for a while. The captain is not pleased with that message, flagging up problems with fuel levels and technical issues.

After Christmas, there are urgent requests for medication to be sent. Over the next few days there are several conversations about sensible next steps. But nothing is sent by fax, so officially there is no movement. Clipper refuses to move without a reduced demand. On 29 December, the pirates' answer finally arrives: US$3.25 million. Clipper counters with US$1 million. Mr Ali and the pirates had confidently expected the new offer to be much closer to US$2 million to converge above US$2 million. But Clipper had now revealed that they were on a completely different curve: much closer to the original intention of convergence at US$1.2 million! Mr Ali's rude outburst in response to this news betrays perplexity, anger, and anxiety. He is very disappointed and afraid of what the pirates will do if when they find out: 'you cannot put that shit in a motherfucking fax...you want to get me killed. Because I told them two million, because you told me so.' Mr S's professionalism is impressive here, he does not lose his calm, but politely tells Mr Ali that he will take all the information back to the board. The introduction to this chapter gives a flavour of the divergence of tones in this conversation. A few hours later, the pirates fax a demand of US$5 million.

Yet the same evening Mr Ali proposes a new idea: more mediators could be brought in, who—for a fee of US$250,000—could get the ball rolling again. Mr Ali is desperate to get off the ship—calling himself the fourteenth hostage. He considers committing suicide. The next day, Mr Ali proposes a deal: US$2.3 million for the ship and US$250,000 for the mediators and 'this thing is going to be finished tomorrow morning'. Have we heard this kind of offer before, somewhere? Clipper—correctly—rejects any possibility of finding that kind of money. The pirates need to come down to a realistic level. Mr Ali concludes bitterly: 'you don't give a damn care about the crew and the vessel, right?'

To Care or not to Care?

Indeed, for Clipper, the best way of caring for its crew was to appear not to care. If the pre-Christmas threats of damaging the vessel and taking the crew away had been successful, they would have been repeated. There was plenty of scope to escalate the threat—from mild physical abuse to mock executions. In other negotiations, Somali pirates went down that route to ratchet up the pressure. Some ship-owners were even told that crew members had died. Everyone was delighted by their mysterious resurrection after the ransom drop. Clipper punished the pirates with a week-long silence after the first threat and seemed surprisingly blasé about the crew members reported sick.

Watching the footage of the tense boardroom meetings and talking to Per Gullestrup it is obvious that crew welfare was foremost on everybody's mind. How did they manage to play it so cool? As a responsible employer, Clipper had made sure that all crew members had recently had full medicals. The company also contacted the crew members' wives, who confirmed that there was no medical history of concern. It did not seem plausible that several crew members would conveniently develop life-threatening conditions at a critical juncture of the negotiation. It is also not unusual for employers to agree code-words before staff enter hostile territory: words to preface false information given on behalf of the kidnappers and a distress signal. If so, the captain clearly did not put real pressure on his company.

A further reason that the company knew that morale on board had not collapsed was that the captain was playing his own cat and mouse game with the pirates. The question of fuel levels had already been raised in the early conversations. It became a theme in the later conversations: would the *CEC Future* have enough fuel to steam out of Somalia after ransoming? Clipper used this as a way of putting pressure on the pirates: you need to let the ship go before it becomes unable to manoeuvre. What would you do with a broken ship? It is your responsibility to keep it safe. However, the captain had misrepresented the problem to the pirates—there was no acute shortage of fuel. The captain's ongoing charade about low fuel levels sent the opposite message to what the pirates intended him to send. Here was a captain who kept his spirits up and acted autonomously in difficult circumstances. Per Gullestrup is still full of admiration for his 'excellent captain'.

The idea of 'theatre', 'performance', and 'role-playing' in ransom negotiations was raised in numerous interviews. One ship-owner argued that the transcript of his negotiation would be of little value for my research: it was 'all merely theatre'. To press home his sense of dislocation and strangeness he then added: 'Kabuki theatre'. This raises the question: do both sides know that this is theatre? Or is the high art of negotiation to play the theatre so well that the other side suspends their disbelief? To care is to appear not to care. To care is to stick to the story, whatever the audience does.

Stalemate

On 30 December, the captain is back on the phone, complaining once more about provisions and technical issues, as Mr Ali goads him on: 'they don't give a fuck about you guys'. The New Year starts with messages about the ill health of the boatswain ('a stroke, a heart attack about 5 minutes ago') and the chief engineer ('bleeding'). The next day Mr Ali reports that he has seen the chief engineer 'tied to a chair and laughing'. The negotiation appears to be stuck. On 2 January, Clipper suggests that the pirates change to a different negotiator. Why not use the previously suggested mediators instead of Mr Ali to get the ball moving again? Mr Ali, however, is adamant that any communication with the pirates must go through him.

In fact, Mr Ali had a different idea: the problem was Mr S, the communicator, who was drawing the negotiation out for his own private gain. The telephone number of Per Gullestrup, the CEO of Clipper Shipping, was readily available on the internet. If Mr Ali could get the real decision maker on the phone and rid himself of the troublesome agent, they could solve this man to man. When would the CEO stop hiding behind Mr S and pick up the phone? Mr Ali had tried so many times already. Mr Gullestrup, worn out and frustrated by weeks of circular conversations, finally picked up the phone on 3 January 2009.

Unfortunately, we don't have a transcript for this spontaneous conversation—the recording system is only set up on 7 January. However, we know from the conversations between Mr Ali and Mr S on the 4 January what was said in the previous day's call. Mr Gullestrup had made several demands. He wanted proof of life for the boatswain and chief engineer, and the captain had to confirm that the electronics and navigation equipment were in good working order and no damage had been done to the ship. Further, the pirates should reduce their ransom demand and anchor the ship to conserve fuel. Mr Ali puts the two crew members on the phone as requested. Both answer proof of life questions and neither mentions a health problem. The captain comes back on to confirm that there is no damage or problem—except the fictitious fuel issue. All is well on board then. However, the pirates are sticking with their previous demand of US$3.25 million. Mr Ali explains that they had gone back up to US$5 million in their last fax and reducing to US$3.25 million again broadly meets Mr Gullestrup's demand. The company should move to US$2 million and then the pirates would move again. Ah—and no, the ship would not be anchored. There are no further recorded conversations in the next two days.

On the morning of 7 January, the captain is wheeled out again. He angrily shouts a catalogue of complaints at Mr S, who interrupts the call. When Mr S accidentally calls the ship a little later, the captain is still on the bridge and calmly answers the phone. Then it is Mr Gullestrup's turn to listen to the litany of woes from the captain: the crew has gone mad, there is no food, and fuel is rapidly running out. Pure theatre? Mr Gullestrup refuses to have that conversation with the captain and asks for Mr Ali. Where is the reduced demand? Where is evidence that the pirates will come below US$2 million so this can be settled? Would an offer of US$1.2 million from Clipper be helpful?

This certainly does not look like the hoped-for sea change. In fact, it could have been a step backwards. The company had revealed that it cared about the crew. The CEO was on the phone and clearly impatient to do a deal. The professional communicator was sidelined. 'Overall, we don't recommend that CEOs take on that role', was all the tight-lipped crisis response consultant would say on the matter. I have never heard him openly criticize a customer. He knows that negotiations are rarely conducted entirely by the book. By ceding control and supporting the CEO's decision to take over the negotiation, the negotiator retained (and perhaps regained) the company's trust. He continued to advise, discuss, and agree the strategy for every call and sat alongside Mr Gullestrup during calls whenever feasible.

The Unexpected Breakthrough

When Mr Gullestrup answered Mr Ali's call and took over the negotiation he had already planned a business trip to Brazil. But, he was also determined to finish the ransom negotiation himself. If the phone calls could be scheduled around his meetings and plane trips, and there was some juggling to accommodate the time difference, he would continue to handle the calls. Thankfully, this was not the message the pirates received. Mr Ali thought that Mr Gullestrup was going on vacation. Here he was, stranded on a ship with pirates he didn't like or trust, trying his very best to find a solution to the stand-off, and the Clipper executives were swanning around the globe. '[Mr Gullestrup] was vacationing most of the time', Mr Ali recollected at interview. 'He went on talk shows and interviews here and there. He didn't care about the thirteen human beings stranded in a hellhole.' So, when Mr Gullestrup warns on 7 January, 'if they don't drop the anchor on that ship and preserve fuel oil, then we are stopping any discussion and we are going to sit back and wait', Mr Ali finally believes him. A few hours later the ship is anchored. When Mr Gullestrup asks for confirmation, the tone of the conversation has changed: 'Yes, Yes, Sir, it is anchored.'

Mr Ali was now completely convinced that the shipping company would outwait the pirates—spurred on by the consultant and communicator. He felt that the professional negotiators had spun out the negotiation to maximize their own fees. The pirates had expected hourly updates at first—but Mr S had rarely called. Clipper had disabled the ship's phone for outgoing calls, frustrating Mr Ali's efforts to mobilize the families and the crewing agent. Now it was up to Mr Ali to make the pirates realize that Clipper was in the driving seat after all. Mr Ali explained to me that the Clipper executives never knew the crew. They had been hired via a crewing agent. 'They were expendables. They were Eastern Europeans. There were no Danish sailors. If there had been, then Clipper would have paid more money in two to three weeks.' Mr Ali was shocked by this lack of empathy and humanity. Although he cursed the arrogance and stupidity of these Westerners, he knew he had to work mainly on the pirates from now on.

The *CEC Future* pirates were a cross-clan venture, led by a senior pirate with a crew of hungry young men attracted by the promise of easy riches. Mr Ali would try to convince the young pirates to cut the negotiation short. The new pirate season was just starting: it was time to get ready to strike again before the next monsoon would confine them to harbour. Even if the junior pirates had been promised a proportion of the final ransom, their share was certainly going up more slowly than their bills. The problem was even more acute for the guards. They had been hired on a flat fee of US$5,000. With supplies arriving on board at cut-throat prices, they would be in debt if the negotiation dragged on. Mr Ali haggled with those who wanted to stay at US$4 million, telling them the US$2 million was a 'mistake', a genuine misunderstanding. If he could sow discord between the clans, perhaps the recalcitrant pirates would depart for their own safety.

Principals and Agents Again

It's time to reassess the principal–agent situation. Initially, Clipper had employed two agents—the response consultant and the communicator—to handle the negotiation. Both derived a significant proportion of their income from the insurance sector. Whoever paid for their work on the *CEC Future* case, their performance would be assessed by their ultimate principal: the insurance industry. The Somali hostage market was in a period of uncertainty. Pirates were pushing for higher ransoms and the responders had to develop responses to the emerging ransom inflation. Sitting tight risked losing the trust of the companies, but letting ransoms escalate would soon make piracy uninsurable. The best the crisis responders could do was to engage in damage limitation. Any advice would be carefully couched in terms of the ship-owners' best interest.

The pirates had also 'employed' an agent, with good English-language skills and prior negotiation experience. Whatever Mr Ali's motivations were at the start, the script shows that after a month on board the ship he was heartily fed up. Initially, Mr Ali believed that whoever had the ship and crew held the best cards. Clipper was rich. He would mediate and after two or three weeks everyone would leave happily. But Clipper sent a different message. Every day Mr Ali updated his beliefs, until he fully trusted that the ship and crew meant nothing to the company.[15] He was getting scared: the pirates would be disappointed with the ransom, and they would take it out on him. Now his best-case scenario was to get away physically unscathed. He would not be sharing in whatever deplorably low ransom this case would settle for.

The conversation between Mr Gullestrup and Mr Ali therefore undergoes a marked shift. Mr Ali has realized that if he is to derive any benefit from his thankless work on the *CEC Future* it will be by working with

Clipper; by mediating rather than demanding. Mr Ali becomes respectful, Mr Gullestrup becomes professionally friendly. Mr Ali addresses his counterparty as 'Sir', but Mr Gullestrup calls him Ali. They chat about Mr Ali's American life and his son. They discuss how they can work on the pirates together. How to structure the give and take to speed up the negotiation. But progress is still slow. On 10 January, Mr Gullestrup starts to lose patience with Mr Ali: 'it only makes sense for me to be involved here as long as we are making progress'. Here is a principal, talking to his agent. The next day the principal is ready to delegate the matter entirely: 'I cannot keep spending my time on this.' 'I will hand over the negotiations to [Mr S], okay. Then you deal with him until [the pirates] come to their senses.' This is the last thing Mr Ali wants—having the principal and decision maker on direct dial is his trump card!

Unfortunately for him, Clipper has also realized this. The cardinal rule of separation of communicator and decision maker has been violated. Mr Ali has too much power to influence the outcome. Mr Gullestrup therefore starts to revise Mr Ali's expectations about his room for manoeuvre: 'my boss has told me that if I cannot make progress then I will be taken off the case'. No, Mr Gullestrup is not the principal—he has a boss. On the morning of 11 January this new layer of hierarchy—who is the CEO's boss?—is explained. The real principal is the board of directors. Mr Gullestrup is not able to make snap decisions. Moreover, he cannot waste his time on the phone discussing the finer points of who said what in a pirate meeting. He is travelling in Brazil and can only be contacted on and off. Mid-day on 11 January, Mr Gullestrup gives his new agent Ali the following instructions: 'Instead of you and I going back at US$50,000 a pop I would rather trust you and say I give you in your back pocket one and a half. That's where we can end up and then I leave you to do the negotiation and try to get this to work.'

The Deal

On the evening of 11 January, Mr Ali comes back, crestfallen. The ransom of the ship that would serve as the pirates' benchmark has crept up from US$1.5 million to US$1.7 million! Mr Gullestrup is asking the impossible with a budget of US$1.5 million. Mr Ali explains: '[The pirates are] just like children you know. If you got that candy they want to have the same candy . . . In regards to the 1.5, I don't think they will go for that. I really don't think they will go for that.' Mr Gullestrup hints at a potential of further compromise: 'we need to end up close to that limit because I simply have my hands tied . . . you work your magic if you can.'

In private, Clipper has resolved to pay no more and no less than the 'market price'. Clipper cannot take responsibility for reversing pirate expectations. When Mr Ali comes back with a demand of US$1.9 million on 12 January, Mr Gullestrup loses patience: 'The [name withheld] is very similar to our ship. Okay, so why do we have to go through this nonsense when they know the [name withheld] was done at 1.7? Why do I have to waste my time at 1.9?' Once more Mr Ali is threatened with the case being handed back to Mr S: 'to use an American expression, it is time for the pirates to shit or get off the pot'.[16] The agent has been put firmly in his place by his principal—but he finally knows the real budget for the ransom. Over the next hours, Mr Ali keeps calling the company to ask them to 'confirm' various (fictitious) offers by fax for the benefit of the pirates.

If there are any lingering doubts about the new principal–agent relationship that formed in this negotiation, they are dispelled in a late afternoon conversation on 12 January. Mr Ali holds out the hope of settling at US$1.7 million. Only one small thing though: 'but, ah, ah, we need an extra hundred'. An unknown sub-contractor apparently demands a small additional payoff and then the deal can be done. 'That is the last thing to happen and actually I'm just being honest with you I'm just sharing the hundred with him.' Mr Gullestrup is sceptical—that's US$100,000 above the market price. Is it worth holding up everything for US$100,000 though? When Mr Ali reveals that the additional payment will be a side-payment into a bank account, and not part of the pirate ransom drop, Clipper is more positive. They are paying the market rate after all. They offer US$50,000, then US$75,000, and Mr Ali agrees.

The question of who received this money was a key issue in the US court case against Mr Ali, but nothing could be proven.[17] What is relevant here is that Mr Gullestrup was convinced that the money would go to Mr Ali. It was only natural that his agent should have a reward—and perhaps Mr Ali would be useful in other negotiations.[18] He had become convincing because he was (and still is) convinced that shipping companies did not care: '97% of sailors are from Eastern Europe, Philippines, Nigeria, Ghana . . . They are worthless to most of the owners.' Even if the initial agreement to make the side-payment was driven by wanting to conclude as fast as possible, the actual payment was not. The payment bounced twice. Clipper successfully made the transfer only after the safe return of the *CEC Future*.

The final conversations in the script are mostly about the organization of the ransom drop and the pirates' surprising decision to refuel the ship. Taking heavy fuel barrels out to the ship on tiny skiffs in high seas and heaving them on board is hard to beat as a gesture of goodwill. The pirates finally left the ship on 16 January. The economist observer refers her readers to the films once more to watch and rejoice with the crew members and their families and breathe a heavy sigh of relief with the Clipper board. There wasn't quite such a happy end in Somalia. The pirates were disappointed and argued fiercely over how the ransom would be split. 'The nasty leader of the old crew' was shot in a firefight as soon as the pirates reached the coast. Mr Ali fled empty-handed, crossing the mountains on foot; relieved to have got away with his life. He resumed the conversation with his new principal once he arrived back in Somaliland, but his career as a negotiator or mediator was effectively over. He could not do much for ship-owners and after a while the unlikely 'friendship' lapsed.

Lessons About Hostage Negotiations

What can we learn from this case study? Because the negotiation occasionally departed from 'the rules', it illustrates the wisdom of the protocol both by example and counter-example. The negotiation was largely shaped by the Lloyd's protocol. When the threats started, Clipper was reassured and eventually came to realize that the pirates' threats were empty. The management adopted the correct strategy to take the crew out of the pirates' firing line. Giving the pirates 'the silent treatment' also ended the threats of damaging or destroying the ship. In the first seven weeks, tightly scripted communications were delivered by a professional communicator. Even after Mr Gullestrup took over, each call and move were discussed in detail with the crisis response expert. The careful handling of the information flow and communication with the families and crewing agent ensured that there was no media drama of the MV *Leopard* type. The apparent conjunction of decision maker and communicator in Mr Gullestrup lasted less than a week.

Regarding the price-setting process, the case of the *CEC Future* confirms that both sides operate with a working hypothesis of converging offer and demand curves. The first few exchanges are critical for signalling the target ransom. If Clipper's intention was to settle at US$1.2 million, then the initial—suitably delayed—offer of US$400,000 was a positive start, but it revealed that Clipper was not a cash-strapped enterprise. However, the next offer at US$700,000 came very quickly and was combined with an ambiguous demand that pirates should come 'below US$2 million', with some of the hijackers aiming for a ransom in excess of US$4 million. The pirates' subsequent demands indicated that they were aiming for convergence well above US$2 million. So, Clipper's next offers were designed to reign back the pirates' exaggerated expectations. Mr Ali's threats and curses in response to the offer of US$1 million when he had confidently expected US$2 million are a natural reaction to his intense disappointment mixed with fear: what if the pirates (literally) shot the messenger? In terms of lessons learned: yes, the curves are malleable, but deviations come at a cost.

The *CEC Future* negotiation also illustrates the empirical regularity that ransom settlements set precedents which shape and constrain subsequent negotiations.[19] The pirates would not easily settle for less than their colleagues across the bay: they would try their best to outdo them. Well-off, caring ship-owners were not prepared to challenge pirates to revise their minimum expectations. Positive deviations from the previous settlement were therefore more likely than negative ones: an upward drift in ransoms was inevitable. Clipper Shipping probably did not drive up ransoms—the side-payment only came to light in the 2013 court case. But even so: US$1.7 million is a lot of money in Somalia. It is highly likely that some people made a profit and provided seed money for the next round of pirate expeditions.

Principal–agent problems were pervasive in this negotiation. The CEO and board were frustrated with the slow tempo of the negotiation. The experience of the consultants ('There is a pace, a rhythm to these things') clashed with the impatience of the ship-owner ('[the pirates] got to wake up and smell the coffee here'). So, the principals (briefly) wrested control from their agents. The *CEC Future* negotiation could have gone seriously off the rails—many others did. Fortunately, the pirate side also had principal–agent problems: their agent switched allegiance. The misunderstanding about the 'vacation' in Brazil completely changed Mr Ali's perception of how this case would best be resolved. One cannot generalize from this one observation, but I was struck by the genuine bitterness and contempt expressed by Mr Ali about the shipping company's treatment of their 'expendable' staff. Possibly, experienced kidnappers are more aware of the theatricality in haggling out a ransom. However, Mr Ali was fully convinced that Clipper did not care—and thereby he became convincing. Even the tried and tested control mechanism of confirming offers by fax failed to contain his entrepreneurialism. In the end game, Mr Ali instructed Clipper when to send their faxes and for how much to ensure convergence at Clipper's final budget line. Clipper agreed that their new agent in Somalia deserved a side-payment—though if he had kept it for himself, he would probably still be in prison today.

Somali piracy presented insurers with a particularly tough challenge. Ship-owners live in a 'time is money' world. The loss of hire, the deteriorating cargo, the reputational cost of missed deadlines, the preoccupation of the board members during a hostage incident, and the cost of repairing a ship soiled after months at anchor dwarfs the cost of the ransom. A piracy incident was likely to be a one-off. Although pirates liked to target the sister ships of ships they already knew, ship-owners learned their lessons and hired armed guards for the next journey. So there was a market for private negotiators who promised to prioritize the needs of the ship-owners rather than insurers. They tried to take a 'time is money' approach with the pirates. Unfortunately, it didn't work. With rampant underemployment, the opportunity cost of haggling and waiting is low in Somalia. Once the infrastructure to avoid death and damage was in place, the pirates could just sit tight and watch the ship-owners panic. Ransoms crept to US\$3 million, then five, then eight, then ten. More time meant more money for the pirates. Each new premium settlement drove up pirate expectations and the ransoms paid by those who could afford them. The crews of ship-owners who could not pay several million dollars stayed in Somalia for years. The laissez-faire hijack for ransom insurance product was doomed to fail at ransoms exceeding US\$3 million and year-long negotiations. Countries stepped up the naval intervention and ship-owners whizzed through the high-risk area guarded by private security companies instead—at a cost of several billion dollars a year.[20]

The *CEC Future* is therefore an excellent case study of successful damage limitation in a grim and tricky environment. I am very grateful to Mr Gullestrup, Mr Ali, and the response consultant for sharing this gruelling yet fascinating experience with us. Crisis response consultants always insist that there is no principal–agent problem in their job. They always do what is best for the victim. The careful analysis of this (and many other) ransom negotiations suggests that they are right. What is best for the victim—accepting the tempo of the kidnapper and meeting his expectations—also works for the insurer: but only if ransom expectations are stable and kidnappers don't make supernormal profits. Ultimately, it is in no one's interest to fuel crime or terrorism by paying excessive ransoms. Hopefully, in future desperate stakeholders will think twice before wresting control from those experienced in price setting in anarchic bargaining situations. Chapter 8 shows that once a price has been agreed, a whole set of new problems arises. Luckily, professional solutions are available.

8

Trading with Kidnappers

We are in the mountains. It's just before dawn, the mist hovers over the meadows and swirls around a small woodland. Shadowy figures move about the hillsides, looking for cover among rocks and shrubs. We know they are heavily armed, their guns are trained on a small clearing and the paths leading to it. For many hours, nobody moves. At dusk, a man sneaks towards the glade. He stumbles; the sounds of snapping branches and muttered curses break the silence. He puts a package on a rock in the centre and sits down at the edge of the clearing. We wait. The moon rises and we see another movement some distance away. Slowly, painfully slowly, two masked people approach from the other direction. One of them is weak, struggling to walk: our hostage—dragged along by a heavy-set thug. The gangster retrieves the package, while the hostage slumps down in the shadows. The contents of the package are examined by torchlight, flickering eerily between the bushes. It seems like an eternity, but eventually the hostage staggers into the clearing as the gangster withdraws. Just then, a startled deer breaks cover: the hillside erupts with gunfire, the hostage tries to run, there is a bloodcurdling scream . . .

The Final Hurdle

We are familiar with hostage exchanges like this one from countless thrillers and films. But what makes a face-to-face meeting under cover of darkness ideal for an adventure story makes it utterly unsuitable as a business solution. The shoot-out and the casualties are the tragic but logical conclusion of a one-shot prisoners' dilemma game. This chapter discusses the ways in which trading with bandits can be made as reliable as possible. Kidnappers and crisis responders have carefully designed protocols, norms, and means to safely deliver ransoms and retrieve live hostages. There are many different approaches—created to facilitate successful hostage releases in different contexts.

A contemporaneous exchange seems attractive at first sight: the kidnappers cannot easily renege on releasing the hostage after receiving the ransom. But a face-to-face rendezvous with a hostage in tow exposes the kidnappers to massive risks: it would be the perfect opportunity for the police to arrest some criminals and intercept the ransom payment. Ideally, the police would also retrieve a live hostage, but hostages are used as human shields and often killed in the rescue attempt. The law enforcers' and the hostage's interests are not perfectly aligned. Some coordination and enforcement problems could be solved by middlemen—but unless they can be carefully monitored, they may add a further layer of complication to the transaction. What if they abscond with the hostage—or all or part of the ransom? We will find that often it makes economic sense to split the transaction into two parts: a ransom drop and a subsequent hostage release.

The tense, lone kidnapper is a negotiator's worst nightmare—especially if his ideas are unhelpfully shaped by watching too many thrillers. The shadow of the future is essential to govern the hostage exchange. If there is an established market for hostages in which many people face the problem of making this tricky transaction work, there is also a demand for business solutions. Once again, we see a market for private governance in which multiple agents develop ways of making reliable and verifiable ransom drops, retrieving hostages, or hosting exchanges in their territory. Diverse agents will come up with a range of offerings, differentiated by their price and reliability. Most of them work for private profit, others to raise their status in their community. If there is the expectation of profitable repeat business, agents build reputations and contracts become self-enforcing.

In the following section, we look at trading with bandits over hostages as another relational contract with prisoners' dilemma characteristics. We then look at resolutions involving contemporaneous exchanges, the case for separating ransom drops from hostage releases, and the role of middlemen in facilitating the exchange. In the final section I analyse how stakeholders should deal with further kidnapper demands after the ransom drop and—having overcome that final obstacle—ultimately the release. This chapter mostly focuses on how to make the hostage trade work. Yet we know that hostage exchanges can fail—often with tragic consequences. We will look at how and why things go wrong in Part III.

The Hostage Exchange as a Relational Contract

As in Chapter 5, we are in a situation where a formal contract is impossible. At this stage, a ransom has been agreed, but there are many unknowns. Is the hostage still alive, and if so in what mental and physical state? Have the police been informed—and what are their intentions regarding the surveillance and possible confiscation of the ransom payment? How do you make a non-traceable payment that is not intercepted by opportunists? Is there scope for negotiating a second ransom after the first one has been received?

The direct, contemporaneous exchange has prisoners' dilemma characteristics. The trade succeeds if the stakeholders appear unarmed with an unmarked ransom and the kidnappers release the hostage to them. Both parties receive their agreed pay-offs. However, if the kidnappers collect the ransom without the hostage, they can restart negotiations for more money or sell the hostage on. Alternatively, they can shoot the hostage after picking up the ransom to silence the witness. They may even ambush the envoy, thereby gaining an additional benefit. However, the stakeholders suffer a substantial loss in grief or prolonged uncertainty. If the kidnapper deals fairly with the stakeholders and brings the hostage to the rendezvous, but the stakeholders have armed support, the stakeholders get the hostage, keep the ransom, and gain satisfaction from punishing the criminals. Meanwhile, the kidnappers have a massive problem: they were caught red-handed with a hostage. If both sides cheat, the stakeholders' grief is marginally reduced by the knowledge that at least they did not fund crime or terrorism. Similarly, a criminal arrested without a hostage can deny having been involved in the kidnapping and the gang can hold on to the hostage until payment is received.

As ever, in the prisoners' dilemma, the dominant strategy in the one-shot game is for both parties to cheat. We cannot rely on the shadow of future transactions to encourage cooperation here. Although the criminals may be serial kidnappers, the stakeholders are in a one-off transaction. Yet this is exactly the premise of our thriller scenario. No wonder the moonlit hills are bristling with snipers and the exchange culminates in a hail of bullets.

We know what security experts think of whistling bullets. Rather than trying to make this most unpromising proposition work, it is better to remove some options. The kidnappers rightly worry about stakeholder opportunism, as stakeholders do not have an incentive to build reputations. But if stakeholders meet hostage-takers in rebel territory, the police are unlikely to come along. Kidnappers can also monitor whether there is an armed escort by sending the ransom delivery guy on a magical mystery tour of shifting locations. But is there really a need to meet at all? Could this not be an arm's length payment? What about an air-drop? How long will it be before ransom demands are made and settled in Bitcoin?[1] The hostages can then be abandoned somewhere

where they can summon help. If the hostage is released to respected religious or political leaders or tribal elders, they can get some credit for bringing them home. Let us look at the options.

Contemporaneous Exchanges

Contemporaneous exchanges are relatively rare—but we have already encountered one case in the introduction to Part I: the Colombian contractor whose rebel counterparty was so secure in the knowledge that he would pay up that they did not even bother to keep the hostage. Indeed, rebel groups, cartels, and mafias who securely control territory and have long time horizons facilitate the smoothest hostage exchanges. Whereas others need to worry about police surveillance, rescue attempts, and the possibility that another gang might intercept the ransom drop, strong protectors exclude all these problems by inviting the ransom-bearers into their own territory. The stakeholders and envoys will be reassured by the protector's reputation for dealing fairly—and the knowledge that the protector would be punished in subsequent transactions for failing to facilitate a smooth exchange.

Crisis responders working in the heyday of the FARC's transnational kidnapping operations recall how stakeholders would send a trusted retainer to designated farmsteads in FARC territory. The envoy would drink a beer with the operatives, while the ransom was counted. Once it was accepted, he could drive straight home with the hostage. The hassle-free hostage exchange was part of the FARC business model. It massively reduced the transaction costs of dealing in hostages. With an indefinite time horizon in the kidnapping business, the hostage trade is more profitable with a reputation for fair dealing, than incurring the costs of one of the more elaborate exchange solutions discussed in this chapter. Crisis responders and local families knew this and the exchanges went ahead.

In some cases, crisis responders can find other ways of raising the kidnappers' cost of reneging. One veteran negotiator was in talks with a central African rebel outfit, when his inexperienced and nervous counterparty threatened to behead the hostage. Researching the group, he found the contact details of their leaders—a government in exile—at a rather nice address in Paris. Communicating to the chiefs how politically awkward it would be if their brothers-in-arms beheaded innocent hostages, the threat was very quickly withdrawn. Buoyed by this success, the negotiation strategy was adjusted. Surely, a reputable political organization would not stoop to demanding a monetary ransom? We thought not—but perhaps they might be persuaded to accept a humanitarian donation for their troubled people instead?

Safe in the knowledge that the 'president' had every intention of continuing his comfortable Paris lifestyle, the negotiator had no qualms about travelling to the rebel stronghold to retrieve the hostage. As a further sign of goodwill, the 'president' sent one of his sons along with him. The young man's presence ensured that the party (including several bearers carrying the components of a second-hand field hospital) was not hassled. Having crossed the Congo River in a dug-out canoe, they were received with full military honours in the rebel camp. The 'army' was put on parade, there was a round of drinks or two with the officers and then the rescue party departed with the hostage. When the kidnappers have nothing to gain by reneging, the stakeholders can travel into their territory. Still, most would probably prefer to send an experienced go-between with nerves of steel.

Another option for a contemporaneous exchange is a private governance solution: a third party offers a 'neutral' location for the exchange. The third party provides a credible assurance to both sides that whichever party breaks the agreement—for example, by preparing an ambush or conducting surveillance operations—will suffer serious consequences. This changes the payoff matrix from a prisoners' dilemma to a cooperative game: the expected punishment is greater than the benefit from cheating. Third-party enforcement only works if the protector has a monopoly on the use of violence. If so, both sides benefit from having a reliable business solution for the tricky hostage exchange. A classic example from Pakistan is a shop with a busy commercial street frontage and a back entrance near a popular place of worship. The envoy with the ransom enters at the front, while a veiled hostage is taken into a dark back room from the rear as crowds of worshippers arrive for prayer. If all is in order, the criminal melts into the multitude as the hostage is brought to meet the ransom bearer. The 'shopkeepers' take a cut from each transaction—and thus have a clear business interest in keeping their locations safe and exchanges trouble-free. Similarly, a stakeholder invited into, for example, FARC territory to retrieve a hostage from a criminal kidnapping gang, would not worry about the reliability of his actual counterparty, but rely on the FARC's reputation for making such trades succeed.

If it is politically opportune that a ransom drop succeeds, government officials may help to facilitate a safe exchange. It is unclear how exactly the Malian government ensured that a multi-million-dollar ransom from Germany billed as 'humanitarian aid' reached its ultimate addressee: an Islamist extremist group holding thirty-two hostages—but it worked.[2] In Somalia, naval forces were involved in creating a safe space for a ransom drop at least once. The planes bringing the ransoms were already on their way when a ship-owner received a panicked call from the pirates: a rival gang was trying to intercept the ransom and their skiffs were converging on the ship. 'Abandon the drop immediately. There are robbers who want to steal our ransom!' the pirate shouted resentfully. But he had a solution. Would the ship-owner petition his government to request that naval coalition headquarters task a vessel to chase off 'those thieves'? He did—and soon afterwards the frigate that had been put on standby to escort the ship home steamed off on its unusual mercy mission. Twenty-four hours later, the ocean was clear for the ransom drop.

The Dead Drop

Many criminal kidnappers do not have access to 'safe' or 'neutral' territory. New kidnapping gangs, whose time horizons, skills, and intentions are unproven, may not be offered a professional service. If they are, they may not want to pay the service provider's fee for organizing the exchange. If the service provider is militarily powerful, only kidnappers who are likely to have a string of hostages over time can rely on the service provider's self-interest to offer fair deals. For high-profile hostages, a local mafia might not be able to guarantee that their thugs would repel (or at least inflict serious harm on) a foreign or domestic special forces unit. If there is no safe place to meet, kidnappers prefer a dead drop.[3] The ransom is left in a specified place and picked up later, eliminating the face-to-face meeting with its prisoners' dilemma characteristics. Even though this option leaves the hostage stakeholders exposed to opportunism by the kidnappers (as discussed below), it is still preferable to something that is almost guaranteed to go wrong.

In a dead drop, the kidnappers have to trade off the risk of being spotted when picking up the ransom with avoiding its interception by a rival gang, the police, or a random passer-by. The busier the place and the longer the gap before the ransom is picked up, the less likely detection becomes—but of course any time lag creates scope for interception. Usually, kidnappers do not specify the drop-off place in advance to eliminate opportunities for covert surveillance or a rival finding out about it and they make sure that the envoy is not followed. If a location is named well in advance of the ransom drop, one can be fairly sure it will be switched at the last minute. In this way, the kidnappers try to eliminate the stakeholder's temptation to involve the police. Any sign of armed guards or police patrols and the drop is abandoned. If kidnappers lose their confidence or temper at that point or want to make a public statement about not being cheated, the hostage is sometimes killed. Lesley Whittle, kidnapped in 1975, was murdered by her kidnapper after a local police patrol car randomly turned up with flashing lights near the agreed rendezvous point and proceeded to take the details of twelve 'illegally parked' Scotland Yard surveillance vehicles.[4] Only stakeholders with the greatest faith in the operational skills, discretion, and coordination abilities of the police choose to take them along for a ransom drop.[5]

The more worried the kidnappers are about the ransom drop, the more elaborate the quest to find the ultimate rendezvous point: the term 'wild goose chase' comes to mind in some cases. Kidnappers often test whether envoys are accompanied by sending them on a long drive across a barren space, where any accompanying vehicle can be easily spotted. At the 'destination' the driver will get a further set of instructions. In former times, there would have been a letter or a call to a public phone booth. Now, the envoy usually receives an anonymous text message with a new set of GPS coordinates. By following the instructions to the letter, the envoy builds trust with the kidnappers. Insiders dealing with Al Qaeda in the Islamic Maghreb say there are usually at least three sets of instructions. Each necessitates a long drive over endless undulating sand dunes, until the fighters finally reveal themselves—sitting cross-legged on a carpet, ready to count the cash.[6] Urban criminals usually prefer the anonymity of a busy public space for the handover of the ransom. Perhaps the envoy takes a convoluted trip on the underground and eventually leaves the bag in an underpass—hoping it will be picked up by the 'right' person.[7] If the envoys are driving, they may be asked to drop the holdall with the ransom at a specific point—or leave it on the passenger seat of a car with the window wound down and walk away from the vehicle. The unlucky ones have to leave the key in the ignition. If anything looks suspicious to the kidnappers, there is an ominous silence or an angry message. Back to square one—at best.

The more careful the kidnappers are about eliminating the risk of the ransom bearer bringing armed support, the greater the stakeholders' fear that the ransom drop could turn into an ambush. But there is an alternative to the family or firm risking direct involvement in the exchange: enter the middlemen.

Middlemen

We are getting used to the idea that when there is a recurrent thorny business problem that people would pay good money to have satisfactorily resolved, someone will offer this service. In this case, we have a neutral third party that acts as a go-between for the stakeholders, delivering the ransom to the kidnappers. If there are many consecutive trades and the middleman earns a substantial fee from each transaction, a reputational solution becomes possible. The stakeholders now hand over the ransom to the specialist in the safety of their own premises. The kidnappers gain from having the ransom delivered to their lair (or their own middleman). Unless the gang's time horizons contract, they have every reason to protect the middlemen in their territory. Middlemen tend to operate in the legal economy or local politics, so breaking their promise to the stakeholders would come at great cost. Overall, they are better off being paid for every transaction than running away with the money once. There is rarely fierce competition in this market and at least in the short term the middlemen can name their price. The expectation of well-paid future ransom drops protects the stakeholders from potential opportunism by the middleman.

Somali piracy serves as an excellent illustration of the development of a market for ransom drop services. For the pirates, there was no fear of detection or official punishment. Everyone knew where the pirates were: on board the hijacked ships anchored in plain view of the Somali coast. However, pirates and stakeholders knew that other pirate groups, rival clans, or roving militias would try their best to intercept anyone bringing a ransom. Initially, pirates used middlemen in Nairobi to take the ransom payments. Usually they would specify a hotel in the city and—at the last minute—change the location to a hotel run by a Somali businessman, where the ransom would be received. The main headache for the stakeholders was how to put together a ransom of hundreds of thousands (and eventually millions) of US Dollars in small-denomination notes in Kenya without alerting the authorities to the grey transaction taking place right under their noses. As you would expect by now, of course there are specialists who have worked out how to do this and can produce any amount of cash within a couple of days.

But as ransoms escalated, a further problem arose: the middlemen became greedy. They had always taken a certain percentage cut of each ransom and did not find it appropriate to change that percentage. When ransoms rose, hundreds of thousands of dollars stayed in Nairobi—rather than tens of thousands—for essentially the same job. Cue angry phone calls to the ship-owners: why was the ransom short? Ship-owners pleaded their innocence and pointed the finger at the greedy middlemen. The pirates decided to pass the buck back to the ship-owners: they could work out for themselves how they would deliver the full ransom to the right address. Soon someone came up with a workable solution: the ransom would be delivered directly to the hijacked ship by tugboat. This was not a low-cost plan: the tugboats would have to be heavily armed to fight their way through the pirate-infested Somali territorial waters from Mombasa, the closest 'safe' port for embarkation. Given the time and danger involved, the cost of this ransom delivery service was around US$1 million—a significant proportion of the total resolution cost. Yet this was what ship-owners did, until a better private business solution became available.

Photos of light aircraft dropping ransom packages on parachutes above hijacked ships became a defining image of Somali piracy—as did the line-up of all crew members on the deck on the first flypast. Ship-owners asked for this final proof of life before the ransoms were pushed out of the aircraft to splash into the ocean next to the jubilant pirates' skiffs. Such ransom drops cost somewhere between US$200,000 and US$300,000. Being much less risky than the tugboat option, ship-owners could also economize on the premium for the 'ransom-in-transit' insurance available at Lloyd's of London. As the underwriters know the market, they price the insurance premium according to who organizes the ransom drop. The best suppliers thus have a large amount of business put their way—if they remain reliable.

When a company becomes careless or unable to cope with the sheer volume of trade, business soon dries up. One company had two planes and US$3.6 million in ransom money impounded in Mogadishu, when the authorities decided to ambush what the company believed had become a routine business operation.[8] It took some time before the firm could negotiate the 'fine' to release their operatives from Somali prison. I hope the irony was not lost on them. In the meantime, a rival business flew the replacement ransoms to the two ships whose ransom money had been impounded by the authorities. Private business interests, competition, and information collated in the Lloyd's underwriting room therefore stabilize a reputational solution to the problem of how to keep a middleman on the straight and narrow. I do wonder though, what story was spun to the pirates to explain how the 'cash-strapped' ship-owners were able to replace the seized ransom money at such short notice.

Firms and people facilitating ransom drops are usually separate from the crisis response consultancies. It would not make commercial sense for each crisis response company to develop the skills or retain the services of a ransom drop specialist for every area of the world. The specialist for downtown Kabul would be unlikely to pass as a local even a few hundred kilometres away. Moreover, stakeholders pretending that they have handed over every last cent to the kidnappers must also feign that the envoy is a trusted retainer or a family friend helping out for free, rather than a highly paid professional who knows how to handle himself in an ambush.[9] If the same Terminator lookalike handles every drop-off, kidnappers will eventually suspect that families spent good money on professional help rather than scraping together the maximum affordable ransom. So, how can you keep a middleman faithful if you can only use him once or twice? It is usually best to subcontract these delicate operations to elite private security companies operating in the relevant area. They can then select different people from their local staff. Their long-term employment contracts ensure that each envoy has the incentive to carry out the mission as intended. The crisis responders in turn know which security companies operate in each market and identify reliable providers to each other.

In some areas, middlemen operate very openly. Kidnaps and their resolutions can then become so well-governed that they appear almost ritualistic. In the 1980s and 1990s the most effective way for Yemeni tribes to petition their government or settle a dispute was to kidnap a foreigner. Each side had their middlemen to conduct the negotiation, while the hostage was treated to endless cups of far too sweet tea in a tent deep in tribal territory. Foreigners should not worry about this, argued the speaker of the Yemeni parliament and leader of Yemen's Hashid tribe in 1997. 'Kidnapping in Yemen is hospitality... an adventure... [T]he tourist will end up learning about the customs of the tribes, as well as their good hospitality.' A former hostage partially concurred: 'They were as polite as one can be when one is pointing a gun at someone...I was treated pretty much like a compulsory guest.'[10] Crisis responders knew how to resolve these tribal kidnaps and which sheikhs would be the most useful middlemen. Companies could some-times accelerate dispute resolution by financially supporting the provi-sion of a new generator for a village or a new minibus service—until 2011 it was uncommon for monetary ransoms to be paid. With the rise of Al Qaeda, civil war, and more recently the arrival of ISIL/Daesh-affiliated militias, respectfully conducted tribal kidnaps that can be resolved for a few thousand dollars have become rare: violence and ransoms have escalated.[11] But even so, tribal norms of treating hostages decently are widely observed and the infrastructure of respectable mediators is still intact. The chosen mediators are acceptable to both sides and are paid handsomely for their services. So, once a deal has been struck, it is in everyone's interest that the ransom for hostage exchange runs smoothly.[12]

The middlemen solution is thus very common in kidnap hotspots, where there is a sufficiently high turnover of hostages for someone to develop a business solution to facilitate payment and release. The costs of doing so are lower when the government tolerates the hostage trade. If law enforcers and elites are complicit in the trade, they can offer the most competitive services, as their costs are partially socialized. This may also explain why rogue governments sometimes enter the market for hostages as mediators (perhaps most famously Colonel Gaddafi). However, middlemen pose significant dangers if they do not have a long time horizon to discipline them or if they fear that one of the parties will cheat them out of their money. We will return to this in Chapter 10.

The Double Cross?

Let us assume that the ransom drop has succeeded. The kidnappers are in possession of the money and contemplate their next step: release, kill, or negotiate another ransom? Only amateurs have a rational reason to kill their hostage—if they have made mistakes such as revealing their identity or location to the hostage and fear that the police will come after them. For any gang with a longer time horizon, the cost of killing the hostage is high: even if the police cannot do much to prosecute the murderers, reneging after the ransom payment will make concurrent and subsequent negotiations much more difficult. When it is known that a gang murders hostages, the high-risk rescue option becomes attractive. In Mexico, civil society groups successfully went after violent kidnap gangs and even galvanized the police into action.[13] Usually, therefore, it is not in the interest of the kidnapper to renege completely—which is why the crisis responders agree to the sequential deal in the first place.

The 'double cross', however, is an ever-present danger. The hours—and sometimes days—after the ransom drop are therefore extremely tense. The kidnappers have to count the money—perhaps multiple times until they are sure everything is in order. Somali pirates often preferred to share out the ransoms on board—inviting the creditors, facilitators, financiers, and militia leaders to the ship that could be defended relatively easily. Then people could make their own arrangements about how to get back to shore with their stash of cash. The pirates only departed when the final bills were settled. So, some delay is expected before the hostages are released. In the double cross, however, the delay ends with a new ransom demand.

Sometimes crisis responders can spot a 'double' before it happens, and the stakeholders can be prepared for a call saying: 'We have received your down payment and now we would like to negotiate the real ransom.' At other times, something happens during the ransom drop that makes the kidnappers suspicious that they have not extracted the maximum ransom. So they try again. Maybe another group has expressed interest in the hostage—should they sell on or go back to the stakeholders for more money themselves? Occasionally the kidnappers manage to open parallel negotiations, and while one is finished the other one still drags on. Perhaps the stakeholders who paid the first ransom can help to accelerate the progress on the parallel negotiation? The poor families and the crisis response team have entered into a loop: everything starts again. Proof of life. Proof of possession. A fantasy first demand, a counter-offer, etc.

Or perhaps not. An experienced negotiator knows to remain calm. What would a family do when they have already given their last cent and their wedding ring to raise the first ransom? Engaging in a debate about a second ransom shows that the kidnappers were right and there is more. 'We gave you everything we had. We want our friend/uncle/father/daughter back. We don't understand why you are saying this. We gave you everything we had.' Often, this is all that is needed—even if it has to be repeated over several hours, days, and perhaps weeks. Eventually, there can be a little more—such scraps as a family that has already maxed out on their credit can raise. Certainly nothing that compensates the kidnappers for the additional time holding the hostage. This will work, as long as no one breaks cover. A well-meant 'save our hostage' fundraising campaign organized via a newspaper or online platform will have the kidnappers sitting back in their chairs awaiting further developments. The former UN employee Colonel Steed who worked to bring home abandoned mariners from Somalia definitely considers these public campaigns counterproductive. 'When the pirates, who monitor social media very closely, hear that families are raising money, they have this expectation that there is more money to come...But of course, the families can only raise a few hundred dollars or a few thousand dollars.'[14] Eventually, in whatever way the double cross is handled, there will be a time where the marginal revenue of holding out exceeds the marginal return. It is time to release.

The Release

Unless the hostage is in bad physical shape and needs immediate medical care, crisis responders don't have interesting stories to tell about releases. Having evaded detection at the critical ransom drop stage, most kidnappers release their hostages without fanfare. Some hostages are pushed out of a car on a remote road or in a busy city street, where they can make their own way to safety. Some are put on a local bus or boat service. Some stakeholders are told where to find their loved ones, perhaps tied to a tree or in a makeshift underground dungeon. Somali pirates just departed from the ships with every valuable that took their fancy, shouting and firing their guns in celebration. Usually, hostages enjoy a degree of protection: the hostage-taker ensures that they are not kidnapped or rehijacked by another group on the way to safety. No released ship leaving Somalia was touched by other pirate groups as they slowly steamed away through Somali territorial waters—despite being easy targets, low on fuel, and crewed by traumatized sailors. This observation demonstrates the strength and reach of informal cross-clan protection arrangements in Somalia.[15]

Another way of providing protection for released hostages is to involve local elites in the 'rescue' process. The hostage is discharged to the local sheikh/leader/mayor who get their five minutes of fame, posing for press photographs. Again: everyone wins. The local dignitaries gain status but have 'no idea' who the bandits might be. The kidnappers save themselves the risk and cost of transporting the hostage to safety, while the hostage spends the journey in relative comfort.

Crisis responders have developed a sophisticated aftercare infrastructure to help hostages settle back into their former lives. The hostages are given a medical examination, and if necessary they are nursed back to health before returning home. Malnourished hostages are carefully reintroduced to tiny portions of rich food. There are fresh clothes, haircuts, baths, and comfortable beds. The hostages get the opportunity to talk about their ordeal with the crisis responders, who want to find out as much as possible about the opposition for future use. Talking confidentially helps the hostages to construct a narrative of their ordeal for the family (and the press if it is a high-profile case). When former hostages who cracked during the negotiations wish to portray themselves as stoic heroes, the crisis responders' lips are sealed: the customer relationship is confidential. What happens on the case stays on the case. Returnees are debriefed by the police where official law enforcement was involved. Hostages are also offered counselling: psychologically it's 'a long way home' and many people struggle to settle back into their relationships after the stress of a hostage crisis.[16] All of these services are standard components of kidnap for ransom insurance. In the unlikely event that hostages still feel short-changed after all these efforts undertaken on their behalf, their firm is also insured against the cost of litigation arising from the case. The probability that a firm which has invested in kidnap for ransom cover will be convicted by a court for negligence is almost nil.

The Importance of Market Concentration

We started this chapter with a thorny trade problem with prisoners' dilemma characteristics. How can two parties that have every reason to distrust each other organize the hostage for ransom exchange to minimize the risk of harm to the hostage, the risk of the ransom being intercepted, and the risk of arrest for the hostage-takers? Unlike in Chapter 7, in the exchange only the hostage-takers are (potentially) in a repeated game, whereas the stakeholders are definitely hoping that this is the last time they deal with the kidnappers. Unless some third party can offer a credible governance solution for simultaneous exchange, the trade will only go ahead if the stakeholders take a massive leap of faith and either take the money into rebel territory or agree to a dead drop. This leaves stakeholders exposed to opportunism: the envoy can abscond with the ransom, the kidnappers can prolong the negotiation (perhaps adding the envoy to their haul), or kill the hostage after receiving the ransom. And yet, the highly unsatisfactory dead drop is the dominant solution to the exchange dilemma.

We observe a similar pattern in other trades where there is a discrepancy between the time horizons of transaction partners. In such situations, the parties with the short time horizons often agree to something that at first sight looks detrimental to their own interests. For example, in early twentieth-century Japan, women entering the market for commercial sexual services often signed indentured labour contracts with brothels. However, the legal scholar Mark Ramseyer's research shows that this was not an intrinsically abusive practice. Prostitutes had low social status but were compensated with relatively high wages. Brothel owners attracted recruits by offering significant advance payments. Bonded labour allowed brothels to commit to high wages by paying them upfront, while protecting their investment from women wishing to renege before paying off their advance.[17] Similarly, the relationship between people smugglers and their customers is characterized by a number of unpleasant practices such as forced labour, confiscation of passports, or kidnap along the way. Nonetheless, millions of migrants employ smugglers. As the people wishing to be smuggled enter a one-off contract, they have to accept that the smugglers protect their investment by constraining their customers' choices until the payment has been extracted. These forms of exploitation may be an integral part of a successful relational contracting relationship.

Having agreed to a dead drop, the successful conclusion of a hostage situation relies on a strong shadow of the future that incentivizes the kidnappers to uphold their end of the bargain, and middlemen to faithfully deliver the promised service. Globally, most kidnaps are local-on-local crimes. Kidnappers victimize firms and families who have failed to make appropriate protection payments, but build a reputation for orderly commercial resolution for cooperative stakeholders. Third parties offer their services in mediation, ransom deliveries, and the extraction of hostages—all of them for private gain. Local firms and families that experience a hostage-taking can obtain all necessary advice and references among their acquaintances. In transnational kidnaps, however, the stakeholders are unlikely to be aware of (or trust) the local resolution networks. Local institutions may not be sufficiently strong to underpin transactions that conclude at prices two or three orders of magnitude higher than the average local deal. For example, an envoy who can be trusted taking a wad of pesos worth two months' local salary to the Don could act quite differently when tasked with delivering a five- or six-figure US dollar ransom.

The transnational hostage trade therefore crucially relies on Lloyd's of London and their network of crisis responders to facilitate the hostage exchange. First, Lloyd's and the elite crisis responders serve as an information hub. Has the counter-party been a reliable transaction partner in the past? How could—or should—we involve the police? Do we need to prepare the family for a double cross? Is there a reliable middleman? Who is best placed to make the ransom drop and retrieve the hostage? As crisis responders are a small, cohesive community and insurers have a joint interest in the smooth functioning of the market for hostages, such advice is freely available. Second, Lloyd's creates a market for profitable business solutions to governance problems. With the collation of information, agents become aware of gaps in the market. If enough people would pay good money for US$1 million in small-denomination notes to materialize in a foreign country without the knowledge of the national central bank or fear of arrest at the border, then it is probably worth finding out how to do it. Who knows someone who would fly a small aircraft over rebel territory and drop a parcel precisely in the right location? There is scope for innovation: how about using a drone to deliver a ransom at a fraction of the price? Who wants to buy a ransom container that will self-destruct unless the recipient enters the correct code? Once the service is up and running, its existence (and success or failure) is quickly disseminated to all interested parties. Third, the free exchange of information leads to the concentration of business in a few capable hands. Creating a monopoly or oligopoly for resolution services raises prices for insurers. However, it is precisely because trusted service providers are profitable that it is in their interest to carry out their promises. Any mistakes, and the business goes elsewhere. Lloyd's thus creates contestable monopolies, providing the optimal combination of reward, incentive, and price discipline for service providers.

This book started with the puzzling observation that around 97.5 per cent of insured kidnap victims return home alive. Most of them were successfully ransomed. This chapter has demonstrated how much thought and resources are devoted to the final stage of the hostage trade. Every successful exchange has overcome strong temptations for both parties to cheat their counterparty. This chapter analysed the institutions underpinning this exchange and what makes them so robust, resilient, and adaptable in a constantly changing marketplace. Chapter 9 takes us back into the underwriting room at Lloyd's to analyse why the market for kidnap insurance is so highly concentrated.

9

Governing Kidnap for Ransom

All hulls end up at Lloyd's
Interview with insurer, February 2013

Private Polycentric Governance

There are a wide range of complex institutional arrangements that do not fit into a dichotomous world of 'states' and 'markets'. Vincent and Elinor Ostrom were the first economists to examine these systems, focusing on the governance of common pool resources and public goods provision.[1] They noted a range of regularities in these systems, which they describe as 'polycentric'—meaning consisting of multiple decision-making centres. Although the various agencies are formally independent of each other, they constitute an interdependent system of relations. Agents may be in competition or rely on formal or informal contracting relationships to cooperate with each other. Governance systems are successful and stable if there are clear rules and norms of behaviour, a central authority to resolve conflicts, and an effective enforcement mechanism.[2]

The system governing kidnap for ransom is clearly one of this type of complex polycentric governance architectures.[3] In Chapters 5, 6, and 7 we examined the work of a large number of what the Ostroms called 'decision-making centres'. The Lloyd's syndicates with their underwriters, loss adjusters, and lawyers. The security consultancies retained by the insurers or employed by firms seeking insurance to minimize the danger of kidnap. The crisis responders who train potential victims, help the stakeholders negotiate a commercial resolution, and manage the successful completion of the ransom for hostage exchange. Within countries we have the helpful sheikhs, mediators, and professional middlemen. There are the mafias providing protection or neutral territory for exchanges, pilots offering air-drops, and intrepid mercenaries willing to trek through urban or primary jungle, mountains, or deserts with a small fortune in a holdall. There are insurers providing cash-in-transit insurance, and financial services specialists who ensure that ransom-bearers are not arrested for smuggling bags full of banknotes through customs and have to be sprung from insanitary prisons.

This chapter examines why the governance system has proved so successful, adaptable, and resilient, by analysing the institutions that enforce the rules and norms in the system. There are three types of overlapping and mutually supporting enforcement mechanisms to incentivize the agents and agencies in the system to provide the best possible service at all times. First, there is the profit motive: reliable service providers are repeatedly employed for good money. Fail and you make a loss. Lose repeatedly and you exit the market. Cheat and you come off the list of reputable service providers. Kidnappers also face clear financial incentives. Threaten to maltreat hostages and ransom increments are substituted for pointless side discussions. Kill, and you can expect a visit from a SWAT team instead of a ransom. Second, people are motivated by status and the respect of their peers. The communities of crisis responders, security consultants, and underwriters at Lloyd's form tightly knit 'epistemic communities'. Their members share a set of norms, beliefs, a common enterprise, and criteria for evaluating new evidence. Shared values and dense social networks facilitate informal communication, cooperation, and—crucially—reputation building.

Third, the system is underpinned by club governance provided by Lloyd's of London. Without the implicit threat of the Lloyd's Corporation to take action against any syndicate that starts to cut corners on its underwriting criteria or the protocol for crisis resolution, the kidnap for ransom governance system would break down. Part III of the book focuses on when hostage trades become problematic and fail. The most problematic hostage market is of course the market for 'terrorist' hostages. I argue that many of the problems arise because when governments negotiate on behalf of their citizens, they lack the rules, incentives, and (crucially) the central enforcement mechanism that stabilizes the market for criminal kidnap for ransom.

Financial Incentives

Private governance is almost always governance for private profit. Whether it is in the commercial world, in the criminal underworld, or in politics, there is a demand for governance and protection. Those who supply it often do so either as monopolists to oligopolists: with few competitors, it is attractive and profitable to provide (good) governance. Some aspects of kidnap for ransom are by their nature monopolistic— criminal market governance in particular is provided monopolistically in each territory in equilibrium. On the legal side, the market for many services could be more competitive than it is. However, fierce price competition often does not create sufficient incentives for firms and people to invest in the skills necessary to provide an outstanding service. A certain degree of market concentration is therefore desirable.

Let us look at the ransom drop as an example of how financial incentives are deliberately shaped to reward outstanding performance. As the ransom negotiation converges, crisis responders begin to organize the ransom drop. They research who can be trusted to deliver the ransom safely to the kidnappers—without themselves becoming a target or a liability. If a responder doesn't yet know the 'go-to' providers, advice is available within their tight-knit community. With bespoke commissions, the price is negotiable. The former hostage negotiator Ben Lopez describes how he identified and tried to hire the local specialist for a ransom drop in Karachi in 2003 for US$5,000 for half a day's work. The specialist was not interested—he claimed he was far too busy with other jobs. Having pleaded and wheedled to no avail, Mr Lopez finally bit the bullet: 'I find that doubling the fees gets the job done.' US$10,000 it was.[4]

Why didn't Mr Lopez just find someone cheaper? If the ransom is sizeable, it makes sense to insure its transit. Once again, Lloyd's of London is the obvious place to obtain such a bespoke product. The insurers' first question is: who will handle the ransom drop? A good reputation is very valuable in the underwriting room. Propose a rookie provider and get an insurance quote of perhaps 45 per cent. Use the undisputed expert and this comes down to maybe 10 per cent. Cash-in-transit insurance thus concentrates the market for ransom drops and discourages stakeholders and crisis responders from experimenting with marginally cheaper competitors to the proven market leader. They lose more in the higher insurance premium than they gain from employing an untried outsider. Deliberate market concentration makes the provision of governance services lucrative. Profitability is important, because it underpins the reputational solutions which are crucial to the success of the system. If my ransom bearer does not expect to make a good living from his profession, chances are that he will abscond with a juicy ransom one day.

However, even if there is a monopoly or a clear market leader in the system, insurers have a strong incentive that the market remains contestable. The history of the Somali pirate ransom drops illustrates that greedy and unreliable providers will be replaced (e.g. the Somali businessmen accepting pirate ransoms in Nairobi), as will reliable but expensive solutions (the armed tug boats). Perhaps the market converges to a dominant solution (e.g. the air-drop, which delivered a final proof of life as well as a reasonably priced, accurate ransom drop). But the market leaders need to stay on their toes: make a mistake and your customers migrate to rival firms. Often different solutions are appropriate for different counterparties: if someone negotiates a four- or five-figure ransom, a six-figure delivery method does not look credible.

Similarly, when insurers encouraged ship-owners to enhance their counter-piracy efforts in the Gulf of Aden and the Somali Basin, they soon had a bewildering menu of options. These ranged from cardboard cutouts of armed figures, water hoses, and barbed wire, to on-board security teams of Mossad-trained snipers. Those of a particularly nervous disposition could consider engaging heavily armed escort vessels ready to blow any approaching skiff out of the water.[5] Through a system of trial and error and reputation building, ineffective, overblown, and unethical 'counter-piracy solutions' were driven out of the market. Evolutionary competition between governance providers is a key aspect of private, polycentric systems.[6] As experts innovate or new entrants suggest superior solutions to existing or emerging problems, those that provide inferior services are found out and are no longer hired. Free entry and exit generates flexibility and adaptability. If part of a private system fails, this creates a market for new governance solutions. Sooner or later (depending on the amount of money on offer) someone will come up with a better solution.[7]

Peer Monitoring

While profits are important, there is also a palpable sense of community among the crisis and security consultants, the underwriters, and the various experts providing hostage retrieval services. They value each other's good opinion and respect for more than just the financial value of their good reputation. Even among informal governance providers, status and the respect of their community matters. Drug bosses may seek to bring welfare and order to the slums they rose from.[8] Clearly, the Yemeni tribesman who incongruously described hostage-taking as a form of enforced hospitality felt bound by his tribe's code of honour. Somali pirate negotiators were just as proud of their track record in bidding up ransoms as the crisis response consultants were for successfully containing criminal aspirations in this arena.[9]

Security and crisis response consultants are mostly recruited from elite law enforcement units and they form a close-knit community. They share the philosophy that prevention is better than cure and that patient negotiation is the best way to resolve hostage incidents. They all have an intense dislike of their criminal opposition, commonly referred to in conversation as 'the baddies'. Individuals' reputations are first built during their military careers. Many subsequently find employment as mercenaries, giving them hands-on experience of managing security risks 'in the field'. Outstanding performers are invited to apply for positions in security and response consulting: the common background and tight network of contacts facilitates discreet communication and close peer monitoring. Consultants socialize both in and out of work—the Special Forces Club in London being regularly mentioned as a meeting place.[10] I already mentioned the crisis responders' evident pride in their track record of resolutions. Yes, a reputation for fast, clean, and cheap resolutions ensures permanent positions for the very best experts and a steady, good income stream for other outstanding negotiators who prefer freelance work. But there is a sense that reputation is about much more than money. It is about recognition within an exacting, high-powered peer group. When someone told me that he recently did a case against Abu Sayyaf, I was impressed, but I didn't know what exactly this entails. Looking at his fingernails, I knew that it was a dreadfully stressful experience, but only his peers can truly appreciate his accomplishment. They know how his ransom settlement compares. The experts take pride in bartering the opposition down, in being trusted with the most difficult cases, and in reuniting families with their loved ones. Yet, the highest accolade is probably being asked for advice by their peers.

Similarly, the underwriters form a tight community. Most of them operate in close proximity on the ground floor of the famous Lloyd's building in Lime Street, London. Choosing what to insure, pricing that insurance, and running a profitable book that meets the syndicate's risk appetite is something of an art form in special risks insurance. Lloyd's is described as a 'wonderfully gossipy' place: people meet over lunch and discuss their cases and how they were resolved.[11] Both success and failure are very obvious—and anyone who has some responsibility for creating a loss (a broker's book of risks that turned sour, a botched negotiation, or a massive security failure) will be very closely monitored thereafter—if they get another chance at all. As in academia, the respect of the immediate peer group is something that is greatly valued, independently of what is directly reflected in one's salary and career opportunities.

The negotiators, security consultants, messengers, ransom envoys, and middlemen at the coalface of the hostage trade have many interesting stories to tell. These stories would have been even more 'exciting' if the experts had not done their job well in anticipating and eliminating the danger. Yet, there are few accounts of the hostage trade written by industry insiders. This underlines that status is not about the admiration of the masses, but about the few peers who really matter. One can think of them as an elite members' club.

Club Governance at Lloyd's of London

At the heart of the governance system for kidnap for ransom is a traditional members' club: Lloyd's of London. The analysis so far has already uncovered several reasons for the unusual concentration in the market for kidnap insurance with around twenty syndicates willing to underwrite kidnap and piracy risks. The system critically relies on pooling and discreetly sharing information among insiders. This can be accomplished in the underwriting room and among the syndicates' associated security and crisis response specialists without compromising customer confidentiality. Second, the concentration of knowledge about the performance of experts is used to restrict competition and occasionally create (contestable) monopolies for expert services. The higher prices incentivize the governance providers to work hard to stay at the top of their game and continue in this lucrative business. Something that would commonly be perceived as a market failure (imperfect competition) is in fact a precondition for the smooth functioning of this unusual market. However, it should be possible to create other lines of communication and perhaps integrate further major players in the insurance industry in the network. Why hasn't this happened?

There is an excellent reason for kidnap for ransom insurance being governed out of Lloyd's of London: insurers need to guard against opportunistic behaviour within the group. The key problem is that containing ransoms, while always in the long-term interest of the market, may not be in the private short-term interest of an insurer faced with a long-running, troublesome hostage incident. The cost of waiting for the kidnappers to converge on the target ransom is significant. The insurer covers the cost of employing all the relevant experts and any costs incurred by the insured agreed under the insurance cover. There is also the potential cost of reduced future business, should the customer come to believe that the chosen negotiators did not act in the best interest of the hostage but that of the insurer. Unless there is a strong disciplining device within the market, it is likely that myopic insurers will occasionally try to settle earlier and more expensively than ideal. But premium ransoms can destabilize kidnappers' expectations in the area and lead them to test future cases at a higher target ransom level.

The Ransom Externality

The problem is that an individual insurer does not bear all the cost of taking a convenient shortcut. A small kidnap insurer with a limited overall business volume might not see another case in the affected region for several years. When one agent's decision creates significant costs that are partly borne by others, we call this an externality. Usually externalities are illustrated in the context of pollution—for example, a chemicals factory releases toxic substances into a river, which compromises the livelihoods of downstream fisheries and salmon farms. Unless the industrialist is forced to consider the impact of pollution on these downstream producers, there will be more pollution than is socially optimal.

If the externality operates through changes in prices, it is called a pecuniary externality. A classic example is an influx of rich city dwellers bidding up the cost of village homes as they acquire second homes in the countryside. This process can put home ownership out of reach for local families—who may protest against the 'unfair' competition for pretty thatched cottages. Yet, price controls would create two other groups of losers: the sellers who cannot obtain the best price for their houses and those who cannot buy their dream house despite having the means to do so. In general, pecuniary externalities are an integral feature of vibrant and efficient markets: there is no economic efficiency argument to prevent them.[12]

However, if impoverished bandits enter negotiations with a ransom demand of half a million dollars and an actual expectation of US$5,000, it is not in the public interest to reveal that some multinationals would pay more than US$100,000 to resolve such cases quickly and smoothly. Not only will every subsequent victim be tested at this threshold (putting all those at risk who simply cannot afford US$100,000), but the twentyfold increase in expected returns would attract further criminals and opportunists to try their hand at kidnap for ransom.

Resolving Externalities

Human ingenuity has found many ways to resolve externalities problems, whether by government intervention (regulation), through the market (pollution permits, integration of upstream and downstream enterprises), or through consensus and informal institutions (resource governance). We can think through potential solutions to the ransom externality by applying the approach pioneered by the economist Ronald Coase. The famous Coase theorem posits that if there are clearly defined and enforceable property rights, the market will resolve externalities problems.[13] If there is a right to pollute then those who are affected by the pollution can pay the polluter to limit the damage—to the point where total joint output is maximized. It does not matter which side holds the property right. If there is an enforceable right to private land, pastoralists will employ herders and compensate farmers for any damage wrought in their fields or vegetable patches. If animals have a right to roam, it is up to the farmers to build fences or pay the pastoralists to control their animals. Either way, enforceable property rights ensure that different economic activities can coexist through optimal investment in damage limitation.

However, Coase went on to analyse what happens if property rights are difficult to enforce. For example, it may not be possible to say with certainty how much damage has been caused—and by whom. There is then an additional information cost to establish what has happened before compensation can be demanded. If outcomes are both variable (by nature) and alterable (by man), the market solution to externalities breaks down entirely. The agent causing the damage can blame 'nature' for the adverse outcome: cheating becomes impossible to detect. In this case contracts are neither self-enforcing nor enforceable.[14]

This is exactly the situation with ransoms: they are intrinsically variable. Ransoms depend on the sophistication, reputation, and patience of the kidnappers. They depend on the perceived financial means of the victims, where insights might be gleaned from identity documents, clothing, the quality of the car—or an internet search. Ransoms also depend on the ability of the stakeholders to raise funds and their ability to manage the expectations of the kidnappers. They depend on whether the stakeholders see the kidnap as a one-off event to be resolved as quickly as possible, or whether they understand the long-term implications of paying premium ransoms. Of course, ransoms are also alterable by the insurers, who can employ persuasive and charismatic consultants to provide excellent advice to stakeholders. The problem is that by looking at the final agreed amount we cannot tell how much effort the insurer devoted to limiting the ransom.

Resolving the Ransom Externality

If one cannot tell whether a ransom was 'unnecessarily high', one cannot enforce a contract wherein insurers 'overpaying' kidnappers must compensate the others. If an agreement or contract is not enforce-able, then it has no disciplining effect. Coase proposes two possible solutions to this dilemma. Either a single firm can form to integrate the interests of all market participants, so kidnap insurance would be supplied monopolistically. Alternatively, a government can impose regulation on the industry, specifying 'what people must or must not do and which have to be obeyed... [and] decree that certain methods of production should or should not be used'.[15]

Indeed, we have a strong precedent for a monopolistic, government-led market structure in the hostage trade. Countries at war used to form ransoming cartels to manage prices and hostage exchanges. Rather than leaving the ransoming of captured soldiers to families, governments set up boards that acted as monopsony buyers of hostages. Ransoms were not set individually but reflected the soldier's rank. This system turned prisoners of war into assets and created incentives to spare lives, and repeated interactions smoothed the path to orderly prisoner exchanges. A monopoly in the hostage trade is an elegant and effective solution to the ransom externality problem.[16]

However, kidnap insurance is not supplied monopolistically. Lloyd's is not a single company, but around twenty providers compete for business in the market for kidnap insurance. Do the Lloyd's syndicates form a ransoming cartel to limit prices for hostages? No: making and enforcing a cartel agreement is challenging. First, the syndicates cannot 'fix' prices. The advantage of the late seventeenth- and eighteenth-century government ransom cartels was that at the time the government effectively owned its soldiers. If a government wanted to change the terms of trade and pay less, it could leave its soldiers in enemy hands for longer. Lloyd's insurers are in a very different position. The insured would not be happy with extended detentions to lower resolution costs for insurers. The norm is therefore that the stakeholders make all the decisions in the perceived best interests of their hostage. The crisis response consultants only provide advice—no one can force the insured to take a particular course of action. As already discussed, this makes ransoms highly variable. Consequently, it would take an expensive and protracted court case to prove that a syndicate paid 'too much' to resolve a case.

However, disputing a case in court would be counterproductive: insurers do not want to reveal who is insured. If kidnappers realize that a firm is insured this increases their ransom expectations for future kidnaps. It is therefore impossible to resolve disagreements in any forum where the identity of insurer or insured becomes public knowledge. It would make the insured's employees particularly attractive targets.

Finally, cartels require a punishment mechanism, should one of the members breach the contract. The regular convulsions of the Organization of the Petroleum Exporting Countries cartel are well known: if some member countries flagrantly breach their quotas, Saudi Arabia raises production, the oil price collapses, and eventually all members come back to the negotiating table. Other price-fixing cartels take recourse to the economic underworld: if punishment for cheating counterparties is meted out by the mafia, cheating is extremely costly.[17] Because the threat of sanctions is credible, there is very little cheating and actual enforcement is usually unnecessary.

To summarize, we are looking for a way of enforcing a cartel-like agreement to contain prices without rigidly setting them. The governance system must work without recourse to a public resolution process. There must be a credible sanction for those who are perceived to be flaunting the rules, even without definitive proof of wrongdoing.

Club Governance at Lloyd's

One excellent solution to this kind of problem is club governance. A private members' club can decide who to admit. Clubs have the legal right to exclude 'the riff-raff': club property is private property. The conditions for membership can be stated in deliberately vague terms—for example: 'open to honourable men and closed forever to notorious cheats'.[18] New members are vetted by the existing members or a committee. New applicants can be rejected without giving a reason. The club designs its own statutes and can levy fines on rule breakers. In case of disagreements between members, a club can create its own private adjudication mechanisms. The ultimate sanction of a club is expulsion. Members can be expelled for relatively vague reasons, such as 'dishonourable and disgraceful conduct'. Once the relevant committee has made its decision, there is no legal appeal.

The City of London is famous for using club governance to order trade. The economist Edward Stringham traces the story of the London Stock Exchange from its coffee house origins to a highly successful rule-enforcing club, whose strict statutes underpin the trust of both buyers and sellers. Similarly, Lloyd's started in a London coffee house as a membership society, in which people would sell and buy insurance and reinsurance. The Committee on Lloyd's was formed to adjudicate disputes about who should pay how much and how any proceeds from salvage might be split. Edward Stringham sees private arbitration as the key governance contribution of Lloyd's: knowing that a fair dispute resolution process existed, people cooperated to prevent the escalation of damage, thereby lowering the cost of insurance for all.[19]

The Lloyd's insurance market operates under the watchful eye of the Lloyd's Corporation. Independent insurance underwriters join Lloyd's as syndicates. Lloyd's members (individual 'Names', limited partnerships, or corporations) provide the capital supporting each syndicate's underwriting business. The Corporation holds the syndicates' assets and members' funds in trust, so they are available to cover the insured risks. A special feature of Lloyd's is that catastrophic losses exceeding the funds of individual syndicates are covered by the 'Central Fund'. This fund consists of the mutual assets held by the Corporation. These can be replenished by calling on all members to make additional subscriptions. Lloyd's strong international credit rating enables relatively small insurance companies to operate in markets with highly concentrated risks.[20]

Lloyd's elaborate 'Chain of Security' thus creates a competitive advantage for its members—but also a danger that individual syndicates attempt to free-ride on the guarantees supplied by the wider membership. Therefore, the Lloyd's Corporation—via its governing body, the Council of Lloyd's—sets required capital levels and commercial standards to ensure that 'underwriters operate in a way that benefits the whole market'.[21] Although syndicates function as permanent insurance operations, legally membership in a syndicate lasts only for one year at a time. Every syndicate must submit an annual business plan for the scrutiny of the Corporation to renew its membership. If a syndicate takes on excessive risk or its business practices undermine the stability or smooth functioning of the market, it can be closed for new business and wound up.

Lloyd's therefore has all the mechanisms in place to enforce a tacit agreement between competing insurers to operate in the long-term interest of the market. There is no need to continuously scrutinize every syndicate's ransom settlements. If a region develops unstable ransom dynamics, however, it is relatively easy to find out which ransoms upset the market and trace them back to their origin. For example, the explosion of Somali pirate ransoms was triggered by the intervention of the Spanish government on behalf of its fishing trawlers and several negotiations conducted by outsiders. They tried to take a 'time is money' approach to resolving 'their' hijacks, leaving everyone else in the lurch. Had a Lloyd's syndicate been responsible for the escalating prices, it would have been advised to review its business practice or exit the Lloyd's market.

Lloyd's membership is crucial for anyone offering kidnap insurance. The Central Fund enables small syndicates to insure concentrated risks.

The Lloyd's Corporation centrally collates information and creates guidelines on legal matters related to kidnap insurance. When someone pays premium ransoms, the market leaders track down the culprit(s) and provide guidance on how to handle such cases in future. For the individuals concerned it probably feels like being sent to the head-master's office—but it helps to stabilize kidnapper expectations. Crisis responders also share information on local experts and reliable inter-mediaries to facilitate the safe return of hostages. Although syndicates compete for business and appreciate that competitors' mistakes will put them at a disadvantage eventually, it is in no one's interest to let ransoms escalate or hostages come to grief by withholding informa-tion. Insurers outside the Lloyd's community cannot take access to this market information for granted, however. Underwriters at Lloyd's do not nurture competing kidnap insurance products, where abduc-tions are not resolved according to the Lloyd's protocol.

Lloyd's membership thus serves several different purposes. The finan-cial guarantee is important to many but not to all members. All members rely on the Lloyd's community of underwriters and crisis responders to share relevant information for the benefit of all. This information advan-tage creates a barrier to entry and raises the profitability of those within the market. Equally importantly, however, Lloyd's membership serves as a commitment device. Club members pay the significant cost of the Lloyd's subscription (including potentially being called upon for add-itional contributions) to signal their commitment to ensuring the long-term stability of the market.

A Club Solution to the Externalities Problem

We return to the Coasean prediction for resolving the externalities problem: either a monopoly or a government regulating the means of production in the interest of the whole market. With Lloyd's we have a solution that is neither a monopoly nor a government. Instead we observe a traditional club at the heart of the City of London that has lost none of its relevance. The club monopolizes the market for kidnap insurance, but its members compete to provide it, engaging in both price and non-price competition. This competition is in the customers' interest. The club functions well, because it has an effective governance structure. The Lloyd's Corporation has been granted the legal right to make and enforce its own by-laws. The Corporation therefore takes on the role which Coase ascribed to the government: it sets standards for all market participants, investigates complaints, and punishes those who act against the interests of others.

As a private members' club, Lloyd's can discipline its members better than a government could. The Lloyd's Corporation does not have to prove a member's wrongdoing in court to suggest a course correction, impose a fine, or close a syndicate that has become a liability to all. We saw that a legal contract to act 'in the interest of the market' was neither enforceable nor self-enforcing. By contrast, the Lloyd's membership contract is enforceable and therefore everyone generally adheres to the letter and spirit of the agreement. In practice, the Lloyd's Corporation rarely takes heavy-handed action against its members. It is usually sufficient to provide 'advice and guidance'.[22]

In fact, with kidnap insurance the informal governance in the underwriting room works so well that the Corporation relies on the market leaders in kidnap insurance to govern their followers. As long as this niche product does not create a problem for the Corporation (i.e. 'the book performs nicely'), there is considerable discretion for the members to govern themselves. So far, kidnap insurance hasn't even acquired its own code in the Lloyd's system, which would be a first step to detailed monitoring. It is a tiny, slightly opaque ('sneaky-peeky'), and unproblematic part of the huge Personal Accidents book. As so often in private governance, a credible threat is enough to discipline the market.

External Threats to Stability

Although the Lloyd's system disciplines its members, and the syndicates in turn discipline the insured, the system can still be threatened by outsiders. Given that that the insured mimic the behaviour of uninsured cash-constrained firms and families, any premium settlement can upset the stability of a local criminal market. Uninsured kidnap victims often fetch premium ransoms: they lack information and experience in negotiating with criminals and are desperate to conclude. If uninsured stakeholders look for professional support, they often encounter negotiators who did not make the cut for permanent employment in the insurance industry. There is no official accreditation system for negotiators, so inept negotiators can privately offer (cut-price) services to desperate folks. More often than not, they fail to deliver a swift, clean return of the hostages, because they lack the experience and connections necessary to craft and deliver a self-enforcing agreement with their criminal counterparty.

One approach to prevent spillovers from uninsured but well-resourced hostages is that crisis responders resolve such cases on a *pro bono* basis. The uninsured party gets free expert advice on how to conduct the negotiation but raise and pay the ransom themselves. A good example is the assistance provided to Judith Tebbutt and the Chandler couple, who were taken hostage by Somali pirates.[23] If their abductors had made a quick buck, tourists in the wider region would have become an attractive income source for anyone able to get their hostages into Somalia. *Pro bono* advice ensured that the hostages returned safely—but the ransom settlements were far below the expectations of pirates. Therefore, the pirate business model was not extended to tourists in Kenya, the Maldives, and the Seychelles—benefitting the regional economies, holidaymakers, and their insurers.

Much worse outcomes arise if uninsured hostage stakeholders turn to politicians for help. Governments do not have hard budget constraints, bureaucrats' careers are not adversely affected by large ransom settlements, and politicians want to resolve hostage incidents quickly to satisfy public or media pressure. This makes them very weak when the 'squeezes' start. Political involvement thus tends to trigger ransom inflation and an escalation of violence—a problem we will revisit in Chapter 10.

A Governance System Under Threat?

The system governing kidnap for ransom is of bewildering complexity—as befits the world's trickiest trade. A multitude of agents have developed specific expertise in response to the needs of the insurance industry. Underwriters craft appropriate and enforceable insurance contracts, which are compared by brokers. Highly specialized experts order transactions with criminals to limit kidnaps and resolve incidents. Overall market order is facilitated by club governance. Information flows freely within and between communities of experts. Repeated interactions mean that transactions can be governed informally: agents do their best to enhance their reputation and do not risk it for short-term gain. The law and the ultimate sanction of losing club membership are only invoked in rare circumstances—but the fact that transgressions could be severely punished is enough to create discipline.

The system manages to repel both opportunism and criminal challenges through a competitive market for governance. The system rewards balanced underwriters, careful syndicates, diligent brokers, circumspect security consultants, and charismatic negotiators. Close-knit communities of experts ensure that inept, overoptimistic, and corrupt operators are weeded out. Experts stand and fall by their reputation within their peer group—because only the peer group can accurately judge their quality. Most insiders do not think about the complex challenges of insuring a transnational crime and ordering trade across the legal/illegal divide. They are experts at solving specific problems. They operate within their own community and interact with their peers, customers, and principals according to the incentives provided by the system. However, jointly they create orderly markets for protection and (failing that) hostages. This facilitates international trade, foreign direct investment, research, news reporting, and humanitarian missions in weakly governed areas around the globe.

By analysing the system as a polycentric governance framework and focusing on how all the crucial regulation functions are fulfilled it becomes clear that (a lack of) ransom discipline is the main challenge to system stability. The system counters this threat among the insiders through rigorous peer monitoring and harsh penalties on those who perform badly or behave opportunistically. However, the system is not immune from outsiders who do not know or deliberately ignore the industry protocol for ordering the trade in hostages. Therefore, this highly effective private order regime occasionally fails to contain a vicious cycle in ransoms and kidnaps. Insurance then becomes unviable unless law enforcement is ramped up. Causing the failure of private governance thus has a tendency to backfire for governments: the cost of enhanced policing or military intervention is generally a multiple of the privately borne cost of insuring a well-contained kidnap problem. Part III analyses when and why things go wrong in the market for hostages.

Part III
When Kidnaps Go Wrong

RIP	Welcome home
Daniel Pearl (US), murdered by Al Qaeda in Pakistan	Jere van Dyk (US), ransomed from Pakistan
Pierre Korkie (SA), ransomed from Al Qaeda, but shot during rescue	Jessica Buchanan (US), liberated from Somalia
Linda Norgrove (GB), killed during rescue from Taliban	Bowe Bergdahl (US), ransomed from the Taliban by prisoner exchange
Martin Burnham (US), shot during rescue operation from Abu Sayyaf	Gracia Burnham (US), liberated from Abu Sayyaf in rescue operation
David Haines (GB), murdered by ISIL/Daesh	Federico Motka (It), ransomed from ISIL/Daesh
John Ridsdel (Can), murdered by Abu Sayyaf	Kjartan Sekkingstad (No), ransomed from Abu Sayyaf
Steve Sotloff (US), murdered by ISIL/Daesh	Nicolas Hénin (Fr), ransomed from ISIL/Daesh
Kenji Goto (Jpn), murdered by ISIL/Daesh	Daniel Rye Ottosen (Dk), ransomed from ISIL/Daesh
Moaz al'Kasasbeh (Jor), murdered by ISIL/Daesh	Javier Espinosa (Esp), ransomed from ISIL/Daesh
James Foley (US), murdered by ISIL/Daesh	Toni Neukirch (D), ransomed from ISIL/Daesh

I have analysed kidnap for ransom as a business and as a tricky market that is amazingly well ordered given the manifold challenges the trade in human lives involves. Thanks to the ingenuity, experience, and expertise of highly specialized service providers, most people insured to live, travel, or work in risky environments are never kidnapped in the first place. If they are, almost all of them come home alive. Yet, the crisis responders who manage these cases and the negotiators who sit with the families or the firms' crisis response teams through the most harrowing and psychologically draining time of their lives barely recognize my view of their world. They take nothing for granted: in their business treasured, precious lives are at stake. Every victory is snatched from the jaws of a horrible defeat. The negotiators' task is to ensure that traumatized and mentally exhausted family members answer the phone calmly to negotiate an orderly commercial resolution that does not put others at risk. To encourage them to think rationally and sometimes act against their gut instinct. To pick up the pieces when a negotiation derails and salvage whatever is possible. To organize the safe retrieval of the hostage. To them, my focus on their ultimate success often seems blasé. The dark sense of humour with which insiders sometimes pepper the conversations about their cases sound inappropriate and uncaring when repeated by an outsider. 'People die, Anja!'

Indeed. Some hostage murders are carefully staged and exploited for maximum publicity. Some victims are shot in cold blood, others are slaughtered in the heat of the moment. A few do not survive the strains of their captivity, others are killed when trying to escape. Some hostages disappear without a trace. All of them leave their families devastated, their friends bereaved, and their colleagues and neighbours saddened (and probably fearful). The final part of the book analyses when kidnapping goes wrong. This is probably the most well-documented aspect of kidnapping in the media: murder is newsworthy.[1] Bereaved families are usually desperate for an answer to why their loved one had to die.[2] Conversely, incidents that are efficiently and cheaply resolved by professionals and covered by insurance are usually only discussed within a tight circle of confidantes. Are there empirical regularities when hostage-taking goes wrong? Is it merely bad luck or a sign of governance failure? I examine three different explanations for extreme violence in kidnap for ransom.

First, it takes time to shape expectations in negotiations: to convince stakeholders that they are dealing with a sophisticated group that could hold hostages indefinitely, and to convince kidnappers that the maximum ransom has been reached. Occasionally, hostages, stakeholders, the police, governments, or kidnappers simply crack under the mental, physical, or political strain. Second, violence can be used strategically to increase the total return on kidnapping. There may be financial, political, and geo-strategic benefits from killing hostages. Unless negotiations are very well managed, abusing hostages encourages rich stakeholders to raise their offers to protect their loved ones. This sets up perverse economic incentives to murder some (relatively low-value) hostages. Third, the orderly market for hostages crucially relies on the shadow of the future. Opportunistic kidnappers may consider a hostage trade as a one-off and try to accelerate or exit the negotiation through torture or murder. Similarly, if negotiators focus solely on the well-being of a specific hostage rather than taking a broad, long-term view, they put others in grave danger. Unless all market participants are disciplined by the threat of higher transaction costs in future interactions, lives are at extreme risk.

The most dreadful and wanton cases of hostage maltreatment and murder occur in 'terrorist' kidnappings. Although one might be tempted to claim that these are 'political' and therefore not kidnap for ransom, I take a different approach. I argue that terrorist kidnap for ransom is so troublesome because of the involvement of some governments in ransom negotiations. Government-led negotiations occur in an institutional framework that encourages kidnapper entrenchment, ransom inflation, and strategic murder. One should therefore seriously question the wisdom of the UN ban on making ransom payments to proscribed organizations. National and international law deliberately sidelines the private governance architecture that usually orders the market for hostages. But rather than ending payments to proscribed organizations, it has increased funding to terrorist organizations. The premium ransoms extracted from some governments more than offset the cost of murdering hostages from nations refusing to make concessions.

10

Why Do Hostages Die?

I really feel that our country let Jim down...As an American I was embarrassed and appalled...Jim believed until the end that his country would come to their aid. We were, you know, asked to not go to the media. To just trust that it would be taken care of. We were told we could not raise a ransom, that it was illegal. We might be prosecuted...I think our efforts to get Jim freed were an annoyance...Jim was killed in the most horrific way. He was sacrificed because of—just a lack of coordination, a lack of communication. A lack of prioritization.

Interview with Diane Foley, CNN, 11 September 2014

My experience is that where governments actively engage, the result is universally sloppy negotiations...[Political interventions] only raise expectations, encourage the villains, create inflation on future release payments and ultimately fuel the crime. This unnecessarily raises the bar for any unrelated, concurrent cases...which is always tedious....[W]here governments...disrupt, confuse or confound family or employer engagement, the results are usually catastrophic for the victims and very traumatic for their families.

Crisis response consultant

Rationality and Irrationality in Kidnap for Ransom

In focusing on the thousands of kidnappings which are quietly and efficiently resolved, I may have created unwarranted faith in the principle of rational exchange. I have assumed that the kidnappers want (or will ultimately settle for) money. Logically calculating perpetrators, hostages, and stakeholders have every interest in a successful commercial resolution. If the assumptions of rational choice hold true, the intricate and complex private governance architecture described in this book will always return live hostages to their families.

But of course, the assumptions of rational choice are not met here. Not every kidnapper is a well-informed criminal mastermind—and some are only tangentially interested in ransoms. There may be political gains from murdering foreign or ethnically different hostages, suspected spies and collaborators, and prisoners of war. Kidnap hotspots are often violent places and kidnappers who were brutalized themselves may enjoy making their hostages miserable. Emotional outbursts are likely on all sides. Offence may be taken where none was intended. Hostages are not 'non-perishable goods' passively waiting to be ransomed: some have pre-existing medical conditions, others fall ill. Some hostages vex their guards and others try to escape. Payments may go astray. Governments with highly trained SWAT teams are often keen to test their mettle against gangs, mafias, insurgents, and terrorists—even if significant casualties are likely. Every single kidnap has the potential to go tragically wrong. Many do, and these are the cases we are most familiar with from the media, books, and blogs. Entire academic papers are devoted to murdered hostages.[3] Even so, professional negotiators employed by specialist insurers almost always manage to steer their highly volatile cases to successful conclusions.

The highly competitive market for consultants selects outstanding negotiators to manage kidnap for ransom cases and there is a wealth of experience to draw on in the network. It is very rare that professionally managed kidnap cases end with a murder. If so, the negotiators retain their jobs because the circumstances were demonstrably outside their control. The outstanding track record of private crisis responders is in stark contrast with the performance of public officials in negotiating with terrorist groups, where both multi-million-dollar ransoms and murders have become the norm in recent years. The next section looks at cases where one or more of the parties involved crack under the pressure of an extended negotiation. We will then examine cases where violence is used strategically, before contrasting the approaches and outcomes achieved by professional negotiators with those of civil servants in comparable situations. From this analysis it becomes clear why terrorist kidnappings resolved by governments so often go wrong.

Accidents Waiting to Happen

In a hostage negotiation, important information is conveyed by the timing of demands and offers. If someone betrays their impatience to conclude, it sends a strong signal that that their price position is negotiable. South American kidnap gangs sometimes waited for months before even making contact with the families. Similarly, stakeholders are encouraged to engage in disruptive bargaining and structure their offers to signal that their funds are limited. Unless the market for hostages is well established and price expectations have converged at a level that everyone can live with, negotiations will take time. If families or firms weaken during this time and reveal their impatience to move on by significantly raising their offer, the result is usually physical or mental torture and perhaps a mutilation to further increase stakeholder impatience. It is rare that torture or mutilations are (accidentally) fatal. There is a rational explanation for kidnappers' predilection for removing earlobes and fingers: other injuries tend to be more difficult to manage. The most common outcome when hostage stakeholders make ill-advised snap decisions is still a release—albeit at a higher emotional and financial cost than necessary. However, it is a different matter if hostages, governments, or kidnappers lose their nerve.

Hostage Morale

For the hostage, the kidnapping is a stressful if not a traumatizing experience. Perhaps they witnessed a killing at close range or are desperately worried about the fate of a friend, colleague, or loved one involved in the ambush. Often the victims are hurt or wounded during the abduction. Almost all are ill-treated and verbally abused by their captors and guards afterwards. A period of 'conditioning' is intended to break the victim's resistance over the negotiation period. If the hostages become passive and compliant, matters tend to improve somewhat—but only within the means of the kidnappers. What filters down about the negotiation is likely to be just as disconcerting and painful for the hostages. As Mr Ali goaded the *CEC Future*'s captain in the begging phone calls: 'They don't give a shit about you!' Whatever realistic story is spun to the kidnappers, it will be upsetting for the hostage, too: the uncaring rich uncle, the callous boss, the called-off wedding, the worthless heirloom, or the wife blowing hot and cold after finding out about the mistress who called to enquire about her lover.

Moreover, as one negotiator put it: 'We don't tend to pay for hostages at the price they value themselves.' If somebody knows his firm has a million in ready cash and there are also good friends who could put their hands in their pockets—why are negotiations stuck at US$50,000? One of the highest ransoms ever paid—US$60 million for the two Born brothers in Argentina in 1975—was negotiated by one of the captives himself: Jorge Born. As a company insider, he knew how much money could be raised, but it still took seven months before his captors were convinced that they had truly squeezed him dry. When it finally arrived, the father felt he had no option but to accede to the memorandum signed by his son and his kidnappers.[4] So negotiators work extremely hard to avoid parallel negotiations and bat away unhelpful interventions from the hostage. It is not surprising that some victims despair.

A common cause of death is an attempted escape—chiefly among young males. Some escape attempts succeed, but it is a risky strategy—especially if it involves attacking guards or if the hostage is held in unfamiliar, hostile territory. One young man overpowered a rebel sentry and escaped into primary jungle. 'Unsurprisingly, his kidnappers knew the jungle better than he did. They found him and killed him in revenge.' Another was fatally shot in the back as he ran away. US army Sgt Bowe Bergdahl only survived his escape bids from Taliban captivity because he was such a valuable asset for his captors—but he was made to suffer. After the first escape attempt, he spent three months tied to a bed to atrophy his muscles. He tried again regardless. For eight and a half days, he lived on grass and what little water he could find in the barren landscape before his captors caught up with him. Sgt Bergdahl spent the remaining three years of his captivity in a six-by-six-foot cage.[5] A violation of the implicit rules of the hostage trade can thus have stark repercussions for the hostage: whether it is a spontaneous emotional outburst, an accidentally fatal shooting, or an attempt to save face or set an example to other captives.[6]

If hostages have any pre-existing medical conditions, captivity is likely to aggravate them and kidnappers are unlikely to have ready access to prescription medicine. In a professionally conducted negotiation, medical issues will be raised very early on to ensure that supplies are not disrupted or restored as fast as possible. Such discussions can help to accelerate a case, as neither side wants to negotiate over a dead body. Only the most sophisticated gangs will attempt to treat major illnesses—such as Al Qaeda trying (at least briefly) to treat the French hostage Françoise Larribe for breast cancer.[7] Even non-fatal conditions provide a useful opportunity to create a cooperative atmosphere—for example organizing the delivery of eye-drops for the treatment of glaucoma. 'We can usually get medication in', say the professionals: whether it is by paying an insider to deliver a package or sending a 4 × 4 laden with hospital equipment to a rendezvous point. Still, despite considerable efforts to manage ill health some hostages die from strokes, heart attacks, diabetes, and local diseases.

The mental health of the hostage also requires very careful consideration. In long cases, dejection (and communicable diseases) are often managed by sending morale-boosting 'goodie-packs'. These always include water-purifying tablets and something to cheer up the hostage. A Brazilian captive—affectionately known to his friends as 'el Gordo' (the fat one)—regularly received parcels containing his favourite Cadbury's chocolate bars. If there is reason to surmise that the kidnappers are smokers (there usually is), in goes a packet of cigarettes: 'It doesn't do any harm.'[8] If a hostage suffers from depression or anxiety, the risk of an escape attempt or a serious medical problem is greatly magnified. Thus, every hostage situation is an accident waiting to happen. Crisis response professionals have carefully honed skills and experience in managing these risks. Where possible, they scrutinize the hostage's medical records and engage professional medical backup when required. They succeed in the vast majority but not in all cases.

Government Rescue Operations

For governments, hostage situations can become an embarrassment if they become public knowledge. If the hostage is a politician, a journalist, an aid worker, a local industrialist, or a celebrity, awkward questions tend to be asked by the media; especially if the hostage is a foreigner. There are interesting cultural differences between nations here. I am always amazed at some of my international (usually French) students' convictions that it is the responsibility of their nation to protect them from mishaps abroad. However ill-advised their adventuring, there is an expectation that they will be rescued. By contrast, British students tend to mutter darkly about the 'Darwin Awards', when hearing about some of the tight spots continental Europeans were retrieved from.[9] With hijacked ships or planes, or multiple hostages trapped in a public building, any government faces international humiliation, adverse business conditions, or political repercussion if it is seen to be weak or indecisive. More than anything, governments want the hostage problem and the negative publicity to end—even if it puts the hostages at risk. Successful rescue missions can pay considerable dividends in the opinion polls for the politicians who authorized them.

Many governments have elite police or military capacity to conduct assaults. Those that don't have their own units may well authorize another country's elite troops to conduct a rescue operation. There is usually a way of declaring a rescue mission 'successful'. If at least some hostages are released and the kidnappers or hijackers are apprehended or killed, further hostage deaths can be portrayed as unavoidable—if regrettable—collateral damage. Many consider the rescue of more than a hundred hostages from pro-Palestinian terrorists by Israeli special forces in Entebbe, Uganda, on 4 July 1976 to be Israel's finest hour. The three hostages killed by friendly fire were well below the rescuers' expectations of twenty-five (!) hostage fatalities. Prime Minister Yitzhak Rabin declared the rescue mission one of the 'most exemplary victories from both the human and moral, and the military-operational points of view'.[10] Yet, a critical evaluation of the records of the mission reveals that the media version of events was tightly edited and heavily spun. The better than expected outcome was mostly due to good luck and the last-minute humanity of the kidnappers, rather than being a true testimony of Israeli military brilliance.[11]

Similarly, few people criticized the Peruvian government for the way its storm troopers ended the Lima embassy siege in 1997: freeing all but one of seventy-two hostages and killing 14 of the rebels.[12] Yet, a professional negotiator recounted this incident to remind me of Supreme Court Judge Carlos Giusti Acuna and the two Peruvian soldiers who died during the operation. Likewise, the death of an innocent cabin crew member during the storming of a Nigerian Airbus in Niamey in Niger in 1993 might have been avoided with a meaningful negotiation, as the idealistic teenage students who had hijacked the plane to make a political statement offered no resistance during the ambush.[13] Even the most efficient military rescue operation puts the lives of innocent people at risk—whereas (according to a seasoned negotiator) 'these things have a tendency to resolve themselves peaceably when the latrines overflow'.

'Friendly fire' is a common cause of death in hostage operations. US Navy Seals famously shot three pirates dead simultaneously as they took Captain Phillips to Somalia in a life raft.[14] But less than a month later, the skipper of the yacht *Tanit* died when French Special Forces tried to free him, his family, and friends from Somali pirates.[15] The Obama administration and US Navy Seals reaped great praise for the daring, pre-dawn raid that rescued the aid workers Jessica Buchanan and Poul Hagen Thisted from their Somali captors.[16] Yet, the painful memory of the assault on the Afghan tribal kidnappers who held the Scottish aid worker Linda Norgrove and three of her local colleagues was still fresh in the public consciousness. This meticulously planned rescue operation, striking the surprised jailers with a highly trained force of twenty-four Navy Seals and twenty US Rangers, ended in tragedy. All four hostages died just after US forces stormed the building—most likely from wounds inflicted by grenades thrown by their rescue party.[17]

Former SAS Deputy Commander Clive Fairweather summarized the danger of rescue missions as follows: 'You've got to accept that in the confusion, in the dark, it's all down to two things—split-second timing and recognition. And on top of that you need a big bit of luck ... I'd say to anyone, negotiate, negotiate. Don't get us involved if you can help it. If you get us involved someone will be dead. It'll either be the hostages, the terrorists or us. Probably all three.'[18] The difference between governments thinking about short-term approval ratings and the negotiators' long-term approach therefore needs careful handling. If governments have special forces they are prone to using them when the public mood turns on a case and there appears to be a window of opportunity for a successful rescue. Managing the media exposure of kidnap cases is therefore critical. If there is no public pressure for action, there is no need to be seen to be doing something.

Spontaneous Homicide

In the academic literature on homicide studies researchers distinguish between planned murders and spontaneous/unplanned murders. Planned homicides are characterized by evidence of preparation: the perpetrators carefully picked the time and place of the murder, selected a murder weapon and style (e.g. the highly symbolic throat-cutting), and made preparations for the disposal of the body (perhaps to preserve the perpetrator's anonymity or to send a warning message to others).[19] In these cases, one assumes that murder has a strategic dimension, which we explore in the following section. However, in kidnapping we also observe homicides where victims are strangled, kicked or beaten to death, or bludgeoned with objects from the immediate vicinity. Such circumstances imply that the murderers did not carefully pre-plan their exit from the hostage negotiation but acted spontaneously. Manual violence also suggests personal hostility and emotional involvement—perhaps the murder occurred in response to a challenge or a perceived insult.

Murders in ongoing ransom negotiations that appear to be driven by emotional outbursts and intentionally caused pain to the hostage are mostly associated with common criminals, rather than organized criminal and radical groups.[20] Indeed, hostage negotiators 'much prefer to deal with people who know what they are doing'. Opportunists sometimes have unrealistic expectations of the ransoms families can raise (even with insurance) and may be angered by the failure to achieve their target. Lone criminals can easily crack under the pressure of a negotiation, while hiding, guarding, and providing for the hostage's basic needs. When more people get involved, but the gang does not have a clear command and control structure, tensions and disagreements can arise between them, regarding the ransom target and negotiation strategy. This can easily boil over into aggression towards the hostage. Unless opportunists can sell the hostage on to a more sophisticated group or fear retribution, a 'falling out among thieves' can have catastrophic consequences. Even so, a killing does not necessarily end the kidnappers' attempts to extract a ransom. Families may be kept on tenterhooks for months until the absence of a further proof of life convinces them that their loved ones have died—or the body is finally found and identified.[21]

Strategic Use of Murder

Some kidnappers develop fearsome reputations by publicizing the torture and killing of hostages to a wide audience. But when is it rational to destroy a financial asset? In *The Invisible Hook*, the economist Peter Leeson analysed the economic logic of pirate tactics and demonstrates why famous pirates (e.g. Blackbeard) deliberately cultivated an image of madness and extreme violence. In the short run, killing hostages and deliberately sinking ships whose crews fought back was costly. However, eventually their terrible reputations undermined the opposition's morale so much that pirates only encountered minimal resistance to their attacks when they hoisted their flags.[22] Today's criminal and terrorist groups employ similar strategies to improve their terms of trade on a range of criminal transactions—including but not limited to kidnap for ransom. There are three broad reasons why a kidnapping gang may be made better off by killing at least some of their hostages—economic, political, and security—and often a mixture of all of them.

Economic Gains from Murdering Hostages

If a group holds multiple hostages, there is a high probability that at least one of the victims will be harmed. By demonstrating their willingness to torture, maim, and kill, the kidnappers signal to the surviving victims' stakeholders that they feel unassailable and secure in their territory. With multiple hostages, there can be a trade-off between violence and time in hostage negotiations. Kidnappers holding several hostages sometimes set an arbitrary, short deadline for some unrealistic concession to be made. After its expiry, they murder one of the hostages and either release the body (perhaps with a note: 'I am a non-payment of ransom'), a video, or a photo of the killing. An example is Al Qaeda's treatment of a British, a German, and two Swiss nationals kidnapped together in Mali in 2009. The terrorists set a deadline for all the governments to make a ransom offer. The British government repeatedly refused to get involved in a ransom negotiation for Edwin Dyer, the

British national. When a further fifteen-day extension elapsed without a positive response, he was killed: 'It seems Britain gives little importance to its citizens', read the terror group's communiqué. His three fellow hostages, however, were released for a ransom of US$8 million in cash. Later that year an additional US$4.4 million of 'humanitarian aid' to Mali, thought to be linked to the hostage case, found its way into the Swiss national budget. A total of US$12.4 million (or even just the US$8 million in cash) would have been a record ransom for four hostages for Al Qaeda in the Islamic Maghreb in 2009—but only three returned. In 2008, Austria had paid US$3.2 million for two hostages and in 2010 Spain paid US$5.9 million for three hostages to the same group.[23] Murdering Edwin Dyer had apparently paid off.

A similar tactic was employed by Abu Sayyaf in the Philippines. Operatives kidnapped two Canadians, a Philippine, and a Norwegian citizen in September 2015. The terrorist group beheaded the Canadians John Ridsdel and Robert Hall in April and June 2016 respectively, as their arbitrary 'deadlines' expired—with the Canadian government holding firm to its commitment not to negotiate with terrorists. The two other hostages, however, were eventually ransomed.[24] Although the ransoms were not publicly disclosed, private hostage negotiators complained bitterly that once again the ransom paid for the survivors did not penalize the kidnappers for murdering two of the original four hostages. 'Sadly, Abu Sayyaf learned the . . . lesson that you can kill half the hostages and still receive a record ransom payment. It was disgraceful.' Thus, if the remaining stakeholders respond to a murder by raising their offers faster and higher, the overall profit of the murderous kidnapper can rise. The improved ransoms of the remaining hostages more than offset the loss from murdering one.

If rebel and organized criminal groups make large territorial gains, they usually lack the resources to guard prisoners taken during their offensives and as they consolidate their rule. Most insurgencies leave death, destruction, and mass graves in their wake. Often the shocking scale of the slaughter is only revealed years later when the graves are found, exhumed, and forensically analysed. Some mass graves contain (uniformed) prisoners of war, while in others forensic scientists reveal the identity of civilians who resisted (or were suspected of opposing) rebel rule. Some contain the mortal remains of entire town or village populations, murdered (apparently) indiscriminately. Can mass murder serve an economic purpose? Kidnap for ransom is usually only a sideline business for groups intent on seizing territory. But the historical record clearly shows that throughout the ages, conquering armies have tended to spare and ransom rich prisoners of war, while putting the poor to the sword. People are only spared if the expected ransom exceeds the cost of feeding, guarding, and trading the hostage.[25] Meanwhile, a reputation for swiftly and indiscriminately executing captured 'enemies' persuades well-off stakeholders to rush forward immediately with sizeable ransoms to rescue their loved ones. This allows rebel groups operating outside their core territory to quickly identify prisoners that are worth keeping alive for ransoming (or political exploitation).

Some groups murder hostages with such apparent relish and inhumanity that one is inclined to write them off as 'nutters' or sadists, who derive personal pleasure from torturing others. For example, members of the Mexican drug cartel Los Zetas regularly make the headlines for barbaric murders and mutilations. Although the perpetrators may be sadists, Los Zetas can also be described as a highly successful, diversified, transnational business.[26] Terrorizing local business owners, honest administrators, politicians, and rivals with gratuitous, sadistic murders can be an effective strategy in gang warfare over lucrative smuggling and trafficking routes. As discussed in Chapter 2, ultimately the business model of mafias is extortion rather than kidnap for ransom. The Zetas' reputation for brutal mutilations and mass killings of hostages makes extortion easier. 'All someone has to do is say he is a Zeta, and the people will pay the extortion . . . because they already know what the Zetas are capable of.'[27] There may even be larger political prizes on the horizon. The annual death toll of the Mexican war on drugs runs into tens of thousands and many people now openly question the wisdom of their government's strategy.[28] The drug kingpins would probably value the improved security from a military draw-down.

Political Gains from Killing Hostages

Sometimes, the non-financial benefits of killing hostages exceeds their monetary value. Extreme political groupings often use kidnap and murder as a strategy to raise their local and international profile. Murders may be carried out for recruitment or fundraising purposes, for intimidation, or to force foreign governments to acknowledge a group's existence. Mass executions of local civilian hostages, suspected spies, and enemy fighters can be used to frighten target populations into submission, to accelerate the out-migration of targeted minorities, and to discourage collaboration with the government.

Some extremist groups also seek to extract political gains from murdering foreign hostages. The videos published by Al Qaeda and ISIL/ Daesh of beheading foreign hostages were intended to humiliate and confront Western governments with their inability to protect their own citizens. For some foreign hostages, kidnappers do not conduct meaningful negotiations. Even if some outrageous demands are made, the point is not to find a resolution but to escalate the situation and generate publicity. It is highly unlikely that the horrific and sadistic murder of the Jordanian fighter pilot Moaz al'Kasasbeh by ISIL/Daesh in 2015 could have been prevented by making concessions. The point was to demonstrate that ISIL/Daesh would gruesomely punish those who bombed its positions and opposed its rule. Although negotiations carried on throughout January 2015, no proof of life had been offered for several weeks. When the shocking video of al'Kasasbeh being burnt alive was released at the beginning of February, insiders surmised that the murder had in fact taken place several weeks previously.[29] Similarly, the Japanese hostages Kenji Goto and Haruna Yukawa were murdered shortly after the Japanese government pledged US$200 million in financial support for the military coalition fighting ISIL/Daesh. It was clear from the outset that ISIL/Daesh's demand of a matching US$200 million ransom was highly unlikely to be met within the announced seventy-two-hour deadline.[30]

Only one of the five US hostages held by ISIL/Daesh was ransomed: the group seemed determined to punish this group of hostages for holding US passports. Fellow captives reported that James Foley was singled out for beatings by his captors because his brother was known to be in the US Air Force.[31] When ISIL/Daesh contacted Peter Kassig's parents, the demand was US$100 million—and the release of all Muslim prisoners in the world. As his mother said: 'Like that was something we were going to be able to do.'[32] The theatrical staging of the executions of US and UK hostages further underlines the political motivation for their murders. Yet, groups that focus on maximizing the political impact of killing some hostages usually also have other hostages, where a monetary resolution is pursued. Of a group of twenty-three foreign prisoners held in the same ISIL/Daesh prison, six British and US hostages were murdered, but sixteen hostages of various other nationalities were ransomed by their governments.[33] As already discussed, a strategy of publicly and gruesomely murdering some hostages for political purposes may help to raise the financial return on other hostages held by the group, whose stakeholders are more forthcoming.

Security Gains from Killing Hostages

Hostages are used as human shields by rebel groups. In the event of a rescue attempt, prize hostages are often deliberately killed by their captors. Unless a group has a proven track record of killing hostages when attacked, prominent hostages pose great dangers (as well as huge opportunities) for their jailers. Political authorization for military rescue missions depends crucially on the probability that a live hostage can be retrieved. This probability (and its perception) can be manipulated by the kidnappers. For example, the Colombian FARC rebels publicized and repeatedly proved their policy of immediately shooting all hostages whenever armed troops approached one of their camps.[34] If the armed forces know that they are dealing with 'nutters, who are ready to go down with their ship', their tactics change. The successful liberation of the FARC's celebrity hostage Ingrid Betancourt and three American contractors only succeeded because the group holding them was tricked into handing them over to an allied rebel group—who turned out to be soldiers in disguise.[35] 'Fire and awe' approaches put the hostages at great risk of murder. Pierre Korkie and Luke Somers were fatally shot by their Yemeni captors as US Special Operations commandoes attacked their camp.[36] Similarly, Boko Haram kidnappers shot their hostages Chris McManus and Franco Lamolinara when a joint British/Nigerian rescue party arrived in their compound.[37] In the Philippines, the Al Qaeda-affiliated Abu Sayyaf group murdered the American hostage Guillermo Sobero to stave off a military 'search and destroy' mission.[38] His fellow captive, Martin Burnham, was killed the following year as the rescue party burst into the group's jungle camp.[39] Even Somali pirates ratcheted up the violence in response to hostage rescue missions, killing four American sailors in 2011 as a US warship approached the scene.[40] Given the twin dangers of friendly fire and last-minute revenge killings by the captors, rescue missions are therefore usually only authorized if there is reliable intelligence that the hostages' lives are in immediate danger already.[41]

Finally, murder may be the best way of preserving the kidnappers' anonymity. If the hostage has information that could lead to the gang's apprehension and capture, hostages are sometimes killed—usually after a concession has been extracted. This happens mostly in areas where governments have partial territorial control and are willing to challenge local criminals and mafias. If armed forces can access and investigate a location described by a released hostage and make arrests, the risk of releasing them rises. If there is no powerful mafia governing the behaviour of criminal gangs and controlling entry into the kidnapping business, there will be more inexperienced, myopic kidnappers making the kind of elementary mistakes that makes killing a hostage optimal—and they won't face extra-legal sanctions for doing so, either. In addition, opportunists without the experience and infrastructure to conduct extended ransom negotiations are also the most likely to make irrational decisions and murder hostages in anger or out of fear. It is not surprising that more than 30,000 people have 'disappeared' in Mexico since the start of the war on drugs in 2006.[42] Where different groups fight over territorial control, no one is in a position to order the market for hostages.

Politics in Hostage Negotiations

Most of the examples of the hostage deaths described in this chapter had a very clear political dimension. This is not accidental. In criminal kidnap for ransom cases, handled by professionals on behalf of insurers, I was reassured many times that 'murder is not part of the strategy'. Illness, dejection, anger, and fear can mostly be managed. Beyond a few tragic accidents, my interviewees had little personal experience to contribute on this topic. Instead, all of them pointed to 'terrorist' kidnap for ransom as the area where negotiations end in tears and disaster. This raises an important question: are terrorist organizations intrinsically different from organizations that are not (yet) on the list of proscribed organizations? Or—do terrorist cases go wrong because they are handled in a different way, by less-experienced negotiators with a different set of constraints and incentives? Does the fact that there is political interest convey unhelpful information to the kidnappers? Let us look at what happens when politicians get involved in criminal cases first—and then at how professional negotiators fared against terrorist organizations.

Governments Negotiating with Criminals

Stakeholders are often tempted to raise the profile of their hostage by soliciting political support or creating media pressure that encourages politicians to help broker a release. Kidnappers generally welcome it when local, regional, or international power brokers take a personal interest in a hostage negotiation. Official interventions—whether undertaken out of personal concern, empathy, or for political gain—are taken as a credible signal that the hostage is a VIP and ransom expectations escalate. Politicians usually face significant pressure to resolve a case quickly— leading kidnappers to entrench themselves more firmly. Occasionally, hostage negotiators have more than one customer kidnapped by the same group at the same time. Such parallel cases can take very different courses if a local politician personally expresses support for one of the hostages (or even worse tries to mediate). Invariably, the politicized cases take longer to settle, are more violent, and/or result in a higher ransom payment. If the criminal opposition is not used to negotiating with governments (or is under time pressure anyway) a premium ransom brokered by officials can lead to a quick release—but such successes are unlikely to be repeatable. A family, firm, or nation that pays premium ransoms makes its members, employees, or citizens attractive targets. The next time, the kidnappers will probe some more—or sell the hostage on to someone who can. If premium ransoms reset kidnapper expectations across the board, they can have dramatic consequences for future kidnap victims.

This is well illustrated by the ransom negotiations between the Spanish government and Somali pirates. In April 2008, Somali pirates hijacked the Spanish fishing trawler *Playa di Bakio* with a crew of thirteen Spanish nationals from the Basque region and thirteen Africans. With Basque fisheries in serious financial difficulty and political arguments over a potential referendum aimed at increased autonomy for the troubled region, Spanish officials swung into diplomatic action. Within a week the vessel was released for a ransom of US$1.2 million—an unprecedented amount for a fishing trawler.[43] It may have been a political necessity, but Spanish trawlers were now an obvious high-value target. When a further Basque trawler—the *Alakrana*—was hijacked in October 2009, the cries of 'save our fishermen' were duly repeated. Yet this time, the negotiations took forty-seven days, with death threats against the crew to pressure the Spanish government to release two recently captured pirates. This concession was avoided, but the case set a further record for a trawler at around US$3.5 million. Prime Minister Zapatero jubilantly announced the 'very good news' of the *Alakrana*'s release, claiming that his 'government did what it had to do'.[44] Unwittingly, he had unleashed a monster. If a rusty fishing trawler is worth US$3.5 million, what is a reasonable price for a cargo ship or tanker? Is there anything more lucrative than maritime piracy in Somalia? With ever more Somali entrepreneurs redeploying their skiffs and skills into hijacking, escalating ransoms, and supporting lengthy negotiations, hijack for ransom was no longer profitable to insure. It took the combined efforts of private security companies, a massive naval counter-piracy initiative, and a substantial investment in strengthening judicial capacity in the region to turn the tide against Somali pirates.[45]

The Spanish government does not bear the sole blame for the explosion of Somali piracy. As discussed in Chapters 6 and 7, impatient ship-owners, media campaigns, and other governments also helped to re-educate pirates about the value Western ship-owners put on the safe return of their ships, crew, and cargo. The ransoms paid for the Basque trawlers merely serve as an illustration how difficult it is to contain expectations if negotiations are conducted by people who do not have demonstrable budget constraints, could make a variety of political as well as financial concessions, are desperate to avoid casualties, and want to conclude quickly. For this reason, it is unusual for politicians to get involved in criminal kidnap for ransom cases—apart from the occasional kind-hearted (and generally counterproductive) interventions of local politicians on behalf of their constituents. Overall, there seems to be an understanding that the private sector achieves superior results. It therefore seems anomalous that in the most sensitive kidnap cases—when hostages are held by terrorists—the private sector is deliberately sidelined.

Private vs Public Resolutions in Terrorist Kidnaps

Several UN Security Council resolutions explicitly forbid the funding of terrorism by making financial transfers to proscribed organizations.[46] Although kidnap insurance is available in areas where terrorist groups are known to operate, professional negotiators cannot offer a monetary concession if there is any cause to suspect that all or part of the ransom will benefit a terrorist organization. The point of reference is the regularly updated record of UN-proscribed organizations and individuals: 'The List established and maintained pursuant to Security Council res. 1267/1989/2253'.[47] Which organizations are included on the list is subject to (sometimes heated) political debate. Some regimes are quick to unilaterally declare political opposition groups as 'terrorists'. It would be terribly convenient to cut off their income from foreign and diaspora supporters by including them on the UN's list. Conversely, if unsavoury groups terrorize the local population but control access to lucrative natural resources, companies trading with them may lobby governments to prevent their listing.

Although some organizations have been proscribed for many years (e.g. Al Qaeda and its affiliates were proscribed in 2001), many governments turned a blind eye to ransom payments. In 2013, however, the political mood changed. The British Prime Minister David Cameron put the issue in the spotlight at the G7 summit at Lough Erne. As he criticized other governments for funding terrorists with multi-million-dollar ransoms, he in turn was slated for Lloyd's insurers facilitating a steady trickle of ransoms to all manner of criminal and militant organizations around the globe. The Lough Erne communiqué of June 2013 affirmed the G7 leaders' commitment to ending ransom payments to proscribed organizations.[48] The UN Security Council adopted Resolution 2133 tackling kidnap for ransom in 2014.[49] In return for other countries' support on the issue, the UK government set out to make its own counter-terrorism law more explicit: 'We want to make it clear to the market that insurers will not reimburse ransom payments made to terrorists under any circumstances. This change will create a new offence which will explicitly prohibit the reimbursement of a payment which they know or have reasonable cause to suspect has been made in response to a terrorist demand.'[50] The UK 2014 Counter-terrorism law applies extra-territorially and includes reinsurance, so that ransom payments cannot be insured via foreign companies who could legally insure ransoms under their own domestic laws.[51] We can therefore examine how negotiations changed when expert crisis responders stepped back from commercial resolutions and bureaucrats and politicians took over.[52]

The Abu Sayyaf group in the Philippines is an interesting example. The group has used kidnap for ransom as a fundraising strategy since its inception in the 1980s. Philippine officials estimate that 90 per cent of the group's funding (around US$35 million between 1992 and 2007) came from kidnapping activities. The proceeds were used to fund the group's highly mobile fighter units conducting raids, assassinations, and bombing campaigns against government and business targets.[53] Although most of Abu Sayyaf's victims were local, crisis responders occasionally acted on behalf of local and international businesses, unlucky tourists, and sailors taken hostage in Abu Sayyaf's piracy operations. Although Abu Sayyaf negotiators knew that other affiliates of Al Qaeda regularly obtained multi-million-dollar ransoms from foreign governments, the private bargaining protocol in the Philippines maintained ransom discipline. Barring attempted rescue missions, foreign hostages were usually released regardless of their governments' (informal) stances on making concessions to terrorists. With Australian and American hostages it is politically awkward to talk about ransoms, but if the 'compensations' for the hostages' board and lodging were revealed, they were in the low six figures. The last set of ransoms one of my interviewees negotiated under the private regime returned a group of hostages for around US$85,000 each.

The very next release, however, blew the low ransom equilibrium apart. In October 2014 Abu Sayyaf received US$5.6 million for the release of two German sailors snatched from their yacht the previous April.[54] Private negotiators hung their heads in despair. How could the families of the Dutch birdwatcher Ewold Horn (kidnapped in 2012) and the Japanese treasure hunter Mamaito Katayama (kidnapped in 2010) possibly meet ransom expectations of a different order of magnitude? Would Abu Sayyaf now change their stance on nationals whose government refused to pay ransoms? Indeed, having failed to draw the Canadian government into a meaningful ransom negotiation for their hostages

John Ridsdel and Robert Hall, Abu Sayyaf copied the tactics of other jihadist groups. Instead of waiting to see whether a private arrangement could be made for the Canadians, they were beheaded. By all accounts, the ransom for their fellow captive, the Norwegian Kjartan Sekkingstad, provided ample compensation.

In Yemen, private negotiators had a long-established network to peacefully settle tribal kidnaps on behalf of businessmen and aid workers. Most could be resolved with a minor political concession, a developmental initiative within the community, or a five-figure ransom. However, with Al Qaeda negotiating ransoms more than two orders of magnitude higher than this, tribal leaders are now better off selling their hostages on.[55] The kidnapping of Edwin Dyer and his travelling companions in Mali had also been carried out by a group of nomadic Tuareg, but the hostages were soon passed on to Al Qaeda. With a political dimension and the Swiss government on the phone, the ransom could be escalated.[56] Once in the hands of a jihadist organization, the victims' outcomes are influenced by their nationality. Hostages from OECD countries whose governments refuse to get involved in ransom negotiations have a significantly higher probability of being killed than hostages from nations that are known to make concessions.[57]

This empirical regularity has led to an interesting twist. Following the public shock and outcry over the beheading of the journalist Daniel Pearl by Al Qaeda in Pakistan in February 2002, the US administration was determined to do 'everything possible to prevent a second Daniel Pearl'.[58] When the CBS journalist Jere van Dyk was kidnapped in the remote tribal areas of Pakistan 2008, his case was scrupulously kept out of the media. Although Mr van Dyk was certain that he had been kidnapped by Islamic extremists, he was repeatedly assured that he had been abducted by a criminal group, not the Taliban. On pressing further, he was told that his captors were 'criminals disguised as the Taliban to confuse [him]'. Mr van Dyk was not convinced. His kidnappers' religious zeal had been so manifest, their preaching so insistent, their religious observance so sincere. 'It sounds like they played their role very well', was the deadpan answer.[59] There is—of course—an excellent reason for this bizarre charade. As long as there was no definitive proof that the kidnappers were affiliated with the Taliban, Mr van Dyk's employers could pursue a private resolution through their insurance company. His life was saved.

Similarly, the British government conducted a detailed review of whether the Al Shabaab group benefitted financially from Somali piracy. Conclusive evidence that ransoms were paid to or shared with a proscribed organization would have ended commercial resolutions. This would have put hijacked ships, crews, and cargoes at massive risk. Ship-owners therefore lobbied for maintaining the 'criminal' regime: 'In a commercial sense, we would rather there was minimum government involvement in the negotiation process. They can help where help is called for, but generally we get it, we understand it, we have a process, and, on a commercial level, it works.'[60] Independent experts involved in the consultation process remember not being pressed particularly hard to provide evidence for a piracy–Al Shabaab link. Thus, although some hijacked ships were anchored in areas controlled by Al Shabaab and locals knew that pirates paid non-interference fees to the group,[61] the Foreign and Commonwealth Office concluded that piracy was essentially a criminal activity.[62] Business as usual then.

Governments Negotiating with Terrorists

The idea behind the UN ban on paying ransoms to terrorists was that proscribed groups would (eventually) stop kidnapping for fundraising purposes. The reduced funding would be reflected in fewer subsequent terrorist acts. Unfortunately, this is not quite how the policy is implemented in practice. As discussed previously, governments differ greatly in their attitude towards making concessions to save their citizens' lives.

The US and the UK government mostly keep to their commitment of not negotiating with terrorists, arguing that a reputation for not paying ransoms will reduce the attractiveness of their citizens as kidnap targets. However, there are exceptions to the rule: occasionally, even the US government negotiates with terrorists. In a controversial deal, Sgt Bowe Bergdahl was released from Taliban captivity in exchange for five prisoners from Guantanamo Bay after nearly five years in captivity.[63] Even if the government is not prepared to engage, there may still be a private resolution. A large majority of citizens agree that in principle it is wrong to pay ransoms to terrorists—but a majority also admits that they would pay a ransom to retrieve a loved one.[64] The uneasy political compromise was that although ransom payments are illegal, neither the US nor the UK government have rushed to prosecute families for privately negotiating with proscribed groups. Officially, however, US families were warned that they might be prosecuted for trying to ransom their loved ones. Such ambiguity can be helpful: if stakeholders are convinced (or can pretend) that they must raise the ransom under the radar of law enforcement, kidnapper expectations will be much lower. Yet, after the

Foley family's despondency and their forceful complaints about the conflicting advice they received, President Obama clarified the position and officially granted immunity from prosecution to families.[65] This opens the door for large-scale fundraising for hostages. Perhaps this will save American hostages' lives—but it completely undermines the stance that US citizens should be 'worthless' as kidnap targets.

Despite these inelegant compromises, there is some evidence that in recent years fewer US and British citizens have been abducted compared to other nationalities.[66] However, this is likely to largely reflect personal decisions (if you think that your passport is a 'death warrant' you will reconsider non-essential travel) and changes in corporate policy. Interviews with NGOs operating in, or close to, areas where designated terrorist groups operate reveal that they take the nationality of their staff members and the approach taken by their home countries towards hostage negotiations into account when deciding on the composition of their local teams.[67] When Jere van Dyk insisted on travelling back to Afghanistan and Pakistan to investigate his own kidnapping, his employer, CBS News, told him that he could not say that he worked for them and eventually ended his contract.[68] Where US and UK citizens are 'non-deployable', the composition of available kidnap targets shifts towards nations whose governments are more inclined to broker deals with terrorists.

The UN regime on banning concessions to terrorists is therefore a paper tiger. In the press release accompanying UN resolution 2133 the Argentinian representative notes that the ban on ransom payments 'should not undermine the possible payment of ransom for hostages'. This is an odd interpretation of a resolution intended 'to prevent terrorists from benefiting directly or indirectly from ransom payments or political concessions'.[69] Unwilling to see their citizens humiliated and gruesomely murdered on video, several governments choose to prioritize the immediate preservation of life over other policy goals.[70] Currently, there is no way of punishing UN member states for disregarding their obligations under the ban. Even though they may be quietly fuming over the latest record ransom, politicians and diplomats generally refrain from 'naming and shaming' their allies. Yet the *New York Times* accused several continental European nations of 'bankrolling Al Qaeda', calculating that the terror group and its direct affiliates received at least US$125 million from various governments in exchange for twenty-two foreign hostages.[71] ISIL/Daesh made between US$35–45 million in the year to September 2014.[72] What explains these huge ransoms?

Why Governments Overpay

When government officials negotiate ransoms, they are unlikely to have comparable experience to private negotiators. Most Western governments regularly rotate civil servants between jobs, so it is rare that one person leads on several comparable incidents during his or her time in post. Unlike private negotiators, officials first have to collect information on the past modus operandi of the opposition and potential intermediaries. Not all of the information may be conclusive, reliable, or up to date. For outsiders, it is often difficult to interpret. Officials will have diplomatic contacts in the relevant country. They will receive many offers of help—solicited and otherwise. They need to find out who might have a bearing on the case and who is trying to insert themselves for private gain. Informal contracting with intermediaries is difficult, because with one-off or infrequent interactions, the shadow of the future is weak. One high-profile foreign hostage was beheaded because the person chosen to deliver the ransom decided to deliver only half of it to the militant group and keep the other half as his 'cut'. The group's leader was so furious about the apparent insult that he snapped. The government had lost both the ransom money and the hostage (but only admitted the latter).

Officials are likely to be aware of the convention of the offer curve of diminishing marginal returns described in Chapter 6, but to construct a plausible curve one needs a credible target ransom. Inexperienced negotiators may not know the local conventions regarding the initial demand: do kidnappers generally settle at around 10, 20, or 50 per cent of the initial offer? Often, civil servants are not aware of private sector ransom settlements but look at previous government-negotiated ransoms as their reference point. This creates ideal conditions for ransom inflation and spillovers among different regions.

Whatever negotiators signal as their maximum ransom, it will be tested. For a family or firm, there is an obvious point at which resources are exhausted. A politician's ransom fund is more fungible: money could be transferred from another budget to avoid the unthinkable. So, what is the absolute ransom limit for an OECD government? Unless the opposition is short of time, there will be significant probing at whatever level was set. How will a bureaucrat react to a long period of silence? How seriously should one take a threat of torture or murder? How should a government react when the threat is carried out? A family approaching their limit cannot offer a massive increment on hearing that a fellow captive was murdered. The killed captive's stakeholders withdraw from the negotiation. However, a civil servant negotiating over the release of, say, four captives cannot credibly impose a financial penalty for murdering one of them. There is no plausible reason to argue that 25 per cent of the previously offered ransom is no longer available because there are now fewer hostages. There are thus no downsides to murdering hostages—but potentially huge upsides if the negotiators raise their offer to save those that remain. Unlike the private crisis response consultant, the civil servant does not face negative career consequences for letting a ransom drift upwards.

Politicians who made the decision to engage in a negotiation in the first place will also care more about their citizens coming to grief than about a higher than average ransom. Hopefully, the next ransom will be another government's problem. It does not help that these negotiations are often conducted in the media spotlight. Even with careful management of press coverage, the internet makes it possible to circumvent national attempts to keep a case largely out of the public consciousness. Begging videos and pictures can be released via unregulated channels. It is extremely difficult to maintain a stance that completely reassures voters at home that their government cares deeply about the fate of its citizens, while at the same time conveying the uncaring attitude that convinces the kidnappers to lower their demand.

Unlike the insurers fearing the reaction of their peers in the Lloyd's underwriting room, governments have not faced significant censure for paying premium ransoms. Usually the payment of a ransom is denied point-blank anyway. Some governments prefer that negotiations are conducted at arm's length by a regional power-broker—who may be officially instructed not to pay a ransom. Theo Curtis (aka Theo Padnos), the only US hostage freed by ISIL/Daesh, was released after mediation by Qatar.[73] Details of the deal are shrouded in mystery, but it is unlikely that ISIL/Daesh gave up a hostage without a concession. Qatar is thought to have brokered several deals with ISIL/Daesh, as well as being involved in the deal that brought Sgt Bowe Bergdahl back from the Taliban.[74] Previously, Colonel Gaddafi of Libya was similarly active in the market for 'political' hostages: a whole stream of foreign hostages was released to Tripoli.[75] Finnish, French, German, and South African former hostages were paraded in front of television cameras to thank the Gaddafi Charitable Foundation for their freedom. Any questions about ransoms or concessions were batted away. In West Africa, the Malian government brokered a number of hostage deals with Al Qaeda in the Islamic Maghreb over the years.[76] Meanwhile, neighbouring governments such as Algeria came to resent these interventions, as rebels have invested the cash into military assets.[77] None of these opaque arm's length arrangements are likely to engender ransom discipline:

the diplomatic payoff is triggered by the safe release of the hostages. Any awkward financial transfers can be hidden in the development aid budget or some other political sweetener.

A Counterproductive Policy

The partial observation of the UN ban on paying ransoms to terrorists has thus greatly enhanced the payoff to hostage-taking for proscribed organizations. In the private, insured regime, kidnappers negotiate with cash-constrained families and firms, advised by experienced, well-informed, and calm experts. There is only one dimension for bargaining: money. Private entities cannot make major political concessions. The system creates strong incentives for ransom discipline: the stakeholders have a ransom limit, negotiators are evaluated on their performance in containing ransoms as well as safely returning hostages, and insurance syndicates have to account for outlier ransoms vis-à-vis their peers. Coordination and information sharing ensures that the expected financial return on torture and murder is negative. Usually, ransoms do not encourage copycat acts across the criminal spectrum: if high ransoms are paid the kidnappers 'earned' the money in lengthy, high-risk negotiations.

By contrast, the public regime is characterized by a lack of information, soft budget constraints, nervous negotiators operating with unclear performance criteria, and a lack of accountability. Due to the absence of a coordination mechanism, murdering (low-value) hostages can have positive financial impact on ongoing and subsequent negotiations—even when the cost of additional rescue attempts is considered. If the kidnappers' negotiators are more experienced than the people acting on behalf of the hostages, psychological tension is deliberately escalated. This encourages stakeholders to pursue short-term emotional and political objectives rather than the long-term public interest. We can no longer assume a rational choice framework for decision making.

In mixed regimes, where desperate families, insurers, and public-sector agents operate in parallel, it is extremely costly for insurers to contain the impact of premium ransoms funded by governments. Inspired by multi-million-dollar settlements for government-negotiated ransoms, criminal kidnappers redouble their efforts to abduct foreigners and do not want to settle for paltry five- and six-figure ransoms. Families forced to seek a private resolution cannot hope to match state-funded ransoms—whether or not they have insurance. Sooner or later, the 'terrorist' and 'criminal' markets intermingle. With the right incentives, a secondary market for hostages develops: whoever is in the position to extract the highest ransom will outbid other buyers. For a proscribed organization, a French or Italian hostage may be the ultimate prize, whereas UK and US hostages may be more valuable to 'criminal' gangs. Alternatively, relatively low-value hostages may be tortured and murdered to improve terrorist kidnappers' bargaining positions in parallel and subsequent negotiations. If local rivalries preclude a market for hostages, there are many other options to blur the distinctions: raiding rivals to steal hostages (hostage-rustling?), pretending to be terrorist (or criminal), and careful political decisions on how to label the opposition. Thus, the current, partially observed UN ban has raised the returns to kidnapping and puts hostage lives at risk. Many areas of the world are no longer accessible to travellers, businesspeople, journalists, and even aid workers.

Who Should Govern 'Political' Kidnap for Ransom?

When we think of kidnap for ransom, usually the tragic cases come to mind first: the murdered, the disappeared, those who succumbed to sickness, the unfortunate victims of failed rescue missions, and those languishing in unknown misery for years. This chapter has showed that every ransom negotiation can end in tears. Yet, in professionally conducted negotiations disastrous outcomes are almost always avoided. Families and firms negotiating without professional support are more likely to fail at some stage of the transaction: negotiating the ransom, preventing escape or rescue attempts, paying the money to the right addressee, or retrieving the hostage. But the dreadful hostage murders etched onto our minds are mostly associated with 'political' kidnappings.

Rather than considering 'political kidnapping' as a distinct type of kidnapping, I have looked at it from an economic point of view. If potentially lucrative trades regularly fail, we must ask whether we have inadvertently generated a set of perverse incentives. Indeed, I have shown that even without invoking intangible political gains or psychological disorders, kidnappers who negotiate directly with governments can improve their terms of trade through 'torture for reputation'. I contrasted the framework under which professional crisis response companies make their decisions with that of civil servants. In the private resolution scenario, hostage-takers are rewarded for cooperation and punished for murder. By contrast, civil servants and diplomats would struggle to impose financial penalties for uncooperative behaviour— and have no personal incentive to do so. As long as some governments make politically opportune concessions, maiming and killing hostages can pay significant dividends.

It is therefore important that governments consider carefully whether a policy of direct (or indirect) engagement with kidnappers of any type truly serves the national interest. Does publicly insuring the (mis)adventures of citizens in complex and hostile territories create moral hazard and hence a higher-than-optimal amount of non-essential travel? The sailor Jürgen Kantner who was hijacked in the treacherous Sulu Sea and murdered by Abu Sayyaf had previously been ransomed from Somali pirates by the German government.[78] Did he feel too safe? Does a reputation for paying premium ransoms lead kidnappers to specifically target one's citizens? Are government-facilitated ransoms really the only way of safeguarding the country's business interests? Could the private sector achieve better outcomes at a fraction of the cost? What are the ethical implications of funding groups that terrorize the populations under their direct control?[79] And what are the implications for national security if well-funded terrorist groups send their operatives to conduct terror attacks abroad? As ISIL/Daesh has proved with its series of attacks on European soil, this final consideration is no longer purely academic.

Unless every government comes to the conclusion that it is truly in the national interest to refrain from paying ransoms (or causing ransoms to be paid on their behalf), the UN ban on ransoms should also be questioned. The ban was intended to cut off an important funding source for terrorist groups and thereby end political kidnap for ransom. Instead, by sidelining the private governance architecture ordering the market for hostages, it has led to the escalation of ransoms. We are now in a situation where the dangers of being kidnapped (and killed) are so acute in the regions where proscribed groups operate that they are effectively no-go areas for OECD (and especially US and UK) citizens without military protection or private security guards.

A comprehensive ransom ban would be the best solution for kidnaps carried out by proscribed organizations. However, a partially observed ban is worse than a well-governed private sector solution for everyone.[80] If it was legal to do so, crisis responders would help families to negotiate and pay ransoms to 'bad people'. They would do so to safeguard treasured lives—at a price that ensures no supernormal returns to kidnapping. If ransoms just reimburse costs, we do not buy our loved ones back at the price of countless innocents slaughtered in the next wave of terror attacks.

11

Debrief

Two expatriate oil surveyors were travelling alone by car along an unfamiliar road when they were stopped at a roadblock. Criminals, who were using the roadblock as a trap to rob passers-by, decided to up the ante when they recognised two foreigners and kidnapped the pair. One surveyor was released along with a $5m ransom demand to take back to the company. The company selected its own security consultant, who was inexperienced and unfamiliar with the territory. The demand of $5m was ultimately paid. However, the negotiation of the safe return of the other employee took almost a year. Ransom payment $5m, Expenses $500,000.

Chubb, 'Kidnap Ransom and Extortion', claims examples[1]

An employee of a multinational mineral extraction company . . . was kidnapped by a group of armed men whilst travelling to a local site . . . Fortunately, the victim was not in possession of information that would have identified his status as a member of the local senior management team and at once began to convince the kidnappers that they had made an error. The kidnappers subsequently . . . found that [his car] was registered to the company. The . . . victim . . . maintained that he was employed as a junior administrative employee and entrusted with the maintenance of the company's fleet of vehicles. During the negotiation process it became evident to the [crisis response] consultant that the kidnappers were not fully aware of whom they had abducted and this paved the way for a negotiating strategy . . . The victim was held for a period of a few days and released after a small ransom was exchanged.

Red24, 'Case Study: Kidnapping in Brazil'[2]

Kidnapping is an intuitively attractive business proposition, wherever there are significant income disparities, easily accessible targets, and a low probability of apprehension and punishment. However, the market for hostages is only profitable where there is governance: norms regarding hostage treatment, protocols or service providers to facilitate the trade, and institutions that encourage all market participants to adhere to the rules. For local hostages in areas outside the reach of law enforcement, such governance institutions often arise spontaneously: kidnappers realize that a reputation for adhering to cooperative norms lowers their own transaction costs and thereby raises their profits. If less bright, short-sighted, or mentally unstable kidnappers defect from the rules and undermine not just the market for hostages but broader economic activity in an area, local elites or the rulers of the economic underworld may choose to intervene and call them to order. If it is in the private interest of insurgents, mafias, or warlords to stop kidnapping in exchange for protection money, they will.

However, when kidnap victims are foreigners, employees of foreign firms, or local VIPs the stakes rise and self-governance can break down—with potentially disastrous consequences for kidnap victims and their loved ones. This book has analysed the private governance system created by a small group of special risks insurers at Lloyd's to order the tricky market for transnational hostages. Kidnap insurance and its related services are extraordinarily successful in managing the risks of operating or travelling in areas where governments are unable to protect their own citizens and struggle to protect foreign investors, expatriates, and travellers. Mandatory security advice and hands-on security management succeed in preventing most abductions of at-risk personnel. When a kidnap occurs, there is an entire infrastructure to facilitate the safe retrieval of the hostage. This is the immediate and absolute priority for anyone working in the industry. But for a stable market, the safe return of one hostage cannot be bought at the expense of putting others at risk. Ransom discipline is therefore paramount.

Counterintuitively, ransom discipline generally also helps the victim: when kidnappers realize that serious money is at stake they redouble their efforts or sell the hostage on to someone who can really put the squeeze on the stakeholders. The two case studies at the start of the chapter illustrate this. The victim in the first case was badly let down by his company. Even though the management was prepared to be magnanimous over the ransom and expenses, it took nearly a year to free him. One also wonders whether the company's employees ever travelled on that remote road again. The second kidnap victim knew or suspected that there was insurance, but he also knew how the hostage market works. He trusted that the kidnappers would not want to upset his company by maltreating or killing him and that he would be safe—even if he claimed that he wasn't worth very much. He helped his company to drive a hard bargain and returned home safely after a few days.

I end this book by offering four reflections: for those who fear they might be kidnapped; for those who are negotiating the release of a hostage or are desperately hoping for somebody's safe return; for policymakers; and on the nature and power of private governance.

Considerations for Potential Kidnap Victims

Ideally, employees are unaware of any insurance taken out on their behalf. However, if people suspect they may be insured, they can use that information wisely. If employees are posted abroad by a firm that is accountable to shareholders, due legal processes, and the media, it is their employers' duty to keep them safe. The chance of being kidnapped on routine business is therefore minimal. If you are given security advice, choose to follow it. If you are told to evacuate, assume that local protection arrangements are no longer secure: it's time to leave. If you have a moral objection to any form of protection money being paid to whichever (corrupt or tyrannical) government, rebel movement, or trigger-happy bullies control a territory, don't go. You may also wish to carefully examine the goods you buy.[3]

If people are abducted by a group deemed to be 'criminal', it is extremely likely that they will be freed. In the meantime, hostages have a choice whether to cooperate with the kidnapper, or the people trying to bring them home safely. In whose interest is it to volunteer the information that your sister is engaged to the nephew of a business tycoon, or that your company has just doubled its operating profit? Whenever a ransom is raised there is a moral dilemma: criminals, rebels, and terrorists are likely to invest their profits in activities that harm innocent third parties. Helping kidnappers to raise cash to step up the oppression of locals or conduct further kidnaps or hijackings is ethically problematic.[4] However, the market for kidnap insurance is based on there being no supernormal returns: in equilibrium, kidnappers just break even. So, if a crisis responder is working hard to barter your jailers down to US$30,000, should you tell your kidnapper that you are 'insured for a million'? If you do, be prepared for a long negotiation and a higher than necessary ransom—which (by the terms of the contract) you are probably no longer insured for.

Recommendations for Worried Stakeholders

It should be completely clear that this book is not a DIY manual on how to negotiate a ransom. Some aspects of the industry protocol for ransom negotiations could be imitated—for example interrupted negotiations, stalling in response to threats, and sending clear signals that financial resources are limited. However, without information on the kidnappers' likely target ransom, it is impossible to develop a strategy to ensure the safe return of the hostage while minimizing the return to crime and the incentive to kidnap again. If the ransom offers are too low, the victim is in danger and the negotiation proceeds at a snail's pace. If the offers are too high or the increments erratic, convergence is also delayed. Paying a premium ransom can put many more people at risk. If kidnapping is profitable more people will be targeted and the family members, co-workers, and co-nationals of the original hostage will become preferred victims. Criminal or insurgent groups flush with cash are likely to invest ransoms in activities that harm innocent third parties.

Professionally conducted ransom negotiations are successful because they are based on the best possible information on target ransoms and kidnapper tactics, drawn from a highly experienced, close-knit group of specialists. The best negotiators are outstanding problem solvers and lateral thinkers. They empathize and build rapport with the stakeholders, to guide them through what is probably the most stressful transaction of their lives. Most negotiators have years of elite military training and experience. They can cope with the pressure of extended conflict situations and many thrive on it. They know the criminal mindset and are aware of the opposition's tactics from their own past cases, from negotiations handled within their firm, and from their peers. These skills come at a price—but insurers are happy to cover this cost for their customers. This implies that looking elsewhere is likely to be a false economy. 'It's just a negotiation... why should this be the preserve of military people?' asked one of my interviewees. But with a track record of letting ransoms escalate without producing early releases, he was on the margins of the business, scouting for the next job. I hope he has now changed career, but without an accreditation system, anyone can offer their services as a ransom negotiator. *Caveat emptor*—buyer beware.

For those observing a professionally conducted ransom negotiation from the sidelines, the process can be puzzling, frustrating, and very frightening. I hope this book has explained why some negotiations are protracted—especially where the ransom equilibrium has previously been upset by impatient negotiators. If the press reports news that flies in the face of human decency or contradicts private evidence: remember that the intended audience may be the kidnappers. Millionaires who disown close family members and long-serving employees, well-known firms reporting sudden financial difficulties, and NGOs that appear to abandon their staff may simply be trying to establish a better negotiating position. Alternatively, such press reports may originate with the kidnappers—trying to shame their counterparty and manipulate more people into contributing to the ransom. If faced with this situation, it's best to think twice about whose purpose a well-meant intervention serves. A scandal or a heart-rending appeal for donations can sell newspapers, but it will also derail the negotiation until the dust settles. Philanthropists occasionally offer to make substantial contributions to retrieve high-profile hostages, but if the kidnappers find out about it, that money is simply incorporated into a revised ransom demand— without achieving anything.

Lobbying the government to take action—and to be seen to take action—is probably the worst possible reaction to a kidnap incident. Yes, the government can (probably) 'Save Our Seafarers!' It has the resources to ransom those that are currently unlawfully detained—but at the price of putting a bull's eye target on other nationals exposed to kidnap risks. If governments do any good at all in the market for hostages, it is because they remain entirely behind the scenes.

Ideas for Public Policy

Scholars of private polycentric governance tend to be enthusiastic about the ingenuity of human beings and the intricate and beautifully adapted systems they create in very difficult circumstances. The system that I have analysed here is particularly interesting in that it has been hidden in plain view for the last forty years. In fact, much of it has even been hidden from the people who helped to create it. It is my hope that, having found out about it, politicians and bureaucrats will recognize its powers and will think very carefully about when to intervene personally on behalf of hostages. If politicians decide that they must interfere, there are options for damage limitation: principally, not getting caught and employing the best private service providers to deal with the most dangerous and volatile opposition. Beware of the well-meaning but inexperienced consultants that did not make the cut in the crisis response world.

In international politics, leaders and opinion-makers should revisit the UN ban on ransom payments to terrorists. Most governments do not want to fund and fuel terrorism and a complete ban on ransom payments would achieve this objective. But as long as some countries intervene on behalf of their citizens, the current ban has unintended and counterproductive consequences. In paying premium ransoms, governments put lives at risk while increasing terrorist funding. Until a strong international consensus emerges to forbid ransom payments that benefit terrorist organizations under *any* circumstances, there are two options.

First, political leaders could design a multilateral governance system to order the trade in terrorist hostages while minimizing ransoms. This book would give helpful ideas on the many issues that would need to be resolved and provide useful examples how they have been tackled by private sector agencies. We don't (quite) have to reinvent the wheel, but it is far from clear how monitoring and enforcement would work in the intergovernmental realm. Without a credible threat of sanctions, it will sometimes be in the interest of states to break the rules—to the detriment of others. It is notoriously difficult to discipline sovereign nations. Even within the tiny circle of the G7, club governance has patently failed to stop ransom payments. Implementing an effective sanctions regime for breaches of the UN ransom ban among the 193 disparate members of the United Nations therefore seems like an impossible task.

Recognizing the human costs imposed on its citizens by the current approach, the US government has already declared ransoming from terrorist organizations to be a private matter.[5] If governments that are known to make concessions to terrorists followed suit, it would reduce the money terrorists can wring from the human misery of the hostage trade. However, this assumes that ransoms are negotiated by the very best specialists in the hostage retrieval business. If I was asked to provide a recommendation, I would (subtly) make enquiries in the underwriting room at Lloyd's. The second option is therefore to realize that the system we need already exists. We know that private negotiators employed by insurers performed well when pitched against 'political' kidnapping gangs. They stepped aside when they were threatened with prosecution.[6] Desperate families and harried politicians have been picking up the pieces ever since. The UN resolutions on ransom payments and the UK Counterterrorism and Security Bill 2014 were written and passed with excellent intentions. However, it is high time to evaluate whether they are really serving their purpose.

Reflections on Private Governance

When I first studied economics, I was taught that markets work well if there is perfect competition, perfect information, and there are no externalities or public goods problems. I learned that if these conditions are not met, governments should intervene to correct the market failure or directly supply the goods that the market fails to deliver. The market for hostages and the market for kidnap insurance turn this textbook wisdom on its head. These markets only work *because* there is a high degree of market concentration *and* crucial information is withheld from key market participants. Because there are so few market-makers, externalities can largely be addressed informally or through club rules at minimal cost. If there is a missing market—such as kidnap insurance for high-risk adventuring and safe houses in conflict zones—this should not necessarily be considered as a market failure. It is probably a sign that the market is working well: certain products simply should not exist—at least temporarily. Stopping the flow of funds to local protectors incentivizes them to re-establish sufficiently stable structures for business to resume. If a government steps in to correct the supposed market failure—e.g. by ransoming adventurous citizens that were denied private insurance—it encourages risk-seeking behaviour, incites people to ignore security advice, and creates a severely dysfunctional parallel market for hostages. Governments paying ransoms fund parties engaged in conflict and thereby risk the escalation and perpetuation of violence. Government failure is *much* more worrying than a missing market.

Insurance specialists at Lloyd's, crisis responders, and security consultants were surprised and concerned when I started to refer to their work as the governance of a criminal market. This is not how insiders see their business. 'But you created an amazingly complex, intricate, dare I say beautiful system to order the world's trickiest market!' No—they see themselves as problem solvers, not as designers. How have special risk insurers at Lloyd's caused this fascinating governance system to come into existence without being fully aware of doing so? Scholars of institutional design show that private governance systems develop through evolutionary competition. This has certainly been a major theme in this book: governance problems arose, bright lateral thinkers proposed solutions, and those that were fit for purpose were adopted. So why did this happen at Lloyd's, and not somewhere else or in several places at once?

The answer is that Lloyd's has created a highly efficient and lucrative market for niche governance solutions. The open plan underwriting room, the small number of underwriting experts, the gossipy atmosphere, and the companionable lunchtimes facilitate the swift recognition of industry-wide problems. Once identified, the problems are presented as a business opportunity to a group of associated problem solvers; often former brothers-in-arms whose complete discretion can be taken for granted. Back in the underwriting room, the solutions are evaluated and relevant information is disseminated. Because of pervasive spillovers arising from poorly managed or failed hostage trades, it is in no one's interest to withhold information about outstanding governance solutions. In fact, the opposite is true: the incentive to innovate and deliver excellent services in these relatively small markets depends on the implicit promise that the winner takes all—and makes a good living.

If private governance systems evolve through evolutionary competition, then Lloyd's is like a state-of-the-art research laboratory. Having identified a problem, Lloyd's syndicates solicit multiple governance solutions and test them in repeated trials. In the meantime, their potential competitors ('out in the field' so to speak) would be lucky to observe one or two naturally occurring examples. Ineffective and unnecessarily expensive approaches immediately impact on the syndicates' profits. They are therefore quickly identified and terminated, while the best solutions go forward to the next round of testing. This is evolutionary competition—but in hyperdrive.

Once a successful protocol has been developed, it can be deployed across a range of similar cases. To somebody experienced in negotiating the safe release of human beings from violent criminals, bartering over the return of a Stradivarius violin, a Picasso painting, or a computer database that has been rendered inaccessible by ransomware probably looks like a familiar problem. Proof of life? Yes. Proof of possession? Yes. Let's talk about the price. I am not surprised that kidnap insurers at Lloyd's also offer art insurance and that crisis responders deal with extortive cybercrime.

To me, this rapidly evolving system—ordering grey transactions with the economic underworld—exemplifies private governance at its most exciting. I am intensely grateful that I was given the opportunity to study it.

Notes

Chapter 1

1. <https://quoteinvestigator.com/2015/03/02/eureka-funny/>, accessed 28 February 2018.
2. *New York Times*, 29 July 2014.
3. Comparing the total number of reported kidnaps per 100,000 inhabitants, in 2006 the world's highest kidnap rates were observed in Turkey, Canada, Kuwait, Swaziland, and Scotland respectively. Mexico was in 37th place, behind Switzerland (13th place) and Iceland (35th place). Clearly, official statistics do not reflect actual kidnap risks. <http://www.nationmaster.com/country-info/stats/Crime/Kidnappings>, accessed January 2018.
4. This book does not study hostage-takings for sexual gratification, kidnappings by mentally disturbed people, or combat and barricade situations in which hostages are used as human shields. However, abductions where political concessions are demanded are within my remit.
5. See for example: <http://www.eglobalhealth.com/kidnap-ransom-extortion-insurance.html>, accessed January 2018 and CMME 2011. Expatriate Risk Management Kidnapping and Ransom.
6. Control Risks April (2016).
7. Key authors in this field are Lisa Bernstein, Avinash Dixit, Avner Greif, Peter Leeson, Mike Munger, and Elinor Ostrom.
8. Leeson (2011).
9. Safer Yemen (2014) p16.
10. Busch (2016), online.
11. Safer Yemen (2014) p18.
12. Key authors are Diego Gambetta, Federico Varese, and David Skarbek.
13. *New York Times*, 5 October 2011.
14. Ochoa (2012).
15. Charles Hecker, senior partner at Control Risks. <https://www.controlrisks.com/riskmap-2018/top-5-risks>, accessed February 2018.
16. *The Times*, 7 January 2012.
17. Loertscher and Milton (2017); Shortland and Keatinge (2017).
18. Control Risks website. Kidnap, Extortion and Threat Response. https://www.controlrisks.com/our-services/resolving-critical-issues-and-crises/kidnap-extortion-and-threat-response accessed February 2018.

Chapter 2

1. Control Risks (2018) <http://riskmap.controlrisks.com/portfolio-view/riskmap-2017-2/>, accessed March 2018.
2. Olson (1993) p6.
3. BBC online, 2 December 2013.
4. Castells (2000) p204.
5. *The Atlantic*, 13 June 2014.
6. Control Risks (2018).
7. Dasgupta (2000).
8. When I use male pronouns, my research indicates that the overwhelming majority of people in that particular role or carrying out that function are men. Clearly, this is subject to review.
9. Olson (1993 and 2000).
10. Lane (1958); Nozick (1974). Intellectual ancestors are Machiavelli (1532) and Hobbes (1651).
11. Levi (1998) dispenses with the Weberian idea that the violence must be 'legitimate'.
12. Border and Sobel (1987).
13. Levi (1998).
14. Tilly (1985).
15. Stasavage (2002).
16. Swiss Info, 12 November 2016.
17. Gambetta (1993); Varese (2001 and 2014).
18. Varese (2010).
19. Dixit (2004).
20. Leeson and Rogers (2009).
21. Gambetta (1993); Varese (2001).
22. Buchanan (1973).
23. Kleemans (2014).
24. Acemoglu, Verdier, and Robinson (2004).
25. Leeson (2007).
26. Reuters, 30 September 2013.
27. This issue is explored in depth in the literature on the 'resource curse': oil, gold, or diamond reserves are more often associated with autocracies or civil war than with thriving democracies.
28. Sivakumaran (2009).
29. Arjona (2014).
30. Bermann (2009).
31. US Army (2006) pA-4/5.
32. Berman, Shapiro, and Felter (2011).
33. Shortland and Varese (2016b).
34. *The Economist*, 4 June 2015.
35. Smith and Varese (2001).
36. Sicilian entrepreneur cited in Frazzica, Scaglione, Punzo, and La Spina (2014).
37. *The Telegraph*, 28 September 2001.

38. Interview with security consultant March 2016.
39. Colombian Centre of National Memory (2014).
40. *The Guardian*, 17 April 2014, 'From Murder Capital to Model City'.
41. Camacho and Rodriguez (2013).
42. Frazzica, Scaglione, Punzo, and La Spina (2014).
43. Interview with crisis responder, March 2016.
44. Control Risks, April 2016.
45. *The Economist*, 17 July 1997.

Chapter 3

1. M&C Saatchi (2017) p20.
2. This chapter draws on consultancy work undertaken for World Bank (2013a) and two joint papers with Federico Varese: Shortland and Varese (2016a and 2016b).
3. For example, there are detailed maps published at <https://www.mar inetraffic.com/en/ais/home>.
4. Shortland and Varese (2016a).
5. BBC online, 27 April 2013.
6. Liss (2014), *Time Magazine*, 22 September 2014.
7. *Chicago Tribune*, 13 October 2000.
8. Gray (2000) pp120–1.
9. Shortland, Makatsoris, and Christopoulou (2013).
10. Little (2003).
11. Umar and Baluch (2007).
12. Stremlau and Osman (2015).
13. Powell, Ford, and Nowrasteh (2008).
14. Menkhaus (2007).
15. Lewis (1994).
16. Dua (2015).
17. Hansen and Bradbury (2007).
18. Dua (2013).
19. NPR, 15 April 2011.
20. Somali Piracy Yearbook For 2009 p157.
21. Gettleman (2010).
22. Somali Piracy Yearbook For 2009 p157.
23. Gettleman (2010).
24. Hadfield and Bozovic (2016).
25. Somali Piracy Yearbook For 2009, chapter 4.
26. M&C Saatchi (2017) p21.
27. Hansen (2009).
28. World Food Programme, 17 October 2013.
29. Hansen (2009).
30. Levitt and Venkatesh (2000).
31. World Bank (2013a).

Notes

32. World Bank (2013b).
33. Dua (2015).
34. World Bank (2013a).
35. Hansen (2009).
36. *Foreign Policy*, 30 May 2013.
37. M&C Saatchi (2017) p21.
38. World Bank (2013a).
39. NPR, 15 April 2011.
40. Shortland (2012).
41. World Bank (2013a).
42. United Nations, 12 July 2013.
43. *New York Times*, 30 October 2008.
44. Gettleman (2010).
45. Marley (2010) p148.
46. Gettleman (2010).
47. Reuters, 17 July 2012.
48. *Washington Post*, 22 April 2009.
49. M&C Saatchi (2017) p18.
50. *The Telegraph*, 21 February 2012.
51. M&C Saatchi (2017) p17.
52. Menkhaus (2009) p24.
53. United Nations, 18 July 2011.
54. *The Guardian*, 16 March 2017.
55. Garowe online, 28 November 2016.
56. Garowe online, 2 February 2017.
57. Pan African Newswire, 23 May 2010; TMT Tracking, 3 February 2017.
58. Dua (2011).
59. Shortland and Varese (2016a).
60. Marley (2010) p153.
61. Garowe online, 22 October 2011.
62. Hansen (2009).
63. Hansen (2009).
64. Somalia: Somali Transitional Charter 2004.
65. Somalia Report, 8 December 2011; Somalia Report, 8 April 2012.
66. *New York Times*, 1 September 2010.
67. *New York Times*, 2 October 2009.
68. BBC online, 27 February 2012.
69. *New York Times*, 16 February 2016; O'Brien (2012).

Chapter 4

1. <http://xlcatlin.com/insurance/insurance-coverage/specialty-insurance/kidnap-ransom-and-extortion-crisis-policy>, accessed February 2018.
2. Lobo-Guerrero (2007).
3. Ostrom (2010).

4. Shortland (2017 and 2018).
5. Shortland (2018).
6. Van Dyk (2017) p286.
7. Heimer (1985).
8. *New York Post*, 21 March 2017.
9. Shortland and Shortland (2017).
10. Clutterbuck (1987); Fink and Pingle. 2014; *The Economist*, 24 August 2006.
11. BBC online, 28 June 2012.
12. Bloomberg, 27 July 2017.
13. Ambrus, Chaney, and Salitskiy (2017).
14. Rodriguez and Villa (2012); Camacho and Rodriguez (2013) p6.
15. All figures from Lewis (2001).
16. Clutterbuck (1987).
17. Campbell (2002).
18. *The Guardian*, 25 August 2014.
19. *The Economist*, 27 June 2013.
20. Shortland (2017).
21. Haufler (1997 and 1999).
22. Lloyd's Syndicate 1414 Annual Report & Accounts 2013, pp21–2.
23. Van Dyk (2017) p286.
24. See for example EU NAvFor's 'BMP4: Best Management Practices for Protection against Somali Based Piracy'.
25. Frey and Buhofer (1988).
26. Clutterbuck (1987).
27. Indeed, in most kidnapping hotspots it is not the rich but local middle-class citizens unable to afford security measures who are the primary victims of kidnapping gangs. Ochoa (2012).
28. Bernstein (1996).
29. Ostrom (2010).

Chapter 5

1. For a primer on how Hawala transfers work, see e.g. Schaeffer (2008).
2. See for example Drive the Americas. 2001. Dealing with corrupt police. <http://www.drivetheamericas.com/wiki/dealing-corrupt-police>, accessed March 2018.
3. These contracts are also called 'implicit' or 'self-enforcing' contracts. Baker, Gibbons, and Murphy (2002).
4. Baker, Gibbons, and Murphy (2002).
5. e.g. *The Guardian*, 22 March 2015.
6. Target Global Security Website accessed January 2018.
7. A similar analysis can be found in Dick (1995), who analyses when illicit firms outsource protection to an organized criminal group.
8. In some countries, the police can be hired for private protection. *The Economist*, 18 March 2010.

9. *Oil and Gas Journal*, 5 February 2016.
10. Reuters, 29 November 2016.
11. Williamson (1979).
12. Hansen (2006) p67.
13. See for example Camacho and Rodriguez (2013).
14. Dick (1995).
15. Oxfam, 20 November 2012.
16. Dalsan Radio, 13 July 2017.
17. Dalsan Radio, 13 July 2017.
18. Sicilian entrepreneur cited in Frazzica et al (2014).
19. This advice was given for fieldwork in rural Puntland in 2011. Please check that it still applies before travelling.
20. Pearce (2007).
21. *New York Times*, 1 January 1997.
22. *New York Times*, 2 December 1992.
23. United Nations Missions in Somalia UNOSOM I, <http://www.un.org/Depts/DPKO/Missions/unosomi.htm>, accessed March 2018.
24. Tripodi (1999).
25. Makinda (1998).
26. FATF (2015) p40.
27. *New York Times*, 16 July 1993.
28. Prince (2014) p44.
29. *New York Times*, 23 October 2014.
30. Reuters, 28 January 2015.
31. Coase (1937); Williamson (1979 and 1989).
32. Coase (1937).
33. *The Guardian*, 30 June 1997.
34. *The Guardian*, 17 October 1998.
35. *The Economist*, 17 July 1997.
36. BBC Online, 1 April 2016.
37. Greif (1993).
38. Bernstein (2017).
39. AIG's private clients for example 'have access to a complimentary resource to screen nannies, housekeepers, drivers, gardeners, chefs, home health workers, private financial advisors and contractors, helping to keep your family and possessions protected'. <https://www-200.aigprivateclient.com/index.php?Page=proactive-loss-prevention>, accessed March 2018.
40. MS Risk Security Advice, 28 August 2017, Burkina Faso.
41. *West Australian*, 25 November 2015.
42. Reuters, 24 January 2017.
43. Aljazeera, 16 March 2016.
44. United Nations Missions in Somalia UNOSOM II, <http://www.un.org/Depts/DPKO/Missions/unosom2p.htm>, accessed March 2018.
45. Channel 4 News, 2 April 2013.
46. *The Telegraph*, 10 March 2010.

47. In Somalia, many charities are now using the Hawala system to deliver cash-aid instead of trying to physically move aid goods to needy populations. See for example OCHA, 22 August 2017.
48. *Platform*, 20 August 2012, p9.
49. Allen (2006); Campana and Varese (2013).
50. For example, Blackwater was renamed XE Services in 2009 and in 2018 traded under the name Academi.
51. *Platform*, 20 August 2012.
52. *The Guardian*, 19 August 2012.
53. Shell, 'Security in Nigeria'. <http://www.shell.com.ng/sustainability/safety/secure-operations-nigeria.html>, accessed October 2017.
54. *Financial Times*, 19 April 2017.
55. Francis, Lapin, and Rossiasco (2011).
56. Santa Fe de Bogota Semana, 14 June 1999.
57. IPI Global Observatory, 12 October 2017.
58. Frynas (2009).
59. *The Guardian*, 3 October 2011.
60. Pearce (2007).
61. See for example *New York Times*, 21 March 2016.
62. *The Guardian*, 26 April 2017. According to Menkhaus (2012) counter-terrorism laws similarly contributed to the massive death toll of the 2011 famine.
63. See for example ODI (2010).
64. Shortland and Keatinge (2017).
65. Control Risks website 2017, 'About Us'. <https://www.controlrisks.com/en/about-us>, accessed December 2017.

Chapter 6

1. *New York Times*, 7 February 2011.
2. Howard (2017).
3. On the hostage's side are the family, employer, and perhaps government(s). The kidnappers may also be able to sell hostages to more sophisticated criminals or political organizations who can extract additional (perhaps non-monetary) value from the hostage.
4. Social norms, local wages, interest rates, and law enforcement capabilities determine who shares in the ransom and how much individuals expect to earn from carrying out, investing in, supporting, or tolerating the crime.
5. For example, Somali pirates initially compelled or recruited English teachers and expatriates to negotiate ransoms. A few turned 'professional' and negotiated a string of ransoms. Somalia Report, 5 March 2012.
6. Families of Western hostages taken in the Kashmir often did not know that their loved ones had died for several years. Hagedorn Auerbach (1998).
7. Terra Firma (2014).

8. *Bankrate*, 22 October 2012.
9. Ochoa (2012); *The Economist*, 4 June 2015.
10. Foreign Policy Centre (2001).
11. *The Economist*, 4 June 2015.
12. Sociological and economic analyses of drug-dealing and prostitution show remarkably low returns at the bottom rungs of the criminal ladder. The seminal paper is Levitt and Venkatesh (2000).
13. World Bank (2013a).
14. *The Economist*, 4 June 2015.
15. Control Risks, 24 November 2016.
16. *New York Times*, 29 July 2014.
17. Control Risks, April 2016.
18. *Shippingwatch*, 4 July 2012.
19. BBC online, 7 September 2011.
20. YouTube, 9 July 2011.
21. *Shippingwatch*, 3 March 2013.
22. *Jylland's Posten*, 5 June 2013.
23. In 2016, the Danish sailors were each awarded US$46,000 in damages. *AP News*, 13 May 2016.
24. *The Guardian*, 14 November 2010.
25. *The Economist*, 4 June 2015.
26. Gambetta (2011).
27. Ambrus, Chaney, and Salitskiy (2017).
28. De Groot, Rablen, and Shortland (2012).
29. *The Telegraph*, 26 March 2015.
30. World Bank (2013a).
31. Communication from crisis response consultant January 2018.
32. Lopez (2011).
33. Klucharev, Smidts, and Guillén (2008).
34. NDTV, 16 April 2011; BNA, 1 December 2011.
35. Lopez (2011).
36. Control Risks, April 2016.
37. Percy and Shortland (2013a).

Chapter 7

1. *SOS—Fanget af pirater* (Taken by pirates). <http://www.imdb.com/title/tt1625551/>, accessed March 2018.
2. *'Kapringen'* in the Danish original.
3. FBI, 21 April 2011.
4. The background of Somali piracy and the pirate/coastguard narrative are brilliantly explored in Dua (2013) and Dua and Menkhaus (2012).
5. Established in 1992, the International Maritime Bureau's (IMB) piracy reporting centre provides a 24/7 service for shipmasters to report any piracy, armed robbery, or stowaway incidents. Locations and short incident summaries are

made available to the shipping community on a website. Details of the incidents are published in the IMB's Annual Piracy Reports.

6. States officially apply similar fines to trawlers caught engaged in illegal and unlicensed fishing.

7. Mr Ali's reasons for coming on board the *CEC Future* and his role in the pirate venture were the subject of a court case in the US. Reuters, 4 November 2013.

8. Percy and Shortland (2013b).

9. Shortland and Vothknecht (2011).

10. Insurance contracts specified exclusions: ships could only be insured if travelling in relatively safe waters. This created heavy traffic on the shortest routes outside the 'war zone'. Location maps generated from signals emitted by the Automated Information System showed busy informal shipping lanes along certain longitude and latitudes: a boon to pirates. In fact, it might have been safer to use a more direct route through the deserted ocean. Shortland and Varese (2016a).

11. Somali pirates almost completely avoided the monsoon seasons. Shortland and Vothknecht (2011); Besley, Fetzer, and Mueller (2015).

12. Shortland and Varese (2016a); World Bank (2013a).

13. Shortland (2012) shows some satellite imagery of Eyl and Hobyo.

14. *The Guardian*, 26 November 2013.

15. This is not entirely unrealistic. One ship-owner said that financially it would have been better for him if the pirates had blown up his ship. For struggling ship-owners, the pay-out on a total constructive loss might have provided a welcome cash injection at a time when the global financial crises had thrown shipping into turmoil.

16. Although this communication style worked well between Mr Gullestrup and Mr Ali, professional negotiators never adopt such confrontational language. Kidnappers can all too easily vent their frustration on the hostages. When kidnap cases end tragically, a significant proportion of killings exhibit the hallmarks of 'spontaneous violence' Phillips (2015).

17. *The Guardian*, 26 November 2013.

18. In addition, Mr Gullestrup was concerned that if he did not pay the full amount, Clipper ships could be specifically targeted by Somali pirates in the future.

19. Studies of Somali pirate ransoms identify a strong time trend and a clear effect of 'reference ransoms' paid for comparable ships. De Groot, Rablen, and Shortland (2012); World Bank (2013a).

20. See, for example, the costs estimated in the annual Oceans Beyond Piracy reports on *The Economic Cost of Piracy* 2010, 2011, and 2012.

Chapter 8

1. In 2017 Bitcoins were used in cyber-extortion, but not in kidnap for ransom as the counterparties were not sufficiently IT-literate.

2. *New York Times*, 29 July 2014.

3. This term is borrowed from espionage tradecraft. Dead drops are used when meeting the counterparty could compromise the spies' operational security.
4. Clutterbuck (1987) p159.
5. Crisis responders generally prefer police to move in after the release. However, sometimes the police insist on monitoring or being involved in the ransom drop, creating a further layer of complication and danger to hostage life.
6. *New York Times*, 29 July 2014.
7. Lopez (2011) describes a classic six waypoint, three-and-a-half-hour wild goose chase ransom drop in Karachi on pp139–42.
8. Reuters, 24 May 2011.
9. See, for example, the colourful description of the messenger Aziz: a man with 'the kind of handshake that could bend pipes, a face constructed from granite, and a square jaw that made him look like a cross between Mike Tyson and the Terminator', in Lopez (2011) p139.
10. *Washington Post*, 16 May 1997.
11. *PRI Global Post*, 3 June 2015.
12. Safer Yemen (2014) p20.
13. Ochoa (2012).
14. VoA, 20 August 2013.
15. Shortland and Varese (2016b).
16. Lopez devotes an entire chapter to the psychological aspects of dealing with the trauma of a kidnap—both for the hostages and their families. Lopez (2011) pp59–84.
17. Ramseyer (1991).

Chapter 9

1. Ostrom, E. (2010).
2. Ostrom, Tiebout, and Warren (1961).
3. Shortland (2018).
4. Lopez (2011) p130.
5. See, for example, Forbes, 23 October 2008.
6. Aligica and Tarko (2013).
7. Shortland and Shortland (2017).
8. Glenny, Misha (2015).
9. Somalia Report, 2 May 2012.
10. Campbell (2002).
11. *The Economist*, 16 September 2004.
12. Holcombe and Sobel (2001).
13. Coase (1960).
14. Allen (2016); Williamson (1989).
15. Coase (1960) p17.
16. Frey and Buhofer (1988).
17. Fiorentini and Peltzman (1995).
18. Morgan and Thomas (1969) p72.

19. Stringham (2015).
20. Lloyd's (2016) chapter 5.
21. HMRC (2016) 'Introduction to Lloyd's—Background'.
22. Interview at Lloyd's 2015.
23. House of Commons Foreign Affairs Committee (2012).

Chapter 10

1. E.g. *New York Times*, 15 February 2015.
2. E.g. *Los Angeles Times*, 31 May 2008.
3. Phillips (2015); Guerette, Pires, and Shariati (2017).
4. Clutterbuck (1987) p158.
5. *Newsweek*, 27 January 2016.
6. Phillips (2015).
7. *New York Times*, 29 July 2014.
8. Interview with crisis responses consultant, 2017.
9. The tongue-in-cheek annual Darwin Awards recognize individuals who came to grief through their own stupidity and—by thus deselecting themselves from the gene pool—contributed to the evolution of *Homo sapiens*.
10. *The Telegraph*, 27 June 2015.
11. David (2015).
12. *New York Times*, 26 April 1997.
13. *Sahara Reporters*, 20 June 2009.
14. *New York Times*, 12 April 2009.
15. *The Telegraph*, 4 May 2009.
16. *Washington Post*, 25 January 2012.
17. *The Telegraph*, 17 October 2010.
18. *The Express*, 12 October 2010.
19. Phillips (2015).
20. Phillips (2015).
21. See, for example, *Los Angeles Times*, 31 May 2008.
22. Leeson (2011).
23. *New York Times*, 29 July 2014.
24. Aljazeera, 17 September 2016.
25. Frey and Buhofer (1988).
26. Correa-Cabrera (2017).
27. *Texas Observer*, 14 September 2017.
28. BBC 4, September 2010; *Business Insider*, 13 February 2017.
29. BBC 4, February 2015.
30. *Japan Times*, 21 January 2015.
31. *Business Insider*, 22 August 2014.
32. *New Yorker*, 6 and 13 July 2013.
33. *New York Times*, 15 February 2015.
34. Reuters, 27 November 2011.
35. *Time*, 2 July 2008.

36. BBC online, 4 December 2014.
37. Reuters, 10 March 2012.
38. *The Telegraph*, 5 August 2001.
39. *Chicago Tribune*, 7 June 2002.
40. CBS, 22 February 2011.
41. *The Independent*, 22 October 2015.
42. CBS, 11 December 2016.
43. Reuters, 26 April 2008.
44. BBC online, 17 November 2009.
45. Shortland (2015).
46. United Nations Security Council Resolution 1267, 15 October 1999, S/RES/1267; United Nations Security Council Resolution 1373, 28 September 2001, S/RES/1373; United Nations Security Council Resolution 1989, 17 June 2011, S/RES/1989; United Nations Security Council Resolution 2133, 27 January 2014, S/RES/2133; United Nations Security Council Resolution 2199, 12 February 2015, S/RES/2199; United Nations Security Council Resolution 2253, 17 December 2015, S/RES/2253.
47. The current sanctions lists can be found at <https://www.un.org/sc/suborg/en/sanctions/un-sc-consolidated-list>, accessed March 2018.
48. G7, 18 June 2014. Extract from Communiqué: The threat posed by kidnapping for ransom by terrorists and the preventive steps the international community can take.
49. UN Security Council Resolution 2133, 27 January 2014, SC/11262.
50. UK Home Office (2014).
51. UK Counterterrorism and Security Bill 2014, Section 17a.
52. Keatinge (2015).
53. O'Brien (2012).
54. Reuters, 17 October 2014.
55. Safer Yemen (2014).
56. *The Telegraph*, 8 December 2010.
57. Loertscher and Milton (2017).
58. Van Dyk (2017) p138.
59. Van Dyk (2017) p138.
60. House of Commons Foreign Affairs Committee (2012) p57.
61. World Bank (2013a).
62. Foreign and Commonwealth Office, 11 December 2012.
63. *Newsweek*, 27 January 2016.
64. YouGov, 4 September 2014.
65. The White House, 24 June 2015.
66. Brandt, Sandler, and George (2016).
67. Shortland and Keatinge (2017).
68. Van Dyk (2017) p174 and p225 respectively.
69. United Nations (2014).
70. Brandt, Sandler, and George (2016); Shortland and Keatinge (2017).
71. *New York Times*, 29 July 2014.

72. UK Home Office (2014).
73. *New Yorker*, 6 and 13 July 2013.
74. *Business Insider*, 20 August 2014.
75. e.g. BBC online, 28 August 2000.
76. *The Telegraph*, 20 August 2003; *New York Times*, 29 July 2014.
77. Ammour (2012).
78. *Newsweek*, 3 August 2017.
79. Howard (2017).
80. Shortland and Keatinge (2017).

Chapter 11

1. <https://www2.chubb.com/uk-en/business/kidnap-ransom-extortion.aspx>, accessed February 2018.
2. <https://www.red24.com/pdf/Case_study_Kidnapping_Brazil.pdf>, accessed February 2018.
3. See, for example, Wenar (2016) and the film *Blood Coltan*, 2007.
4. Howard (2017).
5. The White House, 24 June 2015.
6. UK Counterterrorism and Security Bill 2014, Section 17a.

Bibliography

Acemoglu, D., Verdier, T., and Robinson, J. A. (2004) Kleptocracy and Divide-And-Rule: A Model of Personal Rule. *Journal Of The European Economic Association.* 2:2–3 pp162–92.

Aligica, D. and Tarko, V. (2013) Co-Production, Polycentricity and Value Hetero-geneity: The Ostroms' Public Choice Institutionalism Revisited. *American Political Science Review* 107:4 pp726–41.

Aljazeera 16 March 2016. Attacks on Hotels in Africa.

Aljazeera 17 September 2016. Abu Sayyaf frees Norwegian hostage Kjartan Sekkingstad.

Allen, D. (2016) *Economic Principles: Seven Ideas For Thinking About... Absolutely Anything.* New York: Pearson Education.

Allen, J. (2006) *Hostages and Hostage-taking in the Roman Empire.* New York: Cambridge University Press.

Ambrus, A., Chaney, E., and Salitskiy, I. (2017) Pirates of the Mediterranean: An Empirical Investigation of Bargaining with Transaction Costs. Forthcoming in *Quantitative Economics*; available at <http://qeconomics.org/ojs/forth/655/655-2.pdf>.

Ammour, L. (2012) Regional Security Cooperation in the Maghreb and Sahel: Algeria's Pivotal Ambivalence. *Africa Security Brief* 18/2012.

AP News 13 May 2016. Danish Newspaper to Pay Damages to 2 Kidnapped Seamen.

Arjona, A. (2014) Wartime Institutions. *Journal Of Conflict Resolution.* 58:8, pp1360–89.

Baker, G., Gibbons, R., and Murphy, K. J. (2002) Relational Contracts and the Theory of the Firm. *The Quarterly Journal Of Economics*, 117:1, pp39–84.

Bankrate 22 October 2012. Firms Snatch Up Kidnap and Ransom Insurance.

BBC online 28 August 2000. Philippine Hostages Head for Libya.

BBC online 17 November 2009. Somali Pirates Free Spanish Boat.

BBC online 4 September 2010. Mexico's Drugs Gang 'Death Squad'.

BBC online 7 September 2011. Somalia Pirates Free Danish Family Seized in February.

BBC online 27 February 2012. Colombia's FARC Rebels: End to Kidnap a New Start?

BBC online 28 June 2012. Yemen Car Bomb Victim David Mockett 'Killed by Fraudsters'.

BBC online 27 April 2013. Nigeria's Boko Haram 'got $3m ransom' to free hostages.

Bibliography

BBC online 2 December 2013. Drug Boss Pablo Escobar Still Divides Colombia.

BBC online 4 December 2014. US Hostage Luke Somers and SA Pierre Korkie Killed During Yemen Rescue Bid.

BBC online 4 February 2015. Jordan Pilot Murder: Islamic State Deploys Asymmetry of Fear.

BBC online 1 April 2016. Zimbabwe Clamps Down with its Indigenisation Laws.

Berman, E., Shapiro, J., and Felter, J. (2011) Can Hearts and Minds Be Bought? The Economics of Counterinsurgency in Iraq. *Journal Of Political Economy* 119:4 pp766–819.

Bermann, E. (2009) *Radical, Religious, and Violent: The New Economics Of Terrorism.* Cambridge, MA: MIT Press.

Bernstein, L. (1996) Opting Out of the Legal System: Extralegal Contractual Relations in the Diamond Industry. *Journal Of Legal Studies* 21:1 pp115–57.

Bernstein, L. (2017) Revisiting the Maghribi Traders (Again): A Social Network and Relational Contracting Perspective. Paper presented at the Society for Institutional and Organizational Economics, June 2017.

Besley, T., Fetzer, T., and Mueller, H. (2015) The Welfare Cost of Lawlessness: Evidence from Somali Piracy. *Journal Of The European Economic Association.* 13:2 pp203–39.

Bloomberg 27 July 2017. The Hijacking of the *Brillante Virtuoso.*

BNA 1 December 2011. Somali Pirates Release Singapore Ship, Keep 4 Koreans Hostage.

Border, K. and Sobel, J. (1987) Samurai Accountant: A Theory of Auditing and Plunder. *The Review Of Economic Studies.* 54:4 pp525–40.

Brandt, P., Sandler, T., and George, J. (2016) Why Concessions Should Not Be Made to Terrorist Kidnappers. *European Journal Of Political Economy.* 44:1 pp41–52.

Buchanan, J. (1973) A Defense of Organised Crime? In Rottenberg, S. (ed.) *The Economics Of Crime And Punishment.* Washington, DC: American Enterprise Institute.

Busch, L. (2016) *Taken Hostage: Stories And Strategies.* XLibris (online).

Business Insider 20 August 2014. ISIS Has Been Taking Foreign Hostages Since the Very Beginning—and Getting Paid for Them.

Business Insider 22 August 2014. Nicholas Henin Details Captivity with James Foley.

Business Insider 13 February 2017. After a Decade Fighting the Cartels, Mexico May Be Looking for a Way to Get Its Military Off the Front Line.

Camacho, A. and Rodriguez, C. (2013) Firm Exit and Armed Conflict in Colombia. *Journal Of Conflict Resolution.* 57:1 pp89–116.

Campana, P. and Varese, F. (2013) Cooperation in Criminal Organizations: Kinship and Violence as Credible Commitments. *Rationality and Society.* 25:3 pp263–89.

Campbell, D. (2002) Cozy, Clubby and Covert. Center for Public Integrity. Available at <http://www.mercenary-wars.net/recruitment/cozy-clubby-covert-uk.html>, accessed March 2018.

Castells, M. (2000) *End Of Millennium.* Oxford: Blackwell Publishing.

CBS 22 February 2011. Four Americans on Hijacked Yacht Dead Off Somalia.

CBS News 11 December 2016. 100,000 Dead, 30,000 Missing: Mexico's War on Drugs Turns 10.

Channel 4 News 2 April 2013. The 'Somali Pirates' Who Are Not What They Seem.

Chicago Tribune 13 October 2000. Kidnapping of 10 in Ecuador Seen As Warning from Colombian Rebels.

Chicago Tribune 7 June 2002. American Hostage Dies in Philippines.

Clutterbuck, R. (1987) *Kidnap, Hijack And Extortion: The Response*; St Martin's Press New York.

Coase, R. (1937) The Nature of the Firm. *Economica*. 4:16 pp386–450.

Coase, R. (1960) The Problem of Social Cost. *Journal of Law and Economics*. 3:1 pp1–44.

Colombian Centre of National Memory 2014. *Una Sociedad Secuestrada*. <http://www.centrodememoriahistorica.gov.co/descargas/informes2013/secuestro/sociedad-secuestrada.pdf>, accessed March 2018.

Control Risks 2016. Infographic. Kidnapping Trends Worldwide.

Control Risks 24 November 2016. Kidnapping-for-Ransom: Venezuela's Forgotten Threat for the Year Ahead.

Control Risks (2018) Risk Map 2018. <http://riskmap.controlrisks.com/portfolio-view/riskmap-2017–2/>, accessed March 2018.

Correa-Cabrera, G. (2017) *Los Zetas Inc:. Criminal Corporations, Energy, and Civil War in Mexico*. Austin: University of Texas Press.

Dalsan Radio 13 July 2017. Somalia: Government Issues Stance Warning as Mogadishu's Bakara Traders Admit Paying Thousands of Dollars as Protection Fee to Alshabaab.

Dasgupta, P. (2000) Trust as a Commodity. In Gambetta, D. (ed.) *Trust: Making and Breaking Cooperative Relations*, electronic edition, Department of Sociology, University of Oxford, chapter 4, pp49–72.

David, S. (2015) *Operation Thunderbolt*. London: Hodder & Stoughton.

De Groot, O., Rablen, M., and Shortland, A. (2012) Barrgh-gaining with Somali Pirates. Economics of Security Working Paper #74.

Dick, A. (1995) When Does Organised Crime Pay? A Transaction Cost Analysis. *International Review of Law and Economics*. 15:1 pp25–45.

Dixit, A. K. (2004) *Lawlessness and Economics: Alternative Modes of Governance*. Princeton, NJ: Princeton University Press.

Dua, J. (2011) Piracy and the Narrative of Recognition: The View from Somaliland. SSRC research snapshot.

Dua, J. (2013) A Sea of Trade and a Sea of Fish: Piracy and Protection in the Western Indian Ocean. *Journal Of East African Studies*. 7:2 pp353–70.

Dua, J. (2015) After Piracy? Mapping the Means and Ends of Maritime Predation in the Western Indian Ocean. *Journal Of Eastern African Studies*. 9:3 pp505–21.

Dua, J. and Menkhaus, K. (2012) The Context of Contemporary Piracy: The Case of Somalia. *Journal Of International Criminal Justice*. 10:4 pp749–66.

FATF 2015. *Emerging Terrorist Financing Risks*. FATF Paris, p40.

Bibliography

FBI 21 April 2011. Somali Hostage Negotiator Arrested and Charged With Piracy in Attack on Merchant Ship.

Financial Times 19 April 2017. Nigeria's Cash-strapped Oil Industry Swaps Pipelines for Barges.

Fink, A. and Pingle, M. (2014) Kidnap Insurance and its Impact on Kidnapping Outcomes. *Public Choice.* 160:3 pp481–99.

Fiorentini, G. and Peltzman, S. (eds) (1995) *The Economics of Organised Crime.* Cambridge: Cambridge University Press.

Forbes 23 October 2008. Blackwater Floats Private Navy to Fight Pirates.

Foreign and Commonwealth Office 11 December 2012. Piracy Ransoms Task Force Publishes Recommendations.

Foreign Policy 30 May 2013. The Wild West in East Africa.

Foreign Policy Centre (2001) The Kidnapping Business.

Francis, P., Lapin, D., and Rossiasco, P. (2011) *Securing Development and Peace in the Niger Delta.* Washington, DC: Woodrow Wilson Center.

Frazzica, G., Scaglione, A., Punzo, V., and La Spina, A. (2014) How Mafia Works: An Analysis of the Extortion Racket System. Paper prepared for the ECPR conference available at <https://ecpr.eu/Events/PaperDetails.aspx?PaperID=22389&EventID=14>, accessed March 2018.

Frey, B. and Buhofer, H. (1988) Prisoners and Property Rights. *Journal Of Law And Economics.* 31:1 pp19–46.

Frynas, J. (2009) Corporate Social Responsibility in the Oil and Gas Sector. *Journal Of World Energy, Law And Business.* 2:3 pp178–95.

Gambetta, D. (1993) *The Sicilian Mafia.* Cambridge, MA: Harvard University Press.

Gambetta, D. (2011) *Codes of the Underworld: How Criminals Communicate.* Princeton, NJ: Princeton University Press.

Garowe online 22 October 2011. President of Puntland's Speech at Combating Piracy Week Conference.

Garowe online 28 November 2016. President Ali Signs Deals With a Chinese Company.

Garowe online 2 February 2017. Dozen Foreign Trawlers Arrive Bosasso Port Amid Concerns of Marine Exploitation.

Gettleman, J. (2010) The Pirates Are Winning! *New York Review Of Books,* 14 October 2010.

Glenny, M. (2015) *Nemesis: One Man and the Battle for Rio.* London: Random House.

Gray, M. (2000) *Drug Crazy.* New York: Routledge.

Greif, A. (1993) Contract Enforcement and Economic Institutions in Early Trade: The Maghribi Traders' Coalition. *American Economic Review.* 83:3 pp524–48.

Guerette, R., Pires, S., and Shariati, A. (2017) Detecting the Determinants and Trajectories of Homicide Among Ransom Kidnappings: A Research Note. *Homicide Studies,* online access at <https://doi.org/10.1177/1088767916685367>.

Hadfield, G. and Bozovic, I. (2016) Scaffolding: Using Formal Contracts to Build Informal Relations in Support of Innovation. *Wisconsin Law Review.* 5 pp981–1032.

Hagedorn Auerbach, A. (1998) *Ransom: The Untold Story Of International Kidnapping*. New York: Henry Holt and Company.

Hansen, S. (2006) Warlords and Peace Strategies: The Case of Somalia. *Journal Of Conflict Studies*. SI23:2 pp57–78.

Hansen, S. (2009) Piracy in the Greater Gulf of Aden: Myths, Misconceptions, Remedies. NIBR report 2009:29.

Hansen, S. and Bradbury, M. (2007) Somaliland: A New Democracy in the Horn of Africa? *Review Of African Political Economy*. 34:113 pp461–76.

Haufler, V. (1997) *Dangerous Commerce: State and Market in the International Risks Insurance Regime*. Ithaca, NY: Cornell University Press.

Haufler, V. (1999) Self-regulation and Business Norms: Political Risk and Political Activism. In Cutler, C., Haufler, V., and Porter, T. (eds) *Private Authority in International Affairs*. New York: State University of New York Press.

Heimer, C. A. (1985) *Reactive Risk and Rational Action: Managing Moral Hazard in Insurance Contracts*. Berkeley: University of California Press.

HMRC (2016) Introduction to Lloyd's. <https://www.gov.uk/hmrc-internal-manuals/lloyds-manual/llm1010>, accessed March 2018.

Hobbes, T. (1651) *Leviathan: Or the Matter, Forme, & Power of a Common-Wealth Ecclesiasticall and Civill*. New Haven, CT: Yale University Press (2010).

Holcombe, R. and Sobel, R. (2001) Public Policy Toward Pecuniary Externalities. *Public Finance Review*. 29:4 pp304–25.

House of Commons Foreign Affairs Committee (2012). Piracy off the Coast of Somalia. Tenth Report of Session 2010–12.

Howard, J. (2017) Kidnapped: The Ethics of Paying Ransoms. *Journal Of Applied Philosophy*. 34:3, <http://dx.doi.org/10.1111/japp.12272>.

IPI Global Observatory 12 October 2017. Rebel Networks' Deep Roots Cause Concerns for Côte d'Ivoire Transition.

Japan Times 21 January 2015. Islamic State Likely Gave Hostage Ultimatum Knowing Difficulty of Meeting It.

Jylland's Posten 5 June 2013. Former Pirate Hostage Slams 'Humiliating' Media Coverage.

Keatinge, T. (2015) Kidnap for Ransom: Helpful Clarification or Unnecessary Complication? *RUSI Commentary*, 8 January 2015.

Kleemans, E. (2014) Theoretical Perspectives on Organised Crime. In Paoli, l. (ed.) *The Oxford Handbook Of Organised Crime*. Oxford: Oxford University Press.

Klucharev, V., Smidts, A., and Guillén, F. (2008) Brain Mechanisms of Persuasion: How 'Expert Power' Modulates Memory and Attitudes. *Social Cognitive and Affective Neuroscience*. 3:4 pp353–66.

Lane, F. C. (1958) Economic Consequences of Organized Violence. *Journal Of Economic History*. 18:4 pp401–17.

Leeson, P. (2007) Trading with Bandits. *Journal of Law and Economics*. 50 pp301–21.

Leeson, P. (2011) *The Invisible Hook: The Hidden Economics Of Piracy*. Princeton, NJ: Princeton University Press.

Leeson, P. and Rogers, D. (2009) Organizing Crime. *Supreme Court Economic Review*. 20:1 pp89–123.

Levi, M. (1998) *Of Rule and Revenue*. Berkeley and Los Angeles: University of California Press.

Levitt, S. and Venkatesh, S. (2000) An Economic Analysis of a Drug Selling Gang's Finances. *Quarterly Journal Of Economics*. 115:3 pp755–89.

Lewis, I. (1994) *Blood and Bone: The Call of Kinship in Somali Society*. Trenton, NJ: Red Sea Press.

Lewis, P. (2001) *Guerrillas and Generals: The Dirty War in Argentina*. Santa Barbara, CA: Praeger Publishers.

Liss, C. (2014) Assessing Contemporary Maritime Piracy in South East Asia: Trends, Hotspots and Responses. PRIF report number 125.

Little, P. (2003) *Somalia: Economy Without State*. Bloomington, IN: Indiana University Press.

Lloyd's Annual Report (2016) What is Lloyd's? <https://www.lloyds.com/AnnualReport2016/assets/pdf/lloyds_annual_report.pdf>, accessed March 2018.

Lobo-Guerrero, L. (2007) Biopolitics of Specialised Risk: An Analysis of Kidnap and Ransom Insurance. *Security Dialogue*. 38(3) pp315–34.

Loertscher, S. and Milton, D. (2017) Prisoners and Politics: Western Hostage Taking by Militant Groups. *Democracy and Security*. <https://doi.org/10.1080/17419166.2017.1380523>.

Lopez, B. (2011) *The Negotiator: My Life at the Heart of the Hostage Trade*. London: Little Brown Book Group.

Los Angeles Times 31 May 2008. A Desperate Cry for an Answer.

M&C Saatchi (2017) Independent Qualitative Research on Somali Piracy. <http://piracy-studies.org/wp-content/uploads/2017/06/Tatu-2017-Somali-Piracy-Prison-Survey.pdf>, accessed March 2018.

Machiavelli, N. (1532) *The Prince* (trans. Russell Price, edited by Q. Skinner). Cambridge: Cambridge University Press (1988).

Makinda, S. (1998) Somalia, the UN Experience. In Woodhouse, T., Bruce, R., and Dando, M. (eds) *Peacekeeping and Peacemaking: Towards Effective Intervention in Post Cold War Conflicts*. London: Palgrave.

Marley, D. (2010) *Modern Piracy: A Reference Handbook*. Contemporary World Issues, ABC-CLIO.

Menkhaus, K. (2007) Governance Without Government in Somalia. *International Security*. 31:2 pp74–106.

Menkhaus, K. (2009) Dangerous Waters. *Survival*. 51:2 pp21–5.

Menkhaus, K. (2012) No Access: Critical Bottlenecks in the 2011 Somali Famine. *Global Food Security*. 1:1 pp29–35.

Morgan, V. and Thomas, W. (1969) *The London Stock Exchange*. New York: St Martin's Press.

NDTV 16 April 2011. Somali Pirates Keep Indian Hostages After Ransom.

New York Post 21 March 2017. Stolen Van Gogh Paintings Return to Amsterdam Museum.

New York Times 2 December 1992. Thievery and Extortion Halt Flow of U.N. Food to Somalis.

New York Times 16 July 1993. Italy, in U.N. Rift, Threatens Recall of Somalia Troops.

New York Times 1 January 1997. Cloak-and-Dagger Tale in Bogota has German Accent.

New York Times 26 April 1997. How Peruvian Hostage Crisis Became Trip Into the Surreal.

New York Times 30 October 2008. Somalia's Pirates Flourish in a Lawless Nation.

New York Times 12 April 2009. In Rescue of Captain, Navy Kills 3 Pirates.

New York Times 2 October 2009. Back from the Suburbs to Run a Patch of Somalia.

New York Times 1 September 2010. In Somali Civil War Both Sides Embrace Pirates.

New York Times 7 February 2011. J Paul Getty III Dies: Had Ear Cut Off by Captors.

New York Times 5 October 2011. Taken by Pirates.

New York Times 29 July 2014. Paying Ransoms, Europe Bankrolls Al Qaeda Terror.

New York Times 23 October 2014. Blackwater Guards Found Guilty Over 2007 Iraq Killings.

New York Times 15 February 2015. The Fates of 23 ISIS Hostages in Syria.

New York Times 16 February 2016. Penetrating Every Stage of Afghan Opium Chain, Taliban Become a Cartel.

New York Times 21 March 2016. BP and Statoil Pull Employees from Algeria Gas Fields After Attack.

New Yorker 6 and 13 July 2013. Five Hostages.

Newsweek 27 January 2016. What the Army Doesn't Want You to Know About Bowe Bergdahl.

Newsweek 3 August 2017. How a Love of the Sea Led a German Couple Into the Hands of Pirates, ISIS and Death.

Nozick, R. (1974) *Anarchy, State, and Utopia*. New York: Basic Books.

NPR 15 April 2011. Inside the Pirate Business: From Booty to Bonuses.

O'Brien, M. (2012) Fluctuations Between Crime and Terror: The Case of Abu Sayyaf's Kidnapping Activities. *Terrorism And Political Violence*. 24:2 pp320–36.

OCHA 22 August 2017. Using Cash-based Interventions to Prevent Famine in Somalia.

Ochoa, R. (2012) Not Just the Rich: New Tendencies in Kidnappings in Mexico City. *Global Crime*. 13:1 pp1–21.

ODI (2010) *Good Practice Review: Operational Security Management in Violent Environments*. Humanitarian Practice Network. London: Overseas Development Institute.

Oil and Gas Journal 5 February 2016. TAPI Pipeline Progresses but Future Uncertain.

Olson, M. (1993) Democracy, Dictatorship, and Development. *American Political Science Review*. 87 pp567–76.

Olson, M. (2000) *Power and Prosperity*. New York: Basic Books.

Ostrom, E. (2010) Beyond Markets and States: Polycentric Governance of Complex Economic Systems. *American Economic Review*. 100:3 pp641–72.

Ostrom, V., Tiebout, C., and Warren, R. (1961) The Organization of Government in Metropolitan Areas: A Theoretical Enquiry. *American Political Science Review.* 55:4 pp831–42.

Oxfam 20 November 2012. People in Eastern Congo Forced to Fund the War that Destroys Their Lives.

Pan African Newswire 23 May 2010. Somalia: Pirates or Protectors?

Pearce, J. (2007) Oil and Armed Conflict in Casanare, Colombia: Complex Contexts and Contingent Moments. In Kaldor, A., Karl, T., and Said, Y. (eds) *Oil Wars.* London: Pluto Press.

Percy, S. and Shortland, A. (2013a) The Business of Piracy in Somalia. *Journal Of Strategic Studies.* 36:4 pp541–78.

Percy, S. and Shortland, A. (2013b) Five Obstacles to Ending Somali Piracy. *Global Policy.* 4:1 pp65–72.

Phillips, E. (2015) How Do Kidnappers Kill Hostages? A Comparison of Terrorist and Criminal Groups. *Homicide Studies.* 19:2 pp123–48.

Platform 20 August 2012. Dirty Work: Shell's Security Spending in Nigeria and Beyond.

Powell, B., Ford, R., and Nowrasteh, A. (2008) Somalia After State Collapse: Chaos or Improvement? *Journal Of Economic Behavior & Organization.* 67:3–4 pp657–70.

PRI Global Post 3 June 2015. Chaos in Yemen is Changing the Way Kidnappers do Business.

Prince, E. (2014) *Civilian Warriors: The Inside Story Of Blackwater.* London: Portfolio/Penguin.

Ramseyer, M. (1991) Indentured Prostitution in Imperial Japan: Credible Commitments in the Commercial Sex Industry. *Journal Of Law, Economics, & Organization.* 7:1 pp89–116.

Reuters 26 April 2008. Somali Pirates Free Spanish Boat for Ransom.

Reuters 24 May 2011. Somalia Seizes Planes Carrying Ransoms.

Reuters 27 November 2011. FARC Rebels Execute 4 Military Hostages: Colombia.

Reuters 10 March 2012. Nigeria Hostages Killed in Bathroom During Rescue.

Reuters 17 July 2012. Pirate Kingpins Enjoy Impunity—UN Experts.

Reuters 30 September 2013. Gods Forbid: India's Temples Guard Their Gold from Government.

Reuters 4 November 2013. Mastermind or Translator? Somali Piracy Trial Begins in Washington.

Reuters 17 October 2014. Philippine Militants Free Two German Hostages.

Reuters 28 January 2015. Colombia Investigates Italian Firm Over Bribes to Guerrillas.

Reuters 29 November 2016. Afghan Taliban Offer Security for Copper, Gas Projects.

Reuters 24 January 2017. Somali Militants Ram Car Bomb into Hotel, Kill 28.

Rodriguez, C. and Villa, E. (2012) Kidnap Risks and Migration: Evidence from Colombia. *Journal Of Population Economics.* 25:3 pp1139–64.

Safer Yemen (2014) Changing Tactics and Motives: Kidnapping of Foreigners in Yemen 2010–2014. <http://safer-yemen.com/onewebmedia/Kidnapping-of-Foreigners-in-Yemen.pdf>, accessed March 2018.

Sahara Reporters 20 June 2009. Our June 12 Plane Hijack Story.

Santa Fe de Bogota Semana 14 June 1999. German Role in ELN-Government Process.

Schaeffer, E. (2008) Remittances and Reputations of Hawala Money Transfer Systems: Self-Enforcing Exchange on an International Scale. *Journal Of Private Enterprise*. 24:1 pp95–117.

Shippingwatch 4 July 2012. Hostage-taking Could Bankrupt Shipcraft in 2012.

Shippingwatch 3 March 2013. Shipcraft: USD 6.9 Million Ransom Aided by Private Parties.

Shortland, A. (2012) Treasure Mapped: Using Satellite Imagery to Track the Developmental Effects of Somali Piracy. Chatham House programme paper.

Shortland, A. (2015) Can We Stop Talking About Somali Piracy Now? *Peace Economics, Peace Science And Public Policy*. 21:4 pp419–31.

Shortland, A. (2017) Governing Kidnap for Ransom: Lloyd's as a 'Private Regime'. *Governance*. 30:2 pp283–99.

Shortland, A. (2018) Governing Criminal Markets: The Role of Private Insurers in Kidnap for Ransom. *Governance*. 31:2 pp341–58.

Shortland, A. and Keatinge, T. (2017) Closing the Gap: Assessing Responses to Terrorist-related Kidnap for Ransom. RUSI Occasional Paper, 12 September 2017.

Shortland, A., Makatsoris, H., and Christopoulou, K. (2013) War and Famine, Peace and Light? The Economic Dynamics of Conflict in Somalia. *Journal of Peace Research*. 50:5 pp545–61.

Shortland, A. and Shortland, A. (2017) Governing the Market for Fine Art. *Mimeo*.

Shortland, A. and Varese, F. (2016a) The Protector's Choice: An Application of Protection Theory to Somali Piracy. *British Journal Of Criminology*. 54:5, pp741–64.

Shortland, A. and Varese, F. (2016b) State-building, Informal Governance and Organised Crime: The Case of Somali Piracy. *Political Studies*. 64:4 pp811–31.

Shortland, A. and Vothknecht, M. (2011) Combating 'Maritime Terrorism' in Somalia. *European Journal Of Political Economy*. 27:S1 ppS133–51.

Sivakumaran, S. (2009) Courts of Armed Opposition Groups: Fair Trials or Summary Justice? *Journal Of International Criminal Justice*. 7:3 pp489–513.

Smith, A. and Varese, F. (2001) Payment, Protection and Punishment: The Role of Information and Reputation in the Mafia. *Rationality And Society*. 13 pp349–93.

Somalia: Somali Transitional Charter 2004. <https://peacemaker.un.org/somalia-transitionalcharter2004>, accessed March 2018.

Somali Piracy Yearbook For 2009. Mid-East Business Digest. Lulu Publishers.

Somalia Report 8 December 2011. Himan and Heeb's Antipiracy Plan.

Somalia Report 5 March 2012. The Negotiators: On the Business Side of Piracy.

Somalia Report 8 April 2012. What is Galmudug?

Stasavage, D. (2002) Credible Commitment in Early Modern Europe: North and Weingast Revisited. *Journal of Law, Economics, and Organization*. 18:1 pp155–86.

Stremlau, N. and Osman, R. (2015) Courts, Clans and Companies: Mobile Money and Dispute Resolution in Somaliland. *Stability: International Journal of Security and Development*. 4:1 <http://doi.org/10.5334/sta.gh>.

Stringham, E. (2015) *Private Governance: Creating Order in Economic and Social Life*. Oxford: Oxford University Press.

Swiss Info 12 November 2016. Switzerland Has 'Impressive Results' for Return of Dictator Funds.

Terra Firma (2014) Barking Up the Wrong Tree—Ransom Payments and Sanctioned Organisations.

Texas Observer 14 September 2017. 'Los Zetas Inc.' Author on Why Mexico's Drug War Isn't About Drugs.

The Atlantic 13 June 2014. The Islamic State of Iraq and Syria Has a Consumer Protection Office.

The Economist 17 July 1997. BP at War.

The Economist 16 September 2004. Lloyd's of London: Insuring for the Future?

The Economist 24 August 2006. A King's Ransom: Insuring Against Kidnap and Extortion is a Growth Industry.

The Economist 18 March 2010. Cops for Hire: Police Brutality in Russia.

The Economist 27 June 2013. Kidnap and Ransom Insurance: I'm a Client . . . Get Me Out of Here.

The Economist 4 June 2015. Quickie Kidnappings.

The Express 12 October 2010. Hostage Killing Caught on Film.

The Guardian 30 June 1997. BP's Secret Military Advisers.

The Guardian 17 October 1998. BP Hands Tarred in Pipeline Dirty War.

The Guardian 14 November 2010. British Couple Kidnapped by Somali Pirates Freed After Ransom Payment.

The Guardian 3 October 2011. Shell Accused of Fuelling Violence in Nigeria by Paying Rival Militant Gangs.

The Guardian 19 August 2012. Shell Spending Millions of Dollars on Security in Nigeria, Leaked Data Shows.

The Guardian 26 November 2013. Somali Man Found Not Guilty of Piracy in 2008 Ship Hijack.

The Guardian 17 April 2014. From Murder Capital to Model City.

The Guardian 25 August 2014. The Murky World of Hostage Negotiations: Is the Price Ever Right?

The Guardian 22 March 2015. Colombian Takes BP to Court Over Alleged Complicity in Kidnap and Torture.

The Guardian 16 March 2017. Somali Pirates Release Oil Tanker and Crew After First Hijack for Five Years.

The Guardian 26 April 2017. Anti-terrorism Laws Have 'Chilling Effects' on Vital Aid Deliveries to Somalia.

The Independent 22 October 2015. ISIS Hostage Rescue Mission Frees 70 Prisoners from 'Mass Execution'.

The Telegraph 5 August 2001. Philippines Rebel Kidnappers Behead Nine Christian Hostages.

The Telegraph 28 September 2001. Colombia Factfile: FARC.

The Telegraph 20 August 2003. Germany Accused of Buying Hostages' Release.

The Telegraph 4 May 2009. French Skipper Held Hostage by Pirates 'Shot Dead by Special Forces'.

The Telegraph 10 March 2010. Half Somalia Food Aid is Stolen, UN Report Says.

The Telegraph 17 October 2010. Linda Norgrove: How the Rescue Operation was Bungled.

The Telegraph 8 December 2010. WikiLeaks: Britain Ignored Warnings to Stop Murdered British Hostage Edwin Dyer from being Handed to Al Qaeda Group.

The Telegraph 21 February 2012. Diplomatic Row as India Arrests Italians 'For Shooting Fishermen They Thought Were Pirates'.

The Telegraph 26 March 2015. Why a retired British Army Colonel Has Become the Last Hope for Somalia's Forgotten Hostages.

The Telegraph 27 June 2015. Israel's Raid on Entebbe Was Almost a Disaster.

The Times 7 January 2012. The Piracy Racket Begins Here in the City.

Tilly, C. (1985) War Making and State Making as Organized Crime. In Evans, P., Rueschemeyer, D., and Skocpol, T. (eds) *Bringing the State Back In*. Cambridge: Cambridge University Press.

Time 2 July 2008. Colombia's Stunning Hostage Rescue.

Time Magazine 22 September 2014. The Most Dangerous Waters in the World.

TMT Tracking 3 February 2017. Suspected Scrappage Scam May Have Netted Vessel Owner 1.359 Million Euros.

Tripodi, P. (1999) Mogadishu versus the World. In Tripodi P. *The Colonial Legacy in Somalia*. London: Palgrave Macmillan.

UK Home Office (2014) Factsheet: Counter-Terrorism and Security Bill.

Umar, A. with Baluch, B. 2007. *Risk Taking for a Living: Trade and Marketing in the Somali Region, Ethiopia*. Addis Ababa: UN-OCHA/Pastoral Communication Initiative Project.

United Nations 18 July 2011. Report of the Somalia and Ethiopia Monitoring Group. SEMG S/2011/433.

United Nations 12 July 2013. Report of the Somalia and Ethiopia Monitoring Group. SEMG Report S/2013/413.

United Nations (2014) Security Council Adopts Resolution 2133 (2014), Calling upon States to Keep Ransom Payments, Political Concessions from Benefitting Terrorists. Press release, SC/11262.

US Army (2006) *Counterinsurgency Field Manual*. <https://fas.org/irp/doddir/army/fm3–24fd.pdf>, accessed March 2018.

Van Dyk, J. (2017) *The Trade: My Journey Into the Labyrinth of Political Kidnapping*. New York: Hachette Books Group.

Varese, F. (2001) *The Russian Mafia*. Oxford: Oxford University Press.

Varese, F. (2010) What is Organized Crime? In F. Varese (ed.) *Organized Crime: Critical Concepts In Criminology*. London: Routledge.

Varese, F. (2014) Protection and Extortion. In Paoli, L. (ed.) *Oxford Handbook Of Organized Crime*. Oxford: Oxford University Press.

VoA 20 August 2013. No Ransom No Release for Hostages of Somali Pirates.

Washington Post 16 May 1997. Kidnapping in Yemen is Hospitality.

Washington Post 22 April 2009. Somalia's Muslim Jihad at Sea.

Washington Post 25 January 2012. Navy SEALs Rescue Kidnapped Aid Workers Jessica Buchanan and Poul Hagen Thisted in Somalia.

Wenar, L. (2016) *Blood Oil: Tyrants, Violence and the Rules that Run the World.* Oxford: Oxford University Press.

West Australian 25 November 2015. Welborne Resolute on Mali.

White House, Office of the Press Secretary 24 June 2015. Presidential Policy Directive/PPD-30—Hostage Recovery Activities.

Williamson, O. (1979) Transaction Cost Economics: The Governance of Contractual Relations. *Journal Of Law And Economics.* 22:1 pp233–61.

Williamson, O. (1989) Transaction Cost Economics. In Schmalensee, R. and Willig, R. (eds) *Handbook Of Industrial Organization,* volume 1. London: Elsevier.

World Bank (2013a) *The Pirates Of Somalia: Ending the Threat, Rebuilding a Nation.* Washington, DC: IBRD/The World Bank.

World Bank (2013b) *Pirate Trails: Tracking the Illicit Financial Flows from Piracy off the Horn of Africa.* Washington, DC: UNODC/The World Bank.

World Food Programme 17 October 2013. UN Food Agencies in Somalia Promote Eating Fish to Fight Hunger.

YouGov 4 September 2014. Public: We are Right not to Pay Ransoms.

YouTube 9 July 2011. MV *Leopard* Hostages Beg for Release from Somali Pirates.

Index

Index

Index